VICTORIA
OF ENGLAND

Cresset Women's Voices

Editorial consultant
Rita Pankhurst

Black Country to Red China
Esther Cheo Ying

Constance Markievicz
Sean O'Faolain

Unshackled:
The Story of How We Won the Vote
Christabel Pankhurst

Victoria of England
Edith Sitwell

Cover: *The Marriage of the Princess Royal* by John Phillip (detail)
Reproduced by gracious permission of Her Majesty the Queen

THE OFFICIAL CORONATION PORTRAIT OF
QUEEN VICTORIA

From the painting by Sir George Hayter
National Portrait Gallery

VICTORIA OF ENGLAND

Edith Sitwell

CRESSET WOMEN'S VOICES

London   Melbourne   Auckland   Johannesburg

The Cresset Library

An imprint of Century Hutchinson Ltd

62–65 Chandos Place, London WC2N 4NW

Century Hutchinson Australia Pty Ltd
PO Box 496, 16–22 Church Street, Hawthorn,
Victoria 3122, Australia

Century Hutchinson New Zealand Ltd
PO Box 40–086, Glenfield, Auckland 10,
New Zealand

Century Hutchinson South Africa (Pty) Ltd
PO Box 337, Bergvlei 2012, South Africa

First published 1936
This edition first published 1987

Made and printed in Great Britain by
Richard Clay Ltd, Bungay, Suffolk

ISBN 0 09 172890 8

To
HELEN ROOTHAM
and
EVELYN WIEL

AUTHOR'S NOTE

This book is in no way intended to be a full history of the Queen's reign. It does not attempt to deal with political questions, and is only intended as a portrait of the Queen and of some of her contemporaries, and as a record of certain social conditions. Political questions have been dealt with very fully in other books, and by writers more competent to discuss them.

In the writing of this book, the author would like to express her frequent and inevitable obligations to the late Mr Lytton Strachey. It is a debt which must of necessity occur frequently in these pages; and her thanks are due to the publishers of his *Queen Victoria*, Messrs Chatto and Windus, and Messrs Harcourt, Brace and Co., for the generous permission they have granted her to quote from this work. She owes an equal debt to Mr Hector Bolitho (and R. Cobden-Sanderson, Ltd.) and to Mr Roger Fulford (and Gerald Duckworth and Co., Ltd.) from whose delightful books *Albert the Good* and *The Royal Dukes* she has culled much inestimable information; and to Mr E. F. Benson, whose recent book, *Queen Victoria* (Longmans, Green and Co.), has thrown new light upon various episodes.

If a common stock of information has been drawn upon of necessity, she hopes at least to plead a different treatment of necessarily similar material. Writers on Queen Victoria

[7]

cannot avoid continual quotations from her *Letters* and *Journal*. These are inevitable; and it is only natural that some passages, being the cream of her correspondence, must be quoted in every book that deals with her life. The author would like to record her special debt for the numerous passages quoted, by permission, from *The Letters of Queen Victoria* and the Queen's *Journal*, published by John Murray.

Constant reference has been made to Friedrich Engels's *The Condition of the Working Class in England in 1844*, from which the material contained in the chapter "March Past" has been taken, and the author's thanks are due to the publishers, Messrs George Allen and Unwin, Ltd., for permission to quote. For much useful information, and for permission to quote from his *Flame of Freedom*, she must thank Mr Owen Rattenbury and his publishers, The Epworth Press. She must thank Mr Walter Greenwood, and Jonathan Cape, Ltd., for permission to quote from *Love on the Dole*. She must also thank Mr Frank Hardie and the Oxford University Press for permission to quote from *The Political Influence of Queen Victoria*, and for information contained in some of her later chapters. For information contained in the chapter "The Queen and the Laureate" she is in debt to *Alfred, Lord Tennyson: A Memoir* by his son, Hallam, Lord Tennyson (Macmillan and Co., Ltd.). *Modes and Manners of the Nineteenth Century* by Dr Oskar Fischel and Max von Böhn (J. M. Dent and Sons, Ltd.) has been frequently consulted, and she is especially grateful for the information from it which is contained in the chapter "Fashionable Intelligence".

Certain passages from letters of the Prince Consort are quoted, by permission, from *The Life of His Royal Highness the Prince Consort* by Sir Theodore Martin. Passages from *The Creevey Papers* and from *The Life of Benjamin Disraeli, Earl of Beaconsfield*, by W. F. Monypenny and G. E. Buckle, are quoted by permission of the publishers, Messrs John Murray.

AUTHOR'S NOTE

Other authorities from whom I have drawn my information are Sir Sidney Lee, *Queen Victoria: A Biography* (John Murray); General Grey, *The Early Years of the Prince Consort* (John Murray); *The Greville Memoirs*; *Leaves from the Journal of our Life in the Highlands* and *More Leaves from the Journal of a Life in the Highlands* (John Murray); Lytton Strachey, *Eminent Victorians* (Chatto and Windus); Walter Sydney Sichel, *Disraeli: A Study in Personality and Ideas* (Methuen and Co., Ltd.); André Maurois, *Disraeli: A Picture of the Victorian Age* (John Lane, The Bodley Head, Ltd.); Lord Morley, *The Life of William Ewart Gladstone* (Macmillan and Co., Ltd.); *Letters of Lady Augusta Stanley 1849–1863* (Gerald Howe, Ltd.); and *Early Victorian England,* edited by G. M. Young (Oxford University Press). To authors and publishers I return grateful thanks for their kind permission to use quotations.

My most grateful thanks are due as well to Mr Arnold Freeman for his great kindness in placing his unparalleled learning on social questions at my disposal; to Mr Geoffrey Gorer and Dr Peter Gorer for providing me with much useful information; and to Mr David Horner for his invaluable help and advice in the correction of my proofs.

CONTENTS

CONTENTS

ILLUSTRATIONS

VICTORIA OF ENGLAND

Chapter I

THE DEATH OF THE DUKE OF KENT

The little dry leaves are blowing against the windows of a house near the sea, with a sound like the whispering of small pale ghosts; they are blowing along the parade, over the edge of the century, they are floating away and away into the far-off plantations where the country gentlemen are rooted in the mould.

Here they come, these small ghosts left over, drifting over, from the eighteenth century—dry ghosts like the Beau and Beelzebub or Wicked Shifts, Bogey and Calibre, Gooserump and King Jog, Mouldy and Madagascar and Snipe, and Mr Creevey himself brushing those leaves together with his old hands. Soon there will be no leaves left.

On the 22nd day of January in the year 1820, whilst the threadbare-looking sea beat thinly upon the shore, a man of fifty-two years of age, his once robust and reddish face now yellow, his thin dyed black hair, that had once been shining and carefully brushed (where any remained), now dull with sweat, and with the grey showing through the black and with the skull showing through the hair, lay dying upon a hired bed in Sidmouth.

Downstairs, a damp whining wind drifting aimlessly through an open window blew hundreds of unopened bills across the floor, with a rattling noise like that of rain upon a window-pane; but in the room upstairs there was no sound excepting that of the dying man's breath, struggling now for regularity like the beat of the clocks he had been so interested in making—fluttering unevenly, slowing down. Soon time would stop for him, and all mathematical precision. Turning restlessly with a half-conscious movement towards the stout and usually voluble, apple-cheeked woman, grown so strangely pale and silent, who sat at his bedside, he breathed with some last effort, who knows if produced by that affectionate nature which was at least partly genuine, by his habit of what had been half-unconscious hypocrisy, or by that gift for self-pity which had always been so strong a comfort and excuse, "Do not forget me."

So loud was now the sound of that struggling breath, that there was little room for memory, there was nothing left but that sound, and that last pitiful burst of egotism or affection. There was no place now, in those last moments that were left to him, for the discipline and regularity that had been the gods of his life. Long forgotten in his bloodstained grave lay the soldier whom the Duke of Kent, his commander-in-chief, had ordered to receive nine hundred and ninety-nine lashes as a punishment for some minor offence. Long forgotten was Private Draper,[1] who, because of his desertion and mutiny, had been sentenced by the Duke to execution. Long past was that funeral procession, marching for two long miles to a place outside Quebec, with the Duke at the head, and Private Draper marching behind the soldiers and his coffin, marching upright in his grave-clothes whilst the military band played funeral dirges behind him. When this procession had arrived at the gallows, the Duke stepped forward and, after informing Private Draper that he was now at a very

[1] See Roger Fulford: *The Royal Dukes* (Gerald Duckworth and Co., Ltd.). I am deeply indebted to the chapter on the Duke of Kent for most of the information contained in this chapter.

awful moment and within a few minutes of being judged by his Maker, in the peroration of an extremely long speech, pardoned him. But, as the Duke's biographer, Mr Roger Fulford, remarks, "this was an expensive lesson, as the coffin and the grave-clothes were presumably a slightly gruesome addition to the Prince's debts".[1]

I do not know what was the subsequent fate of Private Draper, if he developed epilepsy or was confined to a mad-house; but now, within a few hours, the bloodstained ghost of one soldier, and perhaps many others—the terrible figure of one marching upright in his grave-clothes, endlessly marching—would rise to denounce this outworn effigy lying upon the bed.

But of these he did not think. Only the clock in his breast counted.

Forgotten was his odd championship of Mr Owen, with his schemes for the bettering of mankind and his cotton-mills on the banks of the Clyde where the workers lived in decent surroundings and where was made some attempt to educate them and to ameliorate the horrors of child-labour. "I know", the Duke is reported to have said in reference to Mr Owen's socialistic theories, "that there will be a much more just equality of our race and an equality that will give much more security and happiness to all." And he added, on a later occasion: "I am fully satisfied with the principles, spirit, and practice of the system which you advocate for new-forming the human character, as far as human means are concerned, and for new-forming the human race, and I acknowledge myself to be a full and devoted convert to your philosophy, in principle, spirit, and practice. But", he continued characteristically, "we must act with prudence and foresight. The English are emphatically a practical people and practice has great influence over them."[2]

It may be true that the Duke had borrowed some hundreds

[1] Fulford, *op. cit.*, p. 157.   [2] Fulford, *op. cit.*, pp. 194-5.

of pounds from Mr Owen, but that does not alter the fact that he was genuinely and benevolently interested in his projects, and had wished, with the Duchess, to visit the mills at Lanark. But now he lay on his death-bed, and the visit would never take place. Nor was the borrowed sum repaid, although, according to Mr Owen's account, the Duke returned from the spirit sphere, after death, not once but several times, in order to confide matters of importance to him. "His whole spirit proceeding with me has been most beautiful," his confidant assures us, "making his own appointments, and never in one instance has this spirit not been punctual to the minute he had named." These spirit-visits must, one imagines, have been the result of the Duke's interest in minor details, for, apart from the vague intimation that he wished "to benefit, not a class, a sect, a party, or any particular country, but the whole of the human race through futurity", his main communication seems to have been that there were no titles in the spirit world—and in this he was backed up by the spirits of President Jefferson and Jeremy Bentham.

The Duke of Kent did not confine his benevolent interests to Mr Owen's scheme; for he supported, both with money and with work, the Westminster Infirmary, the Lying-in Charity for Delivering Poor Women at their own Habitations, the Literary Fund for Distressed Authors, and many other charitable institutions.[1] But now he was too tired to pursue philanthropy any farther. Long past, long forgotten too, were the house in Montreal, and the Lodge at Ealing, where the Duke had lived for twenty-seven years with his faithful Madame St Laurent, who, when Princess Charlotte died, must be discarded so that he might marry and produce an heir to the throne and earn from a grateful country the payment of his debts. How regular had been the life of the royal debtor in the Lodge at Ealing, amidst the pleasant

[1] See Fulford, *op. cit.*, p. 184.

[20]

sounds coming from cages full of artificial singing-birds, musical clocks, and organs with dancing horses. Fountains and running streams played in the water-closets; everything was pleasant, trivial, and orderly, and everything was a matter of routine. The footmen's hair was powdered every day by a hairdresser who lived on the premises and whose work was this, and this alone; and every morning at breakfast the tea-caddy was solemnly unlocked by the Duke, who on one occasion remarked to a guest: "Take a lesson from me—you are just starting in life—never be above attending to particulars, ay, and minute particulars. What is a trifle? Nothing that has reference to our comfort, our independence, or our peace."[1]

In spite, however, of comfort, independence, and peace, the Duke had myriads of debts. But these, if inconvenient, had, together with his sense of duty to the nation, led him into a comfortable and satisfactory marriage, two years before his death. Princess Charlotte, the heir to the throne, was dead, the Prince Regent would never provide another, the Duke of York had no child, the Duke of Clarence seemed unwilling to marry. Was it not, therefore, the duty of the Duke of Kent (remembering, also, that the Duke of York had received a settlement of £25,000 a year on his marriage) to sacrifice himself and produce an heir to the throne of England?

Unfortunately he chose, as a confidant on this project, sly, watchful, spiteful Mr Creevey—partly, I imagine, because he wished the subject to be broached in influential circles. But little did he guess in what a manner everything would be repeated. The interview between the Duke and Mr Creevey took place in Brussels, and the Duke began it with some conversation about trivial matters, then changed the conversation abruptly and came to the point. After referring, gloomily, to the improbability of the rest of the royal family saving him

[1] Fulford, *op. cit.*, pp. 186–8.

from this sacrificial act of producing an heir, the Duke continued: "Should the Duke of Clarence not marry, the next prince in succession is myself, and although I trust I shall be at all times ready to obey any call my country may make upon me, God only knows the sacrifice it will be to make, whenever I shall think it to be my duty to become a married man. It is now seven and twenty years that Madame St Laurent and I have lived together; we are of the same age, and have been in all climates, and in all difficulties together, and you can well imagine, Mr Creevey, the pain it will occasion me to part with her. I put it to your own feelings—in the event of any separation between you and Mrs Creevey....As for Madame St Laurent herself, I protest I don't know what is to become of her if a marriage is to be fixed upon me; her feelings are already so agitated upon the subject." It seemed that one morning at breakfast, only a few days after the death of Princess Charlotte, the *Morning Chronicle* had made some reference to the possibility of the Duke of Kent taking a wife. When he, as usual, had thrown the paper across the table to Madame St Laurent, and had begun to open and read his letters, he "had not done so but a very short time," continued the Duke, "when my attention was called to an extraordinary noise and a strong convulsive movement in Madame St Laurent's throat. For a short time I entertained serious apprehensions for her safety; and when, upon her recovery, I enquired into the occasion of this attack, she pointed to the article in the *Morning Chronicle*." The Duke paused for a moment, then continued in this same noble spirit of duty and self-sacrifice: "My brother the Duke of Clarence is the elder brother, and has certainly the right to marry if he chooses, and I would not interfere with him on this account. If he wishes to be king—to be married and have children, poor man—God help him; let him do so. For myself, I am a man of no ambition, and wish only to remain as I am.... Easter, you know, falls very early this year—the 22nd of

March. If the Duke of Clarence does not take any step before that time, I must find some pretext to reconcile Madame St Laurent to my going to England for a short time. When once there, it will be easy for me to consult with my friends as to the proper step to be taken. Should the Duke of Clarence do nothing before that time as to marrying it will be my duty, no doubt, to take some measures upon the subject myself."

As to his choice of a bride, it seemed that the Duke was in two minds as to whether he should take the Princess of Baden or the Princess of Saxe-Coburg; he was inclined to think the latter, owing to the popularity of her brother, the widower of Princess Charlotte, with the English people. But which-ever bride he chose, he hoped, nay, expected, the grateful nation to do justice to Madame St Laurent. For she was, he assured Mr Creevey, of very good family, and had never been an actress, and, he continued, "I am the first and only person who ever lived with her. Her disinterestedness, too, has been equal to her fidelity. When she first came to me, it was upon £100 a year. That sum was afterwards raised to £400, and finally to £1000, but when my debts made it necessary for me to sacrifice a great part of my income, Madame St Laurent insisted upon again returning to her income of £400 a year. If Madame St Laurent is to return to live amongst her friends, it must be in such a state of in-dependence as to command their respect. I shall not require very much, but a certain number of servants and a carriage are essentials." With this, the Duke reverted to the more im-portant matter of his own settlement, explaining that the Duke of York's marriage settlement ought to be considered as the precedent, since he, too, had made a marriage for the succession, "and £25,000 for income was settled, in addition to all his other income, purely on that account. I shall be contented with the same arrangement without making any demands grounded on the difference of the value of money in 1792 and at present.... As for the payment of my debts," added the Duke, "I don't call them great. The nation, on the contrary, is greatly my debtor."

At the peroration of this address, a clock struck, reminding the Duke that he was due for another appointment. He rose, and Mr Creevey rushed home as fast as his legs would carry him. Great was his excitement, vast was his joy. Here, indeed, was a piece of gossip of the utmost importance. Mr Creevey, having bustled off to communicate the news to the Duke of Wellington, wrote to tell Lord Sefton. The letter arrived just at the moment when a surgeon was sounding his lordship's bladder to discover if it contained a stone. "I never saw a fellow more astonished than he was", wrote the sufferer in reply to Mr Creevey's amazing piece of news, "at seeing me laugh as soon as the operation was over. Nothing could be more first-rate than the royal Edward's ingenuousness. One does not know which to admire most— the delicacy of his attachment to Madame St Laurent, the refinement of his sentiments towards the Duke of Clarence, or his own perfect disinterestedness in pecuniary matters."[1] For alas, the Duke, in spite of all his rather self-conscious virtues, was not a popular figure. Disliked by the Duke of Wellington, who had named him the Corporal, he was even more detested by his brothers, who resented his talent for combining, with a modified version of their own moral be- haviour, frequently expressed moral sentiments of the highest character. His sisters shared their feelings on the subject: "God damme," said the Duke of Wellington to Mr Creevey with a loud horse-laugh, "d'ye know what his sisters call him—they call him Joseph Surface." The Regent adopted this name for him, and called him, in addition, Simon Pure.

[1] *The Creevey Papers*, edited by the Rt. Hon. Sir Herbert Maxwell, Bart., Volume I, pp. 267–71 (quoted by permission of Messrs John Murray, the publishers). *Queen Victoria*, by Lytton Strachey (Chatto and Windus), pp. 9–12 (Phoenix Library edition).

THE DEATH OF THE DUKE OF KENT

The Duke of Kent married, as was his duty, and the new Duchess escaped from one state of poverty to another. And, by a strange coincidence, twelve days after the marriage, which took place according to the rites of the Lutheran Church on the 29th of May 1818 at Amorbach (a second ceremony was performed on July the 11th at Kensington, in the presence of Queen Charlotte, the Prince Regent, and other members of the royal family), the Duke of Clarence followed his brother's example, his bride being the daughter of the Duke of Saxe-Meiningen. It is sad to think that neither of these self-sacrificing men received the Martyr's crown, for the motions to increase their allowances, when brought forward in the House of Commons, were defeated with a large majority. This delighted, though it failed to astonish, the Duke of Wellington. "By God!" he exclaimed to Mr Creevey, "there is a great deal to be said about that. They are the damnedest millstones about the necks of any government that can be imagined. They have insulted—*personally* insulted—two-thirds of the gentlemen of England, and how can it be wondered at that they take their revenge upon them in the House of Commons? It is their only opportunity, and I think, by God! they are quite right to use it." [1] In the end, however, Parliament relented so far as to add £6000 to the Duke of Kent's allowance. As for Madame St Laurent, it is comforting to think that she was neither a burden nor an expense, for, having refused both carriage and servants, she crept away into the shadows of a convent, and troubled the Duke no more.

The new ménage started inauspiciously enough. The Duchess, Victoria Mary Louisa, Princess of Saxe-Coburg-Saalfeld, was accustomed to poverty, but it was a different kind from that endured by the Duke of Kent, her second husband. The sister of Prince Leopold, the widower of Princess Charlotte, she had married when seventeen years of

[1] *The Creevey Papers*, Volume I, pp. 276-7. Strachey, *op. cit.*, p. 12.

age the elderly and impoverished, but resplendent, Prince of Leiningen. Her father and her husband were equally poor; indeed, three years after her marriage, the former died a ruined man, owing to his generosity and his extravagance. Disaster after disaster had befallen him, the Duchy of Saxe-Coburg had been seized by the French, and Mr Strachey tells us, in his *Queen Victoria*, that "the ducal family were reduced to beggary, almost to starvation". Prince Leopold, therefore, that warm-hearted but cautious, ambitious and far-seeing man, had since the age of fifteen been obliged to fend for himself, and had done so very successfully, blending love and ambition in his marriage with the heiress to the throne of England. His sister the Princess of Leiningen, on her side, was forced, by the necessity of poverty and of dealing with a supine will-less husband, into developing a strength of character and, to put it mildly, an obstinacy, which were afterwards to become the despair of King William the Fourth. When her husband died, after eleven years of marriage, she was left with two children, Princess Feodore and Prince Charles, and, as her previous life had rendered her very capable of acting as Regent, she managed the Principality with some success. She was now to be an equally capable wife to the Duke of Kent, moving without complaint from country to country, from Germany to England, England to Belgium, and back again, according to the necessities of ambition or the exigencies of the Duke's debts, cheerful and bustling, voluble and platitudinous, with her short stout body, her rosy cheeks, and her brown eyes and hair set off by her bright-coloured velvets and gorgeous silks. She always, indeed, seemed to be moving, placid-tempered and obstinate, in a hurricane of flying feathers and loud-rustling silks, and this, in after years, added irritation to the dislike with which her brother-in-law, King William the Fourth, regarded her.

After a certain number of wanderings, the royal pair returned to the Duchess's castle at Amorbach; and here the

Duke occupied himself with supervising the battalions of English workmen who had been imported to rebuild and alter the castle, in order to make it fit for him to inhabit (£10,000 had been borrowed by the Duke for this purpose), with drilling the footmen into military precision, with clock-making, locking up the tea-caddy, and other important duties. He had just settled down to this peaceful life[1] when the Duchess announced that she was with child, and the wanderings began all over again. For had not a gipsy at Gibraltar prophesied that, though the Duke was to have a life of many vicissitudes, he would die happy, and his only child would be a great queen? And, if this was so, the child in question must be born in England. The Duchess of Clarence and the Duchess of Cambridge might bear their children in Hanover, but his child must be born in England.

The money for the journey, however, was not forthcoming at first, for the Regent had no wish for his brother's presence, and Prince Leopold was unable to help in the matter. In the end, the Duke's trustee, Mr Allen, sent a certain sum, though it was not large enough to admit of a suitable grandeur in transit. A coach was hired, and what an English spectator called "an unbelievably odd caravan" set off in April, less than two months before the Duchess's confinement, with the Duke sitting on the box and jogging the reins, and with the Duchess, her daughter Feodore, a nurse, a lady's maid, and the Duchess's beloved lap-dogs and song-birds inside—jolting over the stony roads, away and away. The journey was long, exhausting, and uncomfortable; the inns were unendurable, the crossing was rough, but at last in the middle of April they arrived at Kensington, where their reception by the Prince Regent was anything but gratifying.[2]

Yet nothing could alter the Duke's trust in his country's gratitude, however much he might deplore the ingratitude of his brother: "I trust", he wrote to a friend, "my country-

[1] See Fulford, *op. cit.*, p. 191.   [2] See Fulford, *op. cit.*, p. 192.

men will duly appreciate the great sacrifice and exertion made by her" (the Duchess) "in travelling at a period drawing so near her confinement.... With regard to congratulations from a certain quarter, to which you allude, I could say a great deal, but as harmony and peace is my object, I had much rather the world should think that everything was most cordial between us, than the reverse."[1]

On May the 24th 1819, the Duchess of Kent gave birth to a daughter, and the Duke wrote: "As to the circumstances of the child not proving to be a son instead of a daughter, I feel it due to myself to declare that such sentiments are not in unison with my own; for I am decidedly of opinion that the decrees of Providence are at all times wisest and best."[1]

Alas, whether the country was grateful or not, was never known to the Duke. For the Regent, enraged that so soon after the death of Princess Charlotte he should have his failure to provide an heir to the throne brought home to him, furious at his brother's rather smug satisfaction at the situation, refused to allow the public to do anything in the matter. And at the christening, which took place on the 24th of June in the grand saloon at Kensington Palace, he appeared in the rôle of wicked fairy. Resplendent in costume and in manner, he outshone the gold font, part of the regalia of the kingdom, which had been brought from the Tower of London, he put the crimson velvet curtains, which had been imported for the ceremony, in the shade. But it was easy to see that something had made him very angry; the eyes that stared at his brother and sister-in-law seemed more protuberant than usual, the puffiness beneath them was more marked and pinker—a sure sign with the Regent. He had already announced, irrespective of the parents' feelings in the matter, that the Czar Alexander of Russia was to be one of the godparents, and now he arrived at the christening with the fixed determination of thwarting the Duke in every possible

[1] Fulford, *op. cit.*, p. 192.

PRINCESS VICTORIA AT THE AGE OF FOUR

From the painting by S. P. Denning
By permission of the Governors of Dulwich College

way. When, therefore, the Archbishop of Canterbury inquired by what name the child was to be called, the Regent answered "Alexandrina", to which the Duke hastily replied that one name surely would not be enough. The Regent assented blandly: "Georgina", he added. "Or Elizabeth?" suggested the Duke, the memory of a certain reign in his mind. This was too much. The Regent's face looked thunderous. Was he to be reminded in this open manner of the child's future? There was an angry pause, and then, "Very well," said the Regent, "call her after her mother; but Alexandrina must come first."

The incident was over, but not the Duke's troubles, for the Prince Regent continued to ignore the claims of gratitude on the English people. This was made so clear at last that the prudent Prince Leopold offered to provide the money for his sister, her husband, and her children to return to Amorbach. But the Duke refused with some firmness. His child, now that the Duchess of Clarence's baby had died a few hours after birth, was the heir to the throne of England, and in England she should stay, until she was weaned in any case. After that, he hinted, the family would most likely withdraw to Germany, if some signs of appreciation of their services had not been shown before then.

Meanwhile, far away in the yellow stone castle at Rosenau, below the dark pine-haunted Thuringian Forest, the young Duchess of Saxe-Coburg was awaiting the birth of a child. How peaceful and solemn everything seemed, in the lovely August light, thought the Duchess as she looked out of the flower-wreathed windows of her room filled with imitations of Empire furniture, at the beeches, elms, and oaks shining in the late afternoon light, at the clear waterfall and river, the gardens filled with heavy roses, the peaceful fields and the stately virtuous-looking storks.[1] The Dowager Duchess,

[1] See Hector Bolitho: *Albert the Good* (R. Cobden-Sanderson, Ltd.), p. 17.

writing to her daughter in England, said: "Luise is much more comfortable here than if she had been laid up in Coburg. The quiet of this house, only interrupted by the murmuring of the water, is so agreeable...no one considered the noise of the palace at Coburg, the shouts of the children, and the rolling of the carriages in the streets."[1]

At 6 o'clock in the morning of the 26th of August, 1819, a little boy "looked at the world with a pair of jolly eyes", and seven weeks later the Duchess wrote to her great friend Augusta von Studnitz, the eldest daughter of President August von Studnitz of Gotha: "You should see him, he is pretty like an angel, he has big blue eyes, a beautiful nose, quite a small mouth and dimples in his cheeks. He is friendly and he smiles the whole time, and he is so big that a cap which Ernst wore when three months is too small for him, and he is only seven weeks as yet."[1]

The old Duchess, in her delight, exclaimed: "He is just the pendant to the pretty cousin." So time passed, whilst, in England, the troubles of the Duke and Duchess of Kent grew worse and worse, and at the beginning of December, as a matter of policy, the Duke decided to remove with his small family to a hired house at Sidmouth, in order, as he said, "that the Duchess may have the benefit of tepid sea-bathing and our infant that of sea air", and (though on this matter he was silent) because he would be removed from the attentions of his creditors. For himself, he declared, he needed no sea air. His health was so robust that he would say, when speaking of his brothers, "I shall outlive them all. The Crown will come to me and my children."

The new year dawned, and the Duke, always a superstitious man, remembered another gipsy prophecy: in the year 1820, he had been told, two members of the royal family would die. Well, the King was doomed, the Duchess of York was seriously ill, and, as for his brothers, their lives had

[1] Bolitho, *op. cit.*, p. 12.

been most irregular. "I shall outlive them all," he repeated.
But on one soft and insidiously warm and damp day in
January the Duke climbed up Peak's Hill and stood looking
at the view. A sea-mist rose and wrapped him round,
soaked through his skin, soaked through his body to the
lungs. What should such a man, endowed with such
abundant vitality and robust health, do with nursing a cold?
The Duke was impatient of any such restraint, and the cold
was neglected, with the result that it attacked his lungs, and
now, as he lay on his hired bed, the uneven clock in his breast
was slowing down, though its sound was so loud you could
hear it beating through the silence. Prince Leopold and his
devoted friend young Doctor Stockmar rushed to his bedside; the Prince Regent sent flocks of doctors and of messengers, but all was in vain. All was dim now, and cold like the
sea-fog, and nothing counted but the clock in his breast—
that and his wish to be remembered. "Do not forget me,"
he murmured...."May God have mercy upon my wife
and child, and forgive my sins."

During the night he became unconscious, and, when the
dawn broke, this strange blend of the two centuries, this
mixture of warm affection and cold self-seeking, of un-
utterable harshness in discipline and genuine charitableness
and wish to ameliorate the condition of the poor, of self-
indulgence and self-righteousness, hypocrisy and clear-
sightedness, lay dead.

It was Prince Leopold who paid the funeral expenses and
for the journey of his widowed sister and little niece to
Kensington Palace.

Chapter II

EARLY CHILDHOOD

On the 24th of May 1829, an old gentleman was walking very slowly, for though it was still early morning he was tired with the heat, through the world of green shadows that divided Kensington Palace from the labyrinth of fresh and glittering market gardens on the other side. It was a world of various green, of hairy raspberry leaves trilling with dew, of elm-trees floating like islands in the clear gold-powdered air, and of warm beechen shadows. Hearing a sound of high bird-clear laughter, the old gentleman looked through the sharp-scented sweet-briar hedge into the dancing green shadows beyond, and saw a little girl—in a shady straw hat through which dark leafy shadows and sweet golden freckles of the light fell on her kind, honest, homely face and on her dress of white cotton with a darn in it—watering a little garden of her own.

Great clouds of green dew, green light, and green shadows fell like laughter on the shady hat and the little white cotton dress. It was so early that the bright glistening nets of dew still held the dark misty pansies, the large velvety calceolarias, as fat and red and gold-speckled as strawberries, the mustard and cress, the homely pink-cheeked radishes, and the sweet-william, and the little girl ran backwards and forwards like a small bird until the cotton dress was all shining and wet with the dew. There was a flood of laughter and of green water from the watering-can—green from the light under the apple-branches; there was a flood of conversation, of mingled scolding and endearments from a lady who was seated, very upright and watchful, under the apple-branches, with the green light playing like fountains upon her dark parrot-sharp face. A voice floated from a high window in the Palace, calling "Baroness Lehzen, Baroness Lehzen". And the dark figure rose, shutting up her book with a snap, and, driving the little girl before her, returned to the Palace.

This was Baroness Lehzen, dear, kind, severe, watchful Lehzen, who knew nothing and guessed everything, voluble, indiscreet Lehzen, whose god was discretion, Lehzen whose appearance was that of a very soberly dressed parrot, with her sharp black eyes snapping at imperfections in the maids of honour, with her bird-thin mouth that was drawn in because of her habit of eating caraway seeds, with her glossy black head cocked on one side so that her sharp ears might catch any whisper, any rumour of indiscreet conduct, floating up side staircases or out of the high and shadowed, shuttered rooms of the Palace. The daughter of a poor German pastor, now she lived in a palace, and taught a little princess with a darned frock who would one day be a queen; and, too, she bore the title of Baroness, because, when it became necessary, owing to dear faithful Lehzen's incomparable ignorance, for her to share the supervision of the Princess's education with one more learned than herself, Princess Sophia, afraid that the good creature's feelings might be hurt, had suggested to King George the Fourth that this might be obviated if his appreciation of her services was shown by making her a Hanoverian baroness. This was done, and Lehzen became more voluble than ever (if this were possible), living in an unceasing flood of trivial conversation and of caraway seeds that were sent her, done up in mysterious little parcels, from Germany. The caraway seeds roused the derision of the maids of honour, and the Baroness, who was sensitive on the subject, avenged herself by slandering them on every possible occasion.

The Princess, followed by the exhortations of Lehzen, ran quickly over the dew-soaked grass and disappeared into the Palace. Today, happily, there would be no slow and lengthy lessons, for it was her birthday. How happy she had been with all her presents, and a letter from her half-sister, lovely gay Princess Feodore, who was, by now, married to Prince Hohenlohe. "If I had wings," the letter said, "I could fly like a bird, I should fly in at your window like the little robin today, and wish you many very happy returns of the 24th, and tell you how I love you, dearest sister. I should wish to stay with you, and what would poor Ernest say if I were to leave him for so long? He would probably try and fly after me, but I fear he would not get far; he is rather tall and heavy for flying."

There had been the excitement of opening the presents and the joy of opening the letter, and then breakfast had been served on the glittering wide spaces of green in front of the Palace, and every now and then the Princess had run from the table to pick a flower.

It was five whole years since dear Lehzen had first come to the Palace to look after the five-year-old Princess Victoria, but it seemed much longer than that. Until then, as she said in later life, she had been "very much indulged by everyone, and pretty well set *all* at defiance. Old Baroness de Spaeth, my nurse Mrs Brock, dear old Mrs Louis, all worshipped the poor little fatherless child whose future then was still so uncertain."

In those early days, it had always seemed winter or early spring in the Palace rooms, and the little Princess enjoyed leaving them for the warm stillroom, where the winter shadows clustering round the windows seemed dark wide green leaves, and playing with the old housekeeper's little silver-haired dog. Upstairs, when the Duchess of Kent was about, though the Princess was "son amour, ses délices", there was always something that she must not do. One of her earliest memories, indeed, was of crawling on a yellow carpet like the pale early daffodils and the fresh fields of cowslips at Claremont, and of dark voices telling her that if she cried and was naughty her uncle Sussex would hear her and would punish her—for which reason she always screamed when she saw him. Had she known it, the Duke of Sussex was far too busy in his suite above the nurseries, with his eighteenth-century habits and surroundings, his bright-coloured feathered clouds of bullfinches and canaries, and their Scarlatti-like songs, with his small negro page, whom he always called Mr Blackman, with his many clocks which, when the clock of Kensington Palace struck the hour, went off into an explosion of stiff military marches and national anthems, to pay any attention to the screams of a naughty princess.[1] Nor was the Duke of Sussex the only person of whom she was frightened. She had too "a great horror of *Bishops* on account of their wigs and aprons", and, though this was partially got over in the case of the then Bishop of Salisbury, Dr Fisher, by his kneeling down and letting her play with his badge of Chancellor of the Order of the Garter, in the case of another bishop, even his repeated requests to show him her "pretty shoes" had no effect.

So the days melted into evenings when the snow round the eaves was soft and rosy as the feathers of Uncle Sussex's bullfinches, and the gentle household sounds were quiet as their songs. Then the Princess was given a white cloud of milk in a little silver cup, and was put to bed amongst sheets that were cold and sweet as a field of snowdrops amongst the green shadows.

Then Fräulein Lehzen had come, and the Princess soon

[1] See Fulford, *op. cit.*, p. 282.

became greatly in awe of her, though she loved her dearly. At first, Fräulein Lehzen was aghast at the behaviour of her charge. Never had she dealt with such an impossibly naughty child. Gusty squalls of rage greeted any attempt to control her; indomitable will clashed with indomitable will. But then a fresh point struck the Pastor's daughter. The Princess was absolutely truthful. The look in those blue eyes was a look of entire candour. And the will, that could not be moved by any effort of another will, could be guided by affection. In a short time, Lehzen had won the child's devotion, and then it became an easy matter to guide and to train her. Until then, it had been useless to attempt even to teach her the alphabet; now she consented to learn her letters, on their being written down for her. But she still disliked her lessons, for, apart from the trouble of learning to read, there was the greater difficulty of learning to write; the thin straggly letters, that had been like the roots of a water-plant, must be taught to flower. To write was interesting; but it never seemed easy to express oneself: there was so much to say, but it never seemed to leave one's heart, now, or in later life, and for that reason the heart was often heavy. Then there was Geography, with the maps whose lines were clear as Jack Frost's pictures on the window-panes; but the names of the countries—Australia, New Zealand, South Africa, Canada—never sounded in her ears like their far-off seas and winds; they meant nothing to her now, though one day she would be their queen. So she passed the dark wintry mornings, sitting by the fire in her governess's room, whilst outside the country temples of the snow were no longer feather-soft, but sharp and dark green as the dog-haired strawberry leaves they hid—leaves that, too, seemed marked with the maps of unknown seas and lands.

Sometimes in the winter afternoons, another little girl would be popped into a carriage by her grandmother, and whirled away to Kensington Palace to play with the six-year-old Princess Victoria. But, when little Lady Jane Ellice put out a hand to play with the toys, the Princess told her: "You must not touch these, they are mine; and I may call you Jane, but you must not call me Victoria." Some time after this (in 1828) Sir Walter Scott, dining with the Duchess of Kent, was presented to the Princess, and wrote in his journal: "This little lady is educated with so much care, and watched so closely, that no busy maid has a moment to whisper 'You are heir of England.'" But he added: "I suspect, if we could dissect the little heart, we should find that some pigeon or bird of the air had carried the matter."[1] This same pigeon, I imagine, was responsible for the treatment of Lady Jane Ellice at the winter tea-parties.

Soon after the appearance of Fräulein Lehzen at Kensington Palace, traces of her influence appeared in many of her tiny charge's sayings, sounding strange in that childish mouth; for this character, that was so strong even in earliest childhood, was intensely malleable as to moods, though never as to deeds. There was, as well, the influence of a voice, which though different, sterner, wiser, was equally given to platitudes—the voice of dear good Uncle Leopold. How happy were the days spent at Claremont with that wise and beloved being, who never talked to her as if she were a child, but always as if she were as experienced as himself...who talked to her of goodness, moral worth, duty, self-knowledge, piety. She thought she could never have enough of it. The King of the Belgians, as he was soon to become, had in her a docile pupil. Nor was she the only one. Far away, in the fairy-tale castle on the edge of the dark Thuringian Forest, and at Coburg, the little boy who had been described as "the pendant to the pretty cousin" was being trained for his duty, moulded for the high fate that was his. King Leopold had

[1] John Gibson Lockhart: *Memoirs of the Life of Sir Walter Scott.* *Queen Victoria: A Biography*, by Sir Sidney Lee (John Murray), p. 24.

seen his opportunity of controlling the destiny of England by means of his wife slip through his fingers, but with these two children a new chance had arisen, and he and wise, watchful Dr Stockmar had begun to form these two very different characters from their babyhood.

From the very first, Prince Albert had shown a touching sweetness of disposition, a shy gentleness that was both moving and appealing. "Whilst still very young," wrote Count Mensdorff, "he was feelingly alive to the sufferings of the poor." Indeed, when he was but six years of age, "he raised funds to rebuild the house of a poor man who had lost his possessions in a fire". Mr Hector Bolitho, from whose charming book *Albert the Good* I culled this information, tells us also that "when ten years of age, the Prince wrote of his sadness that the world should be governed with so little morality". And, according to the same authority, the methodical habits which were so remarkable in after life were shown at the age of six, when this lonely little boy began keeping a diary:

"1825. 21st January—When I got up this morning I was very happy; I washed myself and then was dressed, after which I played for a little while, then the milk was brought, and afterwards dear Papa came to fetch us for breakfast. After breakfast, dear Papa showed us the English horses. The little white one can trot very fast, but the chestnut one is rather clumsy....

"Now I am sleepy, I will pray and go to bed."

"23rd January—When I woke this morning I was ill. My cough was worse, I was so frightened that I cried. I did a little drawing, then I built a castle and arranged my arms; after that I did my lessons and made a little picture and painted it. Then I played with Noah's Ark. Then we dined and I went to bed and prayed."

"26th January—We recited and I cried because I could not say my repetition, for I had not paid attention. I was not allowed to play after dinner, because I had cried whilst repeating."

"11*th February*—I was to recite something, but I did not want to do so; that was not right, naughty!"

"28*th February*—I cried at my lesson today, because I could not find a verb; and the Rath (his tutor) pinched me to show me what a verb was. And I cried about it."

"4*th April*—After dinner we went with dear Papa to Ketschendorf. There I drank beer and had bread and butter and cheese."

"9*th April*—I got up well and happy. Afterwards I had a fight with my brother."

"10*th April*—I had another fight with my brother; that was not right." [1]

But there were moments when his good uncle's exhortations to the higher life were forgotten, and we see only a little boy lonely and longing for affection, peeping shyly at us from the pages of a diary, and of letters, written over a hundred years ago:

"Our finches", he told his father, "have such a fine house to live in. Think of me very often and bring me a doll which nods his head. Your little Albert." [2]

The spring and summer time in England brought to the little Princess other delights than those known by her cousin on the edge of the Thuringian Forest. Every morning, when she was not watering her garden, the Princess would ride on a virtuous and gentle-tempered donkey that had been given her by her uncle the Duke of York, who, as she wrote later in her life, was always very kind to her, and she added that she remembered him well, and that he was tall and rather large, very kind, but extremely shy. Stockmar described him, at the time, as being "very tall, with

[1] *The Early Years of the Prince Consort*, by Lieut.-General the Hon. C. Grey (John Murray), pp. 32–5. Bolitho, *op. cit.*, pp. 27–8.

[2] Bolitho, *op. cit.*, p. 28.

immense *embonpoint* and not proportionally strong legs",
and as holding himself "in such a way that one is continually afraid he will tumble backwards". He had, indeed, the appearance and gait of an enormous toy, one that
is meant to overbalance and that keeps in an upright position
with some difficulty. He did not fit well, either physically or
mentally, into the century that had just begun, he did not
fit well into the long tight trousers which were the principal
portents, from his point of view, of that century. He was
used to eighteenth-century manners, habits of thought, and
clothes. He *could not* get used to those pantaloons, and on
one occasion, when paying a visit to his father at Windsor,
frightened that royal lunatic out of his harmonium-playing
and ghostly bird-high unceasing chatter by catching his spur
in the strap of those magnificent pantaloons and falling with
a crash to the ground.[1] When he walked, he drew up his
feet as if the dead Duchess's forty dogs were still yapping at
his heels; he turned corners as sharply as if he were trying to
escape from the crowd of urchins crying "Duke and Darling"
instead of "Heads and Tails"—a cry that was one of his
minor punishments for the scandal of Mrs Clarke and the
sold army-honours. Even in his way of walking, he showed
that fear of his past life, that nervousness of the future, that
beset him. But, of the two fears, that of the future was the
greater. Yet, ridiculous as he was from many points of view,
his niece loved him, because of his kindness. Had he not
given her a donkey, and, though he was very ill, did he not
arrange a Punch and Judy show for her in his garden? Under
the trees floated the high shrill sounds of the puppets; but
these were not more unreal than the personages who surrounded her—strange puppets and effigies left over from the
last century, but not relegated to the Palace attics: on the
contrary, surrounded by pomp.

It was not until the year 1826, when the Princess was seven

[1] See Fulford, *op. cit.*, p. 67.

years old, that the most magnificent puppet of all drew her towards him. For King George the Fourth had needed the space of those years to come between him and the resentment he had felt at "Joseph Surface" or "Simon Pure", as he had called his brother, providing an heir to the throne. Until then, as the Queen said, later in her life, he took hardly any notice of the poor widow and little fatherless child, who were so poor at the time of the Duke of Kent's death that they could not have travelled back to Kensington had it not been for the kindness of Prince Leopold.

Now, however, seven years after this event, the First Gentleman in Europe invited his sister-in-law and niece to Windsor for the first time.

The King lived at the Royal Lodge with Lady Conyngham and her husband and children, whilst the other members of the royal family and the general visitors stayed at Cumberland Lodge. On her arrival, the King, holding out his large hand, staring with protruding eyes at the little niece whose age was too small, whose heart was too large, to mock at his changed figure, said "Give me your little paw."

This swollen effigy of what had once been a human being, and possessed of much beauty, wore, as his niece tells us, "the wig which was so much worn in those days; he was large and gouty, but with a wonderful dignity and charm of manner." "Prinny", wrote coarse, watchful Mr Creevey, "has let down his belly, which now reaches his knees. Otherwise he is said to be well." Mr Creevey watched, he waited, for the time when that proud figurehead, with the terribly distorted body, that poor dropsy-stricken hulk of a king, would hide itself, in its transit through the streets, in a carriage with closed windows. The streets must be cleared, that the King might pass unseen. Mr Creevey watched, he waited, he knew. "Oh Prinny, Prinny, your time will come, my boy, and then your fame and reputation will have fair play too." Indeed only the other night, according to

Mr Creevey, poor Prinny had "crept into town in the dark, when nobody could see his legs or whether he could walk". But the attempt to hide was soon to be frustrated, since there was to be a council, and Lord Rosslyn had promised to "keep a sharp look-out on the legs".

But here there was none to watch, and the King remembered his reputation as First Gentleman in Europe, and ogled the lovely eighteen-year-old Princess Feodore, whose manners he much admired. Indeed, some people even believed he might marry her.

Every day brought fresh pleasures for the Princess Victoria. One lovely morning, the young and beautiful Lady Maria Conyngham, who was afterwards Lord Athlumney's first wife, and Lord Graves, who afterwards shot himself on account of his wife's conduct, were desired to take her for a drive to amuse her. So away they went with Fräulein Lehzen, in a pony carriage drawn by four grey ponies, and were driven about the Park and taken to Sandpit Gate where the King had a menagerie with wapitis and gazelles and chamois. Away they went and away—over pale grass, over the long and light summer land, with the huge gold sun shining down on the ladies' parasols, each like a gold sun reflected in the water.

Next day, the Princess, with the Duchess of Kent and Lehzen, went through the dark woods, where waterfalls tumbled from the rocks like clear showers of wistaria, pale clematis, and banksia roses, to Virginia Water. And there they met the King, who was driving in his phaeton with the Duchess of Gloucester. And the King said, "Pop her in," and she was lifted in and placed between her uncle and aunt, and her mama was very frightened, though the Duchess of Gloucester held the Princess tightly round the waist. The child was much excited, and full of admiration for the scarlet and blue liveries (the rest of the royal family must be content with scarlet and green.) The phaeton galloped round the nicest part of Virginia Water, and then stopped at the Fishing Temple. Here there was a large barge, and everyone went on board and fished; and in another barge there was a band playing, and great crowds of people watched the royal party from the bank. The King asked his niece what was her favourite piece of music, and the seven-year-old child replied, "God Save the King".

Then, after everyone was tired with fishing, the Princess and Lehzen drove to Page Whiting's cottage—for he had once been in the Duke of Kent's service; and there they ate a great deal of fruit, and the Princess amused herself with cramming Page Whiting's little girl with peaches.

It was sad when the summer day was done; it had passed too quickly. The days at Windsor were soon over, and now it was time for the Princess to return to Kensington Palace. But she took with her a beautiful miniature of her uncle the King, set with diamonds, and attached to a blue ribbon so that she might wear it on her left shoulder.

And amongst the many impressions she retained there was one that was particularly curious—a fleeting impression it seemed at first, but one which was repeated over and over again until at last it became of importance in her mind. On her return to Kensington Palace she asked Fräulein Lehzen "Why do all the gentlemen raise their hats to me and not to Feodore?" The great moment had come. Fräulein Lehzen made no reply, but next day the child found a royal genealogical tree amidst the pages of her history book. "I will be good," said the future Queen of England, and then, in a voice that might have been Lehzen's own, yet with an alien greatness in it: "Many a child would boast, but they do not know the difficulty. There is much splendour, but more responsibility."

Chapter III

LATER CHILDHOOD

In the early dawn of the 29th of May 1829, any belated ghosts, wandering homeward under the fading moon, must have been considerably startled to see two little girls in gauzy white dresses, one wearing a Portuguese Order, being ushered from the courtyard of St James's Palace, each accompanied by a separate retinue. One little girl, who looked like a white water-lily floating on the dark waters of the dawn, was the Princess Victoria; the other, who preceded her, and was followed by a retinue of dark-complexioned and grave-mannered gentlemen, was the ten-year-old Queen Maria II da Gloria of Portugal, in whose honour the First Gentleman in Europe had given a children's ball. The Queen and the Princess were driven away, and immediately afterwards there was a sound like the twittering of a myriad drowsy little birds, and a crowd of little girls and boys were ushered through the doors of the Palace, and whirled away in their own carriages through the sleeping Park.

Her Majesty of Portugal had arrived in state, with her suite following her in two carriages, and after being received with full military honours by the King's Guard she was shown into the presence of the King, who was resplendent in a blue

Field-Marshal's uniform covered with stars—the Insignia of the Garter and all the principal Russian, French, and Prussian Orders. After the two monarchs had had some conversation, the Queen and the Princess danced quadrilles to the sound of the bright sharp military music (one quadrille, we are told, had a particularly fine and long passage for trumpets), and watched children who were not of royal rank dancing waltzes.[1] But now it was dawn, and the little Queen and the still smaller Princess must be taken home and put to bed. And at midday there would be, for the latter little girl, lessons again with deep-voiced cawing Mr Davys, the Dean of Chester, rook-like and glossy in his black ecclesiastical clothes, and the exhortations to virtue and affectionate scoldings of dear watchful Lehzen. Signorina Taglioni, the great ballerina, would come to teach the Princess dancing, Mr Sale, the organist of St Margaret's, Westminster, would arrive to give her a singing lesson, the smooth pastel melodies sounding thin and crumbling and even paler than their natural hues in her childish voice. Then Mr Richard Westall, R.A., would instruct her in the art of drawing—eventually the famous Mr Landseer himself became her tutor in this accomplishment—and over each lesson Baroness Lehzen presided, and the Duchess of Kent was, as well, present for part of the time.

It was felt, however, that the teaching of religion and the inculcation of moral virtues were even more important than either learning or grace, and so, when the Princess had reached the age of eleven, she went through an examination by the Bishops of London and of Lincoln, who professed themselves as highly satisfied with her progress. "In answering a great variety of questions proposed to her," ran the report, "the Princess displayed an accurate knowledge of the most important features of Scripture History, of the leading truths and precepts of the Christian religion as taught by the

[1] See the *Morning Post*, 30th May 1829.

Church of England, as well as an acquaintance with the chronology and principal facts of English History, remarkable in so young a person. To questions in Geography, the use of the Globes, Arithmetic and Latin Grammar, the answers which the Princess returned were equally satisfactory."

The Duchess was delighted, for she had already told the Bishops that, when the Princess "was at a proper age, she commenced attending Divine Service regularly with me, and I have every feeling that she has religion at Her heart, that she is morally impressed with it to that degree, that she is less liable to error by its application to Her feelings as a Child capable of reflection." And she added: "The general bent of Her character is strength of intellect, capable of receiving with ease, information, and with a peculiar readiness in coming to a very just and benignant decision on any point Her opinion is asked on. Her adherence to truth is of so marked a character that I feel no apprehension of that Bulwark being broken down by any circumstances."[1] Constantly watched, reflected the Duchess, under perpetual supervision, how could any faults spring up in her child's character? Why, she even slept in her mama's room, nor was she allowed to walk down the stairs without somebody holding her hand.

Two or three years after this satisfactory examination, lectures of the most alarming kind were instituted, and the small Princess, with her large blue eyes fixed on the lecturer, mastered at least the names of the subjects, and noted them in her diary. We find from this that on December the 30th 1833 Mr Walker lectured, and the following subjects were broached: "Properties of Matter—Particles infinitely small,

[1] These, and subsequent passages denoted *Letters*, are quoted, by permission, from *The Letters of Queen Victoria*, edited by A. C. Benson and Viscount Esher (John Murray). Volume I, pp. 14–17. Strachey, *op. cit.*, p. 26.

divisible and hard, Cohesion, Capillary attraction, etc. Repulsion exhibited in various ways, as counteracting the preceding influences, Recapitulation, Mechanics, Gravity considered, its effects on descending and projected bodies, National weights and measures—Mechanical Powers explained by various machines, application, etc....Draft of Horses, Defect of wheel carriages, road, etc...pointed out." [1]

It is a comfort to know that on the same evening Her Royal Highness was taken to see *Old Mother Hubbard and her Dog: or Harlequin and Tales of the Nursery*.

Such was the life at Kensington Palace—a life of lessons and an occasional pantomime. But there had also been, in the past, happy peaceful holidays with dear Uncle Leopold at Claremont. How much she enjoyed listening to him while he, with his eyes half closed and that peculiar smile of his, spoke to her of the duties of royalty, of goodness and truth. Now, alas, he had left England [2] to become King of the Belgians, and, instead of those long talks about Virtue and Prudence, there were only letters to be looked forward to; it was true that those letters were as long as the conversations, but the comfort of the King's bodily presence was taken from her, Princess Feodore had gone far away to be married, and only dear good Lehzen was left—"the best, the truest friend she ever had". For though she was very dutiful to her mama, and was fond of her—oh yes, of course she gave her mama a great deal of affection—it was Lehzen who was nearest to her heart, it was Lehzen who controlled her likes and dislikes. All these feelings and the simple pleasures of her life were recorded in her childish handwriting in her diary—which, like her letters to the King of the Belgians, throws at moments, unwittingly, a strong light on certain aspects of her character.

"It was a delightful ride. We cantered a good deal.

[1] The Queen's *Journal*, 30th December 1833.
[2] In 1831.

LATER CHILDHOOD

SWEET LITTLE ROSY went BEAUTIFULLY"—a significant entry, for in her gentle yet obstinate nature there was, throughout her life, a strong vein of impatience; she never could bear to go slowly, though she learned at last to wait for events to shape themselves. She had at all times this un-conscious gift of self-revelation, as when, much later, at the age of seventeen, she told the King of the Belgians in a letter: "I like Mrs Hutchinson's life of her husband only comme cela; she is so dreadfully violent. She and Clarendon are so totally opposite that it is quite absurd, and I only believe the juste milieu." It was the *juste milieu* that ruled her life. She was not, however, so developed in character at the time of the canters on dear little Rosy, and the opinions in-herited from Lehzen find their way more often than not into the diary—her dislike for pertness, for instance, and her ideas on good breeding: "Read Mrs Butler's Journal" (Fanny Kemble). "It is certainly very pertly and oddly written. One would imagine by her style that the authoress must be very pert and not very well-bred; for there are so many vulgar expressions in it. It is a great pity that a person endowed with so much talent as Mrs Butler should turn it to so little account and publish a book which is so full of trash and nonsense which can only do her harm.... The Bishop of Chester's Exposition of the Gospel of St Matthew is a very fine book indeed! Just the sort of one I like, which is just plain and comprehensible and full of truth and good feeling." [1]

Far more delightful, however, than reading even the Bishop of Chester's Exposition of the Gospel were the concerts, and hearing Malibran sing in *Norma,* and seeing Taglioni dance in a ballet, looking very pretty in a kind of Swiss dress. She first appeared, it seems, in a petticoat of brown and yellow, as bright as the artificial sunlight on the stage, with a gay little Swiss hat and with long plaits of her hair

[1] *The Girlhood of Queen Victoria*, edited by Viscount Esher (John Murray), Volume I, p. 129. Strachey, *op. cit.*, p. 30.

hanging down; and dressed like this she danced like a water-fall among the trellised wooden bridges and staircases formed by the orchestration, and the pastures full of wild flowers transformed into melodies. Her second dress was of scarlet and yellow silk, with a white apron, and the dancer wore a wreath of flowers in her hair, and her smile was brilliant and flashing as water.

Reading this diary, we can almost hear the childish treble voice of the little Princess who wrote it a hundred years ago, and the melodies of Donizetti, budding like wild flowers or floating down like the songs of naïve birds among the green and babyish leaves of an unfading spring.

Since the visit to Windsor, peace, or at least an armed neutrality, had existed between the Duchess and King George the Fourth, for the First Gentleman in Europe understood very well how to restrain the Duchess's natural exuberance without letting her know that this was being done. But, on June the 26th 1830, poor Prinny, with his "dramatic royal distant dignity", died of that terrible disease whose symptoms had excited the derision of Mr Creevey, and was succeeded by his brother the Duke of Clarence, who was scarcely able to conceal his delight; and from that moment a season of warfare, ever increasing in violence, succeeded the calm, for the Duchess of Kent aroused all the latent irritability of that very excitable, choleric, good-natured old gentleman, with his popping, bobbling gestures, his habit of exploding into a room rather than entering it, his obstinacy allied so strangely with extreme changeableness, his ideas that floated in and out of his mind as if they were blown by a sea-gale, his head shaped like a pineapple, and his eyes that floated on the surface of his face as if they were bubbles. Mr Greville remarked that "King William had considerable facility in expressing himself, but what he said was generally useless and improper"; and His Majesty put this gift of facility to full use when dealing with his sister-in-law.

For some time before his brother's death, according to his biographer Mr Roger Fulford,[1] the Duke of Clarence had been preparing for his inheritance, and had taken precautions as well against any chance that might deprive him of it; for the Duke of York had died in 1827, leaving debts to the tune of £200,000, and no one excepting King George the Fourth now stood between him and the throne. Remembering the fate of the Duke of Kent, he always wore "a magnificent pair of goloshes", he gargled every morning, with a view to disposing of germs, he marched up and down in his study at Bushey on wet days in order to be in a good condition when the affairs of state would make a sedentary life necessary; he even took a pleasure in the voluminous correspondence, because, as he explained, it would keep his hand supple for his future task of signing "William" on endless documents.

Early in the morning that the news of his brother's death was brought to the Duke of Clarence at Bushey, the people of Putney and Chelsea were much astonished by the spectacle of "an elderly gentleman with a long piece of black crape flowing from the crown of his white hat, whirling through the streets in his carriage, and grinning and bowing to all and sundry",[2] for the news of King George's death had not yet reached them, and not many people knew King William by sight. The new King was on his way to St James's Palace for his first Privy Council, and the Privy Councillors were nearly as much astonished at the behaviour of His Majesty as had been the people in the streets, when the door of the Council Chamber burst open, and a short, explosively energetic red-faced personage dashed into the room, and rushing straight up to the table, without acknowledging in any way those present, "seized a pen and signed 'William R.' with a bold splutter".

From the moment of his accession the battles began, for

[1] See *The Royal Dukes*, pp. 122–3.
[2] *The Royal Dukes*, pp. 123–4.

His Majesty could not endure his exuberant, voluble sister-in-law, and now that he had become King he found her perpetual reminders of her daughter's position as heiress to the throne galling in the extreme. He insisted, however, on his niece's attendance at Court, even at this very early age, on all state occasions; and this attendance led to fresh battles. It is true that at the first of these functions,[1] when the eleven-year-old Princess, dressed in the deepest mourning in memory of the late King, with a court train attached to her tiny figure and a long black veil which swept the ground, followed Queen Adelaide at a Chapter of the Order of the Garter, no outbreak occurred. But when, on February the 24th 1831, a Drawing-room was held in honour of the Queen's birthday, His Majesty's attention was attracted, and held, by the fact that the Princess watched him with a stony stare. In vain did kind, gentle Queen Adelaide try to smooth him down, changing the subject and directing his attention to other matters; His Majesty had remarked that stare and he remembered it.

The Duchess returned the King's dislike fully, and she was determined that her daughter should go to Court as seldom as possible. She, the Duchess of Kent, was the mother of the heiress to the throne, and it was not for her to propitiate a foolish old man who behaved more like a sea-captain than a king, who had several illegitimate children and no legitimate child, and who was always growing touchy about one thing or another. He was King, it was true, but one day her child would be Queen, whether he liked it or not. The rarity of the Princess's appearances at Court naturally formed a fresh grievance; and when, on the occasion of the King's Coronation on September the 9th 1831, neither the Princess nor her mother was present, His Majesty's wrath was thoroughly aroused. Indeed, their absence caused so much comment that a question was asked in Parliament as to the cause of this

[1] 20th July 1830.

phenomenon, a question that was met with the discreet and evasive answer that His Majesty was perfectly satisfied with the reason. Actually, the Duchess had refused to come or to allow her daughter to be present, because a wrangle had occurred between the King and herself as to what place the Princess should occupy in the procession. The King, who had no clear ideas about this matter, wished her to follow, instead of precede, his brothers; the Duchess insisted clamorously that her daughter was heiress presumptive to the throne, and must therefore walk immediately after the monarch. Neither side would on any account give way, so the Princess was not allowed to attend the Coronation, and spent that day, and many days before, in tears. "Nothing could console me," she told her children many years afterwards, "not even my dolls."

The Duchess was, by now, determined to annoy His Majesty as much as possible by insisting on and emphasizing his niece's position, and His Majesty, on his side, was determined that the position in question should be kept well within bounds. When, therefore, in August 1831, the heiress to the throne and her mother, who were on their way to the Isle of Wight, received a royal salute from the ships stationed at Portsmouth, King William asked the Duchess to forgo these honours and, when she refused, gave orders that they should not be paid in future. Later, he was to become still more infuriated by what he called the Princess's "royal progresses"—in which, accompanied by her mother, she visited manufacturing towns and other public places, and received addresses. Or rather, the Duchess of Kent, all smiles, feathers, and rustling silks, received them, keeping well in the foreground and making speeches. The King, enraged by this exuberance and assertiveness, by the public speeches in which the Duchess spoke of "the future Queen", adding, with a tactful smile, "I hope at a very distant date," and by the behaviour of her major-domo Sir John Conroy, who arranged those speeches, rather in the manner of a Prime Minister, exclaimed, "The woman's a nuisance, the woman's a nuisance." And the nuisance grew worse, not better. Nor were matters improved by the profound dislike which existed between King William and the King of the Belgians, a dislike that had been much enhanced on King William's side by King Leopold's unfortunate addiction to drinking water instead of wine. "What's that you're drinking, sir?" inquired King William one night at dinner. "Water, sir," was the reply. "God damn it, sir! Why don't you drink wine? I never allow anybody to drink water at my table."[1] Marquis Peu-à-Peu, as his father-in-law King George the Fourth had called him, made no reply; but he missed no opportunity in the future of warning his niece against the dangers of ill treatment to which she and her relatives would be exposed if they did not use caution in their dealings with King William.

The Princess, on her side, was never weary of her beloved uncle Leopold's advice, both in conversation and in his letters: "To hear dear uncle speak on any subject", she exclaimed in her diary, "is like reading a highly instructive book; his conversation is so enlightened, so clear. He is universally admitted to be one of the first politicians now extant; he speaks so mildly, yet firmly and impartially, about politics." Nor about these alone; His Majesty was even firmer, more highly instructive, about moral worth, duty, self-examination, etc. . . .

As time went on, the Duchess's visits to the Court grew rarer and rarer; she did, however, make a slight attempt to propitiate His Majesty by giving a large dinner party in his honour on April the 24th 1832, at which his niece, exhorted to virtue and caution beforehand by dearest Lehzen, made but a brief appearance. As a return for this politeness, the

[1] *The Greville Memoirs* (Silver Library edition), Volume III, p. 377. Strachey, *op. cit.*, p. 37.

King gave a children's ball for the Princess on her birthday in the following year, though neither of their Majesties was present—owing, it was said, to indisposition. And the Princess and her mother were invited to a Royal night at the Opera, where they were observed by watchful Mr Creevey, who wrote: "Billy 4th at the Opera was everything one could wish; a more *Wapping* air I defy a King to have—his hair five times as full of powder as mine, and his seaman's gold lace cock-and-pinch hat was charming. He slept most part of the opera—never spoke to any one, or took the slightest interest in the concern....I was sorry, not to see more of Victoria: she was in a box with the Duchess of Kent, and of course, rather under us. When she looked over the box I saw her, and she looked a very nice little girl indeed."

Their Majesties were present at their niece's Confirmation at St James's Palace on the 30th of July 1835—an occasion on which she was shaking with fright and bathed in tears. As the little Princess, dressed in a white lace frock with a white crape bonnet and a wreath of white roses round it, drove in the chariot with her dear mama, followed by Lady Flora Hastings, Lehzen, the King and Queen, the Duke and Duchess of Cambridge, the Duchess of Gloucester, the Duke of Cumberland, the Duchess of Weimar, the Duchess of Northumberland and her husband, Lord Conyngham, Lord Denbigh, and Mr Ashley, the heat was so great that the sun had drunk all the water from the leaves, and there was a white mist through which the breath of the horses came in little curls like the buds of lilies of the valley. The heat had turned the faces of the children who crowded round the carriages into those of negresses, but their hair seemed the long gold hair of planets, as they stared at the little Princess in her white dress like the heat-mist or the gauzy white roses that decorated the chapel. When they arrived at the chapel, the King advanced first, leading his niece, then came the Queen leading the Duchess of Kent.

When, at a quarter to two, the service was over, and the Princess returned to Kensington Palace, the King gave her a fine set of emeralds, her dear mama gave her a lovely bracelet enclosing a piece of her hair, and a beautiful set of turquoises, whilst dear Lehzen was also given a bracelet in honour of the occasion. But even then all the excitements of the day were not over, for that very night the Princess heard that her beloved sister Feodore had given birth to a daughter. And in four days' time the expected letter from her beloved uncle reached her.

In this, after complaining that "*Hypocrisy* is a besetting sin of all times, but *particularly* of *the present,* and many are the wolves in sheep's clothes. I am sorry to say, with all my affection for old England, the very *state of its Society and politics* renders many in that country essentially *humbugs and deceivers*", he comforted his niece by assuring her that whilst "others may tremble to have at last their real character found out, and to meet all the contempt which they may deserve, your mind and heart will be still and happy, because it will know that it acts honestly, that truth and goodness are the motives of its actions."[1]

The King of the Belgians, with commendable restraint, failed to name the actual identity of the wolf in sheep's clothing, the humbugs and deceivers, the "others" who may tremble to have at last their real character found out, and to meet all the contempt which they may deserve; but we are left with a feeling that he *could* have named "them" had he wished, and that the plural number was used only from a sense of politeness.

[1] *Letters;* 4 August 1835.

Chapter IV

EARLY GIRLHOOD

In a room at Kensington Palace, shuttered against the flaunting heat, Baroness Lehzen sat writing a letter to her sister in Germany; scratching away busily, her pen covered the pages with long descriptions of the Princess's progress in goodness, of the Duchess's veiled unkindness to the writer, of Sir John Conroy's rudeness, and the queer way in which, when Lehzen entered a room, she invariably found the Duchess and Sir John sitting in close proximity, and talking in low voices. But most vivid of all was the Baroness's description of what she had suffered from Lady Flora Hastings, the Duchess's lady-in-waiting—the sharp looks and the sharp remarks and the derision at the caraway seeds which, as the recipient of the letter very well knew, brought back such happy memories of dear Germany to the writer. Ah..h.h... the Baroness's lips were drawn into a still tighter line as she remembered one particular sneer....Let her wait...the Baroness had eyes in her head, she knew the kind of person that Lady Flora was, with that flippancy and that bird-sharp brightness. It was only a question of waiting....

At this point, a high clear sound of youthful laughter was heard, and in ran the little fourteen-year-old Princess in her darned white frock, and two boys, the Princes Alexander and

EARLY GIRLHOOD

Ernest of Würtemberg, the sons of the reigning Duke and the Duchess's sister, who were paying a visit to their aunt at Kensington Palace. The Princess noted in her diary that both the Princes were *extremely* tall, Alexander was *very* handsome, and took such care of his cousin when getting out of a boat, and Ernest had *a very kind expression* and was equally assiduous. "Both these young gentlemen were EXTREMELY *amiable*," and Her Royal Highness, chaperoned by the ubiquitous Lehzen and her enemy Sir John Conroy, shared with her cousins the great experience of hearing, for the first time, Signor Paganini play the violin. "He played by himself, some Variations most WONDERFULLY," she stated in her diary, and added of this physical mimicry of all-conquering Death: "he is himself a curiosity."

The Princess was very sad when these cousins returned to Würtemberg; standing on the beach with Lehzen she watched them sailing away in their barge, and for many days afterwards longed for their company.

Two years after this time, two other cousins came, who were almost more delightful—the Princes Ferdinand and Augustus—dear Ferdinand who elicited universal admiration from all parties, who was so very unaffected, and had such a very distinguished appearance and carriage, who was handsomer than Augustus because his eyes were so beautiful and he had such a lively clever expression. There was something *quite beautiful* in his expression when he spoke and smiled, and he was *so good*. But then dear Augustus was very amiable too, and, when known, showed much good sense. The Princes spent a great deal of time with their cousin, who noted in her diary that "Dear Ferdinand came and sat near me and talked so dearly and sensibly. I do *so* love him. Dear Augustus sat near me and talked to me, and he also is a dear good young man, and is very handsome."[1]

[1] *The Girlhood of Queen Victoria*, Volume I, pp. 150-3. Strachey, *op. cit.*, p. 32.

But oh, most wonderful, most exciting of all, was the first visit paid to Kensington Palace by her dear cousins Prince Ernest and Prince Albert, the sons of the Duke of Saxe-Coburg. She loved all her dear cousins, but much the most precious, the dearest of all, were Ernest and Albert.

Their visit took place in May 1836, when the Princess was just seventeen years old; and King William, who was perfectly aware that King Leopold had determined from the moment that his nephew Albert was born that he should become the husband of the future Queen of England, decided to annoy that water-drinking monarch by inviting various other young men in order that they might serve as rivals to the Saxe-Coburg Princes. He accordingly invited King Leopold's enemy the Prince of Orange and his two sons, and the youthful Duke of Brunswick, to stay at St James's Palace, at exactly the time of Prince Ernest and Prince Albert's visit to Kensington. The Prince of Orange had a particular antipathy to the King of the Belgians, of whom he said, "Voilà un homme qui a pris ma femme et mon royaume," for he had wished to marry Princess Charlotte; the King of the Belgians cordially returned this dislike, and the visit was designed to annoy King Leopold to the full. It led to an endless flow of grumbling, an outpouring of complaints from King Leopold to his niece.

"I am really *astonished*", he wrote[1], "at the conduct of your old uncle the King; this invitation of the Prince of Orange and his sons, this forcing him on others is very extraordinary.... Not later than yesterday I got a half-official communication from England insinuating that it would be *highly* desirable that the visit of *your* relatives *should not take place this year*.... The relations of the Queen and the King, therefore, to the God-knows-what degree, are to come in shoals and rule the land, when *your relations* are to be *forbidden* the country, and that when, as you

[1] *Letters*, Volume I, pp. 47–8. Strachey, *op. cit.*, pp. 36–7.

know, the whole of your relations have ever been very
dutiful and kind to the King." His Majesty hoped this out-
rageous behaviour would rouse his niece's spirit, for "Now
that slavery is even abolished in the British Colonies, I do not
comprehend *why your lot alone should be to be kept a white little
slavey in England*, for the pleasure of the Court, who never
bought you, as I am not aware of their ever having gone to
any expense on that head, or the King's ever having *spent a
sixpence for your existence*. I expect that my visits to England
will be prohibited by an order in Council. Oh, consistency
and political or *other honesty*, where must one look for you?

"I have not the least doubt that the King, in his passion
for the Oranges, will be excessively rude to your relations.
This, however, will not signify much; they are your guests
and not his, and will therefore not mind it."

The Princes arrived with their father, bringing the little
Princess a present of "a most delightful lory", which was so
tame that it would sit on her hand, and would never bite if
she put her finger inside its beak. Its plumage was very
brilliant, and the colours scarlet, blue, brown, yellow, and
purple; and Kensington Palace now echoed with the sound
of happy youthful laughter and of Haydn duets. "Ernest",
wrote his cousin, "has dark hair and fine dark eyes and eyebrows, but the nose and mouth are not good; he has a most
kind, honest and intelligent countenance, and has a very good
figure. Albert, who is just as tall as Ernest but stouter, is extremely handsome; his hair is about the same colour as mine, his
eyes are large and blue, and he has a beautiful nose with a very
sweet mouth and fine teeth; but the charm of his countenance
is his expression; which is most delightful." A few days later,
the Princess's journal tells us that she sat between her two
dear cousins on the sofa and they looked at drawings; that
both of them drew very well, but particularly Albert, and
that they both played very nicely on the piano. And, three
weeks after this time, we learn that "Dearly as I love Ferdi-

nand and good Augustus, I love Ernest and Albert more than them, oh yes, MUCH *more*. Augustus", she added, with a faint touch of youthful priggishness, "was like a good affectionate child, quite unacquainted with the world, phlegmatic and talking but very little; but dearest Ernest and dearest Albert are so grown up in their manners—Albert always used to have some fun and some clever witty answer at breakfast...he used to play and fondle Dash so funnily too."[1]

When her dearest beloved cousins and her dear uncle left England, the future Queen wrote: "I cried bitterly, very bitterly." Then, when she had dried her tears, she sat down and wrote with a curious mixture of egotism and warmheartedness to her dearest uncle, of whose plans she was perfectly aware, thanking him for "the prospect of great happiness you have contributed to give me, in the person of dear Albert....He possesses every quality that could be desired to make me perfectly happy. He is so sensible, so kind, and so amiable too. He has, besides, the most pleasing and delightful exterior and appearance you could possibly see.

"I have now only to beg you, my dearest Uncle, to take care of the health of one now so dear to me, and to take him under your special protection. I hope and trust that all will go on prosperously and well on this subject of so much importance to me."[2]

Prince Albert, on his side, remarked merely that he found his cousin "very amiable", and then turned his thoughts to other matters. Pursued by his uncle's exhortations to virtue, his recommendations to develop "an earnest frame of mind, which is ready of its own accord to sacrifice mere pleasure to real usefulness", haunted by Baron Stockmar's homilies on the subject of the whole duty of princes, he, with his brother Ernest, went to complete his education at Bonn University,

[1] *The Girlhood of Queen Victoria*, Volume I, pp. 157–61.
[2] *Letters*, Volume I, p. 49.

where they speedily became renowned for their virtues. Prince Albert's biographer, Mr Bolitho, tells us that an Englishman, who was at the University at this time, in after years described Prince Albert's costly banquets, "to parties of between twenty and thirty students, selected entirely for their personal worth and talents". It appears, also, that "the Princes themselves could hardly be said to partake of the rare luxuries provided for the occasion, so rigidly temperate were they both, and more especially Prince Albert".[1]

Meanwhile, from both Belgium and England, the sound of new grumbling, fresh quarrelling arose. The King of the Belgians, it seems, was perpetually being affronted, not only by the King of England, but by the English people, and in especial by the newspapers: "An infamous Radical or Tory-Radical paper, the *Constitutional*," he wrote to his niece on the 18th of November 1836, "seems determined to run down the Coburg family. I don't understand the meaning of it; the only happiness poor Charlotte knew was during her short wedded existence, and there was but one voice on that subject, that we offered a bright prospect to the nation.

"Since that period I have (though been abused and vilified merely for drawing an income which was the sequence of a Treaty ratified by both Houses of Parliament, and that without one dissenting voice, a thing not very likely to happen again) done everything to see England prosperous and powerful. I have spared her, in 1831, much trouble and expense, as without my coming here very serious complications, war and all the expensive operations connected with it, must have taken place. I give the whole of my income, without the reservation of a farthing, to the country; I preserve unity on the Continent, have frequently prevented mischief at Paris, and to thank me for all that, I get the most scurrilous abuse, in which the good people from constant practice so much excel. The conclusion of all this is scurrilous

[1] Bolitho, *op. cit.*, p. 49.

abuse of the Coburg family. I should like to know what harm the Coburg family has done to England? But enough of this."[1] To which his niece replied: "My most dearly beloved Uncle, you cannot imagine how happy you have made me by your very dear, kind, long, and interesting letter of the 18th.... Your letter is so interesting and instructive I could read it over and over again."...Curiously evasive, thought His Majesty, as he read this letter for the second time. What could the dear child have in her mind? Had he but known it, that evasiveness would be found more than once in the dear child's answers to her uncle's letters, after she became Queen of England.

In England, the quarrelling between the Duchess of Kent and the King of England grew worse and worse, so that it became obvious that before long there would be an open battle. The August of 1836 was particularly hot, and the weather inflamed the tempers of both the parties concerned. The Duchess was aggrieved because, owing to the fact that she had received the royal salute from ships in the Solent, the King had forbidden the firing of these to be accorded to any ship unless the reigning monarch or his consort were on board. The King was enraged by the "royal progresses" on the part of the heiress to the throne and her mother, to which I have already referred—for during the last four years she had presented prizes at the Eisteddfod, laid the first stone of a boys' school near Plas Newydd, and as a result of her tour in Wales Princess Victoria was the theme for the poetic competition at the Cardiff Bardic Festival.

It must be admitted that, much as the King resented these "progresses", they were a cause of endless excitement to his niece, who on the occasion of the Eisteddfod visited Sir Richard and Lady Bulkeley; and who chronicled the minutest details in her diary. "We were received at the door", she wrote, "by Sir Richard and farther on by Lady Bulkeley

[1] *Letters*, Volume I, p. 53.

whose dress I shall describe. It was a white satin dressed with
blonde, short sleeves and a necklace, ear-rings, and sevigne of
peridots and diamonds with a wreath of orange-flowers in
her hair. We then went upon the terrace and the band of the
Anglesea Militia played 'God Save the King'. We then
presented all the bards and poets with medals.... At 5 we went
to dinner which was in a temporary building, which was lined
in the inside with pink and white linen. The dinner was
splendidly served, and the china was rich and beautiful. The
fruit was magnificent. After dessert was over Sir Richard
made a speech and brought out a toast in honour of Mama and
me. We then went upstairs into Lady Bulkeley's pretty little
dressing-room. Her toilet table was pink with white muslin
over it trimmed with beautiful lace and her things on the toilet
table were gold. We then went downstairs and took coffee
and Lady Williams' famous dog, Cabriole, played tricks."
Then she had visited Chester and had declared open a new
bridge over the River Dee, naming it "Victoria Bridge". She
had visited Strutt's Cotton Mills at Belper, and on every occasion her bustling self-important mother had been more in the
foreground than she. The King resented all these activities, and
his anger grew deeper still, when in this hot August weather
he invited the Duchess and the Princess to stay at Windsor on
the 12th of August for eleven or twelve days, during which the
birthdays of both the King and Queen were to be celebrated,
and the Duchess refused to come before the 20th. This put the
King in a fury, and matters were made still worse, for as soon
as they had arrived the King went to London for the day in
order to prorogue Parliament, and whilst there, the idea flew
into his head that he might as well pay a visit to Kensington
Palace in order to find out what "that nuisance of a woman is
doing". He found out! She had just gone into occupation
of a suite of seventeen rooms, in spite of the fact that he had
directly forbidden her to do so. His Majesty's wrath now
knew no bounds, and the excited Mr Greville tells us that

"when he arrived at Windsor and went into the drawing-room (at about 10 o'clock at night) where the whole party was assembled, he went up to the Princess Victoria, took hold of both her hands, and expressed his pleasure at seeing her there, and his regret at not seeing her oftener. He then turned to the Duchess and made her a low bow, almost immediately after which he said that 'a most unwarrantable liberty' had been taken with one of his palaces; that he had just come from Kensington, where he found apartments had been taken possession of not only without his consent, but contrary to his commands, and that he neither understood nor would endure conduct so disrespectful to him! This was said loudly, publicly, and in a tone of serious displeasure."

This was bad enough, but the next day was to be the occasion of a far more violent outbreak. The scene was the banquet in honour of the King's birthday, and a hundred or more guests were present. The Duchess of Kent, looking sulky, and fidgeting restlessly, sat on the King's right hand, the Princess sat directly opposite. At the end of dinner His Majesty rose to reply to the toast of his health—and then came the deluge. Scarlet in the face with anger, in a loud violent voice the King denounced his sister-in-law. In nine months' time, he said, the Princess would come of age; he hoped, he prayed, that his life might be spared for that nine months in order that there should be no danger of the regency of "a person now near me, who is surrounded by evil advisers and who is herself incompetent to act with propriety in the station in which she would be placed. I have no hesitation in saying that I have been insulted, grossly and continuously insulted, by that person—but I am determined no longer to endure a course of behaviour so disrespectful to me. Amongst many other things I have particularly to complain of, is the manner in which this young lady has been kept away from my Court; she has been repeatedly kept from my Drawing-rooms, at which she ought always to have been present; but I am fully resolved this shall not happen again. I would have her know that I am King and I am determined to make my authority respected, and for the future I shall insist and command that the Princess do upon all occasions appear at my Court, as it is her duty to do."

At the end of this tirade, a complete silence fell. The hundred and more guests, aghast, held their breath; gentle Queen Adelaide blushed until she was as red as the King; the Princess burst into tears. But the Duchess, pale with humiliation and anger, said not a word.

This silence remained unbroken until the company had left; then the Duchess, beside herself with fury, jumped to her feet and called for her carriage; she would return that night to Kensington, she declared. It was only after some time and with considerable difficulty that she was induced, at last, to remain at Windsor till next day.[1]

From that moment, the detestation in which the King held his sister-in-law, the intense dislike she felt towards him, were perfectly undisguised. And even with her departure from Windsor she could not find peace, for there was her own household to contend with. Lehzen was always interfering and making mischief or contracting grievances, Sir John Conroy and she quarrelled almost unceasingly. And then came the final blow. The Duchess had grown more fond of Sir John Conroy than her position and his marriage rendered desirable; there were affectionate passages between them, and one day Princess Victoria interrupted a scene of the kind. Much shocked, she told the Baroness, and the Baroness's greatest friend, Baroness Späth.... Lehzen pursed her lips and pondered. So she *had* been right in her suspicions! But Baroness Späth did not give herself time to ponder; she was just as voluble and not so discreet as Lehzen; not only did she gossip, but she actually went to the length of re-

[1] See *The Greville Memoirs*, Volume III, pp. 374-6. Strachey, *op. cit.*, p. 38.

proving the Duchess, with the result that she was instantly dismissed. But to dismiss Baroness Lehzen was a very different matter. She remained irritatingly non-committal, her manner, her speech were obstinately respectful, and what she thought, she kept to herself. And the King, too, would have to be dealt with if Lehzen were sent away. He thoroughly approved of her conduct and of the way in which she had brought up his niece, and he would hear nothing against her. She remained; and, from that day, Kensington Palace echoed with the sound of warfare. The Duchess, it is true, had Sir John Conroy, his affection, and his advice to rely upon, and she had the devotion of Lady Flora Hastings, who could always be relied on to be amusing at Baroness Lehzen's expense. But then, as against this, there was the strange silence of Princess Victoria; the curious hardness that from time to time replaced the usually mild expression of her eyes, when she looked at her mother. The Duchess knew only too well that she could hope for no support from her daughter, whose youth and whose natural tendencies made her regard moral slipshodness without a trace of pity, and who, as well, was devoted to Späth who had been dismissed, and to Lehzen whom the Duchess would have liked to dismiss. The Duchess felt hot with mortification. How could she have let herself wander into such an impasse? For there was no help for it; she had lost ground with the Princess—that she knew—she whose hold upon her had been largely founded on religious teaching, and the stern moral outlook which the Duchess, aided by the Dean of Chester and Lehzen, had inculcated.

In the midst of these troubles, and only a few days before the Princess's eighteenth birthday, the news reached Kensington Palace that the King was desperately ill. His will-power, however, and his strong constitution carried him through this illness, so that the Princess was able to celebrate her birthday, the plans for which included a visit to the Royal Academy, a Drawing-room, and a state ball.

EARLY GIRLHOOD

Early in the morning, the Princess was awakened by an *aubade*, performed outside the Palace by the villagers of Kensington, and then received her birthday presents, which included a grand piano sent by the King. After this, as Sir Sidney Lee remarks, gloomily, "addresses from public bodies were presented to her mother". The Duchess, forgetting her troubles in the excitement of the moment, was as voluble, as bustling, and quite as indiscreet as ever. She made a long and elaborate speech, prepared for her by Sir John Conroy, in answer to an address presented by the Corporation of London, in which she referred to her daughter's "royal progresses" and her knowledge of all classes of society, and in which she complained bitterly about the slights put upon her by the royal family. The rest of the speech, which might have been delivered by a reigning monarch, dealt with the "diffusion of religious knowledge, the preservation of the constitutional prerogatives of the Crown, and the protection of popular liberties as the proper aim of a sovereign".

After the addresses had been presented and the deputations had gone, lighter joys were indulged in. The Princess visited the Royal Academy, whose exhibition was then held in the building which is now the National Gallery, in Trafalgar Square. Here she was welcomed by vast crowds of her uncle's subjects; she shook hands with and had a conversation with Mr Rogers the poet, and, on being told that Charles Kemble the actor was in the room, asked that he should be presented to her. And that evening, greatest joy of all, the Court Ball was given in honour of her coming of age, though neither the King nor Queen was able to be present, owing to the state of the King's health. At this ball, Count Eugène Zichy, "renowned", as she told the King of the Belgians, "for his magnificent turquoises and his famous valsing", and who was "a good natured elegant", was presented to her, and she noted, afterwards, that he was very good-looking in uniform, but not in plain clothes. Count Waldstein, too, was presented, looking remarkably handsome in his splendid Hungarian uniform. But, alas, the Princess could not dance with him, although she would have liked to do so, because he could not dance quadrilles, and in her station it was unsuitable that she should waltz or galop.

The day passed happily, and even the Duchess forgot her resentment at her own indiscretion. But, a few days later, a fresh humiliation was in store for her. Lord Conyngham, the Lord Chamberlain, arrived at Kensington Palace bearing a letter from the King to the Princess. When he was ushered into the room where the Princess and the Duchess were sitting, the latter at once put out her hand to take the letter, but Lord Conyngham with a grave air begged her pardon, saying he had received instructions to give the letter to nobody excepting the Princess herself. The Duchess, with a thunderous look, drew back and the Princess opened and read the letter. It contained the King's offer to make the Princess an allowance of £10,000 a year, a sum which was to be for her own use, and which might not be disposed of by her mother. The Duchess was furious. Was it for this, she inquired, that she had brought up her daughter with such admirable simplicity? £4000 a year would have been ample as an allowance for the girl and, as for the remaining £6000, it would only have been just and right if it had been offered to the Duchess.

As for the King of the Belgians, he wrote an excited letter to his "dearest child", saying: "You have had some battles and difficulties of which I am completely in the dark. The thing I am most curious to learn is what the King proposed to you concerning your establishment....I shall reserve my opinion till I am better informed, but by what I heard I did not approve of it, because I thought it ill-timed....Two things seem necessary: not to be fettered by an establishment other than what will be *comfortable* to *you*, and then to avoid any breach with your mother....I am very curious to know what he proposed; you will have it in your power to modify his proposition, as it will be difficult your approbation should be dispensed with."[1] For, thought His Majesty, should his niece have an establishment of her own, might it not be a little more difficult to keep that watchful parental eye over the thoughts and doings of the future Queen of England? But the "dearest child" had, before she received this letter, written to King William, thanking him for his kindness and accepting his offer. And as she did so that strange look came once more into her eyes. Her mouth was set in a by now not unfamiliar line.

His Majesty, meanwhile, seemed to have recovered temporarily from his illness, although it had left traces upon him which resulted in the Court becoming even duller than before. Lady Grey, who paid a visit to Windsor Castle at about this time, told Mr Creevey, "in her own distressed manner", that "she was really more dead than alive". She said[2] "all the boring she had ever endured before was literally nothing compared with her misery of the two preceding nights. She hoped she never should see a mahogany table again, she was so tired with the one that the Queen and the King, the Duchess of Gloucester, Princess Augusta, Madame Lieven and herself had sat round for hours—the Queen knitting or netting a purse—the King sleeping, and occasionally waking for the purpose of saying—'Exactly so, ma'am!' and then sleeping again."

But this recovery was not for long. The poor rather kindly old man, of whom his niece had said that he was "odd, very odd and singular", but that "his intentions were often ill-interpreted" and that "he was always kind to me", suddenly collapsed; and soon it was known that he was dying. The King of the Belgians, in a state of great excite-

[1] *Letters*, Volume I, pp. 67-8.
[2] *The Creevey Papers*, Volume II, p. 262. Strachey, *op. cit.*, p. 41.

ment, wrote to his niece: [1] "*Be not alarmed* at the prospect of becoming perhaps sooner than you expected Queen; aid will not be wanting, and the great thing is that you should have some honest people about you who have your welfare *really at heart*. Stockmar will be in this respect all we can wish, and we must hope that *useful* occupation will prevent his health from suffering"—for the King knew that his friend was, to some degree, a *malade imaginaire*.... The next letter, written a week later, contained these lines: "You may count upon my faithful good offices in all difficulties, and you have at your command Stockmar"—and he added, for a sense of humour was not His Majesty's strongest point: "my object is that you should be no one's tool." The King of the Belgians could indeed hardly resist coming in person to supervise the conduct and policy of his niece; but it would be better, it *would be wiser*, he felt, if he did not give way to this impulse. "The result of my *examen*", he wrote, "is that I think it better to visit you later. If, however, you wanted me at any time, I should come in a moment. People might fancy I came to enslave you, while I glory in the contrary; and thirdly, they might be jealous, or *affect* it at least, at my coming, as if I thought of ruling the realm for *purposes of my own*."

Meanwhile his former enemy, the poor good-natured old sailor King, with his "Wapping air" and his "quarter-deck gestures", was dying fast. On Sunday the 18th of June, the dying man, awakening with the memory that this was the anniversary of Waterloo, said to Dr Chambers: "Let me live over this memorable day—I shall never live to see another sunset." Dr Chambers said "I hope your Majesty will live to see many." "Oh that's quite another thing, that's quite another thing," replied the King.

That evening, when the Archbishop of Canterbury entered the King's room, he was greeted by a feeble voice which said "I am sure the Archbishop is one of those persons who

[1] *Letters*, Volume I, p. 70.

pray for me," and as he left, the King, crossing his hands upon his breast, said: "God bless thee, dear, excellent, worthy man; a thousand, thousand thanks." Next morning, though he was within a few hours of his death, he whispered to the Queen: "I shall get up once more to do the business of the country," and when being wheeled in his chair from his bedroom to his dressing-room, he turned round and waved his hand with a kindly smile to the Queen's attendants who were standing in tears near the door.... Though the last flicker of life was nearly extinguished, he could still find strength to comfort those about him; that night, when the Archbishop performed the service for the Visitation of the Sick in the dying man's bedroom, the King, seeing that the Queen was, for the first time since his fatal illness, giving way unrestrainedly to her grief, said to her comfortingly: "Bear up! Bear up!"

As the night wore on, the Queen, as she knelt by the bed-side, still holding her husband's hand, felt that hand still warm in hers, and could not believe that he had left her for ever.

Chapter V

TWO DAYS IN JUNE

At 5 o'clock in the morning of Tuesday June the 20th 1837, two gentlemen of grave and distinguished aspect might have been heard knocking vainly at the door of Kensington Palace. It was with difficulty that they were able to rouse the porter, and when they had done so, and explained that they were the Archbishop of Canterbury and the Lord Chamberlain, and that they must see the Princess immediately, the porter refused point blank to disturb her. At length, however, after an hour had been passed in heated argument, he consented grumblingly to rouse Baroness Lehzen, who fluttered downstairs with a rustling sound like that of a bird dashing through leaves, breathless with excitement and curiosity, and who, on hearing the news, flew to the Duchess. Together, the ladies awoke the Princess, and in a few moments a little figure, with a shawl wrapped round her dressing-gown, her fair hair streaming down her back, and her tiny feet thrust into bedroom slippers, walked downstairs alone for the first time in her life; the door of the room where the Archbishop and Lord Conyngham were waiting was opened, and the eighteen-year-old Queen of England entered the room. Lord Conyngham dropped on his knee, kissed her hand, and spoke in a low voice of the King's death: the Archbishop followed suit, and the little Queen, with tears in her eyes and her hands clasped, spoke of her aunt the Queen Dowager, inquired if she was broken with grief, asked what could be done to comfort her.

She had been fond of her bustling, self-important, but good-natured old uncle, who had always been kind to her—once her "stony stare" had been forgiven—and who had wished to make her an allowance of £10,000, so that she should be independent of her mama; the fact that Mama and Uncle Leopold had spent much of their time quarrelling with him had seemed to her no reason why she should dislike him; and so there were tears of grief in the Queen of England's eyes as she walked upstairs to dress in the plainly furnished little room leading out of the bedroom which she shared with the Duchess of Kent. They were tears springing from real grief; but she was eighteen, her vitality was of an extraordinary character, and who can be surprised if the excitement of this, the greatest event of her life, filled her with a kind of exultation, mingling with the grief. There would be no more darned muslin dresses, no more scoldings from Mama—she would never sleep again in a bed in Mama's room, for the Queen of England would have a room of her own. An odd hardening changed for a moment the little sweet but self-willed mouth, the blue childish eyes seemed for a fleeting while more prominent—but perhaps this change was only due to the summer sunlight drifting through the half-closed shutters in dust like that of the sweet lime-bloom. It was a look, however, that was to be seen many times in after years by Sir Robert Peel, once by Prince Bismarck, and, above all, most often by Lord Palmerston.

She dressed quickly and ran downstairs into a room flooded with happy living sunlight, to find that breakfast was laid already, and that dear kind Baron Stockmar, her uncle Leopold's great friend and adviser, was waiting for her, grave-faced because he had heard the news, but with a strange quiet look of triumph too. The Baron, on his side, had eaten even less breakfast than usual, because the sudden excitement—and, of course, sorrow for the death of the late King—had brought on symptoms which threatened a return of the dyspepsia from which he suffered; but he was full of kind advice, and he was at once respectful and fatherly to the little Queen.

After breakfast a hasty letter to her dear uncle, so far away in Belgium, must be written, and another to her sister, and then, before the big clock in the tower had struck 9 o'clock, the Prime Minister, Lord Melbourne—such a handsome and at the same time fatherly man—wearing full court dress, sought an audience with his sovereign. "It has long been my intention", she said to him in her lovely youthful voice, "to retain your lordship and the rest of the Ministry at the head of affairs." Lord Melbourne left her presence, and then came the moment to write a letter of condolence to her dear aunt Queen Adelaide, who had always been so kind to her. This was scarcely finished, when the Duke of Sussex, her uncle, arrived, and would have knelt before the new Queen, but she would not allow it and, putting her arms round him, kissed him warmly. Then came the great, the venerable Duke of Wellington, and all were so respectful, so kind to her; she was no longer the little Princess Drina, she was Alexandrina Victoria, Queen of England.

But the excitements of that busy day were not yet over. At 11 o'clock, Lord Melbourne reappeared, and sought a fresh audience of his sovereign, and at half past eleven came the greatest moment of that most sad yet wonderful day: the Privy Council, hastily assembled, waited for the presence of their Queen. Her uncles the Dukes of Cumberland and Sussex, elderly ministers of state, grave bishops and generals, all were waiting: then, as Mr Strachey[1] wrote: they "saw the doors thrown open and a very short, very slim girl in deep

[1] *Queen Victoria*, p. 44.

plain mourning come into the room alone and move forward to her seat with extraordinary dignity and grace". Being seated, she read a speech that had been carefully prepared by Lord Melbourne. She spoke of "this awful responsibility imposed on me so suddenly and at so early a period of my life"; she said that she had been "educated in England under the tender and enlightened care of a most affectionate mother; she had learned from her infancy to respect and love the constitution of her native country."

She not only filled her chair, said the Duke of Wellington, a few hours after the Council, she filled the room; and not only the Duke, but all who were present, Sir Robert Peel, Lord Melbourne, even bad-tempered Mr Croker and cross, grumbling Mr Greville, were overcome with astonishment at the perfection of the queenly manner. The lovely bird-like youthful voice read the speech aloud, and then, to quote Mr Strachey once more, "they saw a small figure rise and, with the same consummate grace, the same amazing dignity, pass out from among them, as she had come in, alone."[1]

Her Majesty crossed the anteroom leading from the Council Chamber, and found that most affectionate mother, under whose tender and enlightened care she had been educated in England, waiting for her daughter. At last, thought the Duchess, swelling with pride, the triumph, the power for which she had waited during those eighteen weary years of battles and of making two ends meet, were within her grasp. Her daughter entered the room and paused: "And now, Mama," inquired her dutiful child, "am I really and truly Queen?" "You see, my dear, that this is so," replied the eager woman. "Then, dear Mama, I hope you will grant me the first request I make to you, as Queen. Let me be by myself for an hour."

As her daughter spoke, a slight shadow fell over the Duchess's heart, a little feeling of chilliness in spite of the

[1] *Queen Victoria*, p. 44.

heat of the June day. What had happened to the child, that she should insist on her position as Queen to her own mother?—say that she must be alone, she who had never known what solitude meant, even for half an hour.... The Queen smiled at her mother, she walked through the door, and when she reappeared at the end of an hour it was to order that her bed should be removed from her mother's room.

When the Duchess heard the order, her plump, rather inexpressive hands sank into her lap apathetically, her feathers, her silks no longer flew like banners on a wind of hope. It was for this, then, that she had laboured for eighteen years, for this that she had dedicated her life to the moulding of her daughter's character. She had hoped, she had intended to be virtual ruler of England; it was because of this hope that her daughter had been educated with such rigidity, watched over with so much care.

With disillusioned eyes, the Duchess looked at a vision of the future. That she would be treated with all the respect due to the mother of the Sovereign, she knew—she would have nothing to complain of on that score; but she knew, too, that a door had been shut, and would never more be re-opened.

So much the Duchess foresaw, as she passed a handkerchief over her trembling mouth. "Il n'y a pas d'avenir pour moi," she told Madame de Lieven, "je ne suis pour rien." Her forebodings were justified. She who had given eighteen years of her life to her child—"mon amour, mes délices"—scolding for the child's good, nudging and snatching, was now to be relegated to a position far from the child's life. Lehzen, quiet respectful Lehzen, had the confidence of the Queen of England, Lehzen was told everything. And when, a short time afterwards, the household of the Queen was removed to Buckingham Palace, the mother of the Queen was given a suite far removed from that of her daughter, whilst Lehzen occupied the bedroom next to that of the Queen.

VICTORIA MARY LOUISE, DUCHESS OF KENT

From an engraving after the painting by F. Winterhalter, 1849

British Museum

TWO DAYS IN JUNE

Upstairs, the child in question was scratching away in her diary: "Since it has pleased Providence", she wrote, "to place me in this station, I shall do my utmost to fulfil my duty towards my country. I am very young, and perhaps in many, though not in all things inexperienced, but I am sure that very few have more real good will and more real desire to do what is fit and right than I have."[1]

Late that night, as she lay in her narrow little bed, in a room far removed from that of Mama, looking at the moonlight as it shone through the curtains, she heard the distant sound of music, or could it be only her imagination?...How strange it sounded, as it spoke of many things! Romance—love—the greatness of her country. Now it sounded still farther away, and seemed only the sound of the faint summer wind in the trees.

The next day, there was a new life from the moment she awoke till the moment, very late at night, when she blew out her candle. She must drive in state to St James's Palace to attend the proclamation of her accession to the throne, in the morning of the glittering June day. Standing at the open window of the Privy Council Chamber, between Lord Melbourne and Lord Lansdowne, she looked across the courtyard at a sea of faces whilst the heralds spoke their announcement, and the immense crowd of her subjects, touched by the sight of this youthful and gentle-looking little creature, cheered and waved their handkerchiefs. "At the sound of the first shouts, the colour faded from the Queen's cheeks", wrote Lord Albemarle, the Master of the Horse, "and her eyes filled with tears. The emotion thus called forth imparted an additional charm to the winning courtesy with which the girl-Sovereign accepted the proffered homage." And perhaps the old gentleman's thoughts went back to a lovely day in May, eight years before, when

[1] *The Girlhood of Queen Victoria*, Volume I, pp. 195–6. Strachey, *op. cit.*, p. 43.

looking through a sweet-briar hedge he had seen a little girl in a darned muslin frock watering a little garden of her own, in which grew sweet-williams, dark velvety pansies, mustard and cress, and pink-cheeked radishes.

The proclamation had been made, and Her Majesty, returning into the shadow of the room, granted an audience to the Lord Chancellor; and the Commander-in-Chief; then, at noon, she held her second Council—this time at St James's Palace—and later in the day the proclamation was repeated at Trafalgar Square, Temple Bar, and the Royal Exchange.

The summer day seemed too short for all the excitements, all the events that must take place, and the Duchess of Kent's tightened mouth, her reddened eyelids, dusted over carefully with powder, her sudden gestures of reproof checked almost before they were born, passed unnoticed. Victoria was Queen of England, and, as Mr Strachey says, "Among the outside public there was a great wave of enthusiasm. Sentiment and romance were coming into fashion; and the spectacle of the little girl-queen, innocent, modest, with fair hair and pink cheeks, driving through her capital, filled the hearts of the beholders with raptures of affectionate loyalty."[1]

"We have had glorious female reigns", said Lord John Russell, the Home Secretary in Lord Melbourne's government, shortly after this time: "those of Elizabeth and Anne led us to great victories. Let us now hope that we are going to have a female reign illustrious in its deeds of peace—an Elizabeth without her tyranny, an Anne without her weakness. By the total abolition of slavery," he added, "by a more enlightened method of punishing crime, and by the improved education of the people, the reign of Victoria might prove celebrated among the nations of the earth and to our posterity."[2]

[1] Strachey, *op. cit.*, pp. 45–6.
[2] *The Life of Lord John Russell*, by Sir Spencer Walpole, Volume 1, p. 284. Lee, *op. cit.*, p. 55.

Soon the name Victoria was to be the symbol of all that was good and beautiful. When a light carriage was invented, soon after the Queen's accession to the throne, it was named after her; a great water-lily, which was brought to England from Guiana in 1838, blooming for the first time in 1849, when Her Majesty was presented with the faultlessly shaped and glamorous flower, was given the name of Victoria Regina. But most wonderful of all, the terminus of the London, Chatham, and Dover, and London, Brighton, and South Coast Railways was honoured with her name in the year 1846.

Chapter VI

EARLY DAYS

With the accession to the throne of the child of the Duke of Kent—that strange epitome of the faults and virtues embodied in the century which was past, that foreshadowing of the century which, during his lifetime, had only begun—a new age (which had, it is true, been preparing for almost eighty years past) sprang into being —an era of the middle class and of middle-class virtues and vices, an age of capitalism and of commercial values, a world inhabited by machinery, engines supplanting horses, spinning-jennies supplanting men. This, indeed, was to be the age of the industrial era which, according to Friedrich Engels, was of the same importance for England as had been the political revolution for France, the philosophical revolution for Germany. "The Reform Bill of 1831", wrote the same authority, in *The Conditions of the Working Class in England in 1844*, "had been the victory of the capitalist class over the landed aristocracy," and the reign of Victoria was to see the complete triumph of the capitalist class and its ideals, mingled, strangely enough, with exaggerated ideals of personal virtue, exalting domestic misery, of no matter how degraded a character, as long as that misery and degradation could be supposed to be the result of a sense of duty.

EARLY DAYS

With the invention of steamboats, with the forming of canals and the building of railways, began the industrial age, already foreshadowed seventy-eight years ago, when the first grand canal in England—that reaching from Manchester and the coal-mines of the district to the mouth of the Mersey —was constructed by James Brindle. Then the steamboat (this new invention had appeared first on the Hudson River in 1807) was launched in Britain, on the Clyde, in 1811. Finally, the first great railway, that which ran from Liverpool to Manchester, was opened in 1830.

It was not, actually, until the revival of trade after the crisis of 1847 that the industrial epoch was in full flower.[1] Then, after the repeal of the corn laws and the subsequent financial reforms, there was a great growth of commerce. The Californian and Australian gold-fields were discovered; the Colonial markets were developed with extraordinary rapidity, and consequently English manufactured goods were absorbed. In India, millions of hand-weavers were crushed out by the Lancashire power-loom. China was opened up. But, above all, the spinning-jenny, and the new means of communication introduced at the close of the preceding period, the railways and ocean steamers, were now worked out on an international scale.

The great and glorious industrial revolution had begun; and each ragged and hungry scarecrow, who stood for fourteen or sixteen hours a day, or sometimes for as long as from thirty-six to forty hours at a stretch, in a dingy hell of steam and fetid odours for the sum of one penny an hour, each huddled bundle of rags and bones that stalked through the slums without even the blessing of that meaningless toil (since machines had replaced, to a great extent, the labour of men), must bless these great inventions.

[1] See Engels: *The Condition of the Working Class in England in 1844*, translated by Florence Kelley Wischnewedzky (George Allen and Unwin, Ltd.).

But these were early days. Twelve years before the accession of the young Queen had seen the earliest appearance in Parliament of the great Railway Movement, and old Mr Creevey had been appointed a member of the committee to deal with the bill of the Liverpool and Manchester Railway Company. On this occasion, he found that his friends, Lord Derby and Lord Sefton, "like most territorial magnates, reviewed the designs of the railway engineers with the utmost apprehension and abhorrence". "I have come to the conclusion", he told Mr Ord, on March the 16th 1828, "that Ferguson is insane. He quite foamed at the mouth with rage in our Railway Committee in support of this infernal nuisance—the loco-motive monster, carrying eighty tons of goods, and navigated by a tail of smoke and sulphur, coming thro' every man's grounds between Manchester and Liverpool. He was supported by Scotchmen only, except a son of Sir Robert Peel's, and against every landed gentleman of the country, his own particular friends, who were all present, such as Lord Stanley, Lord Sefton, Lord George Cavendish, etc." It is pleasant to know that on June the 1st Mr Creevey was able to announce that "this devil of a railway is strangled at last".

Nine years after this time, however, a certain difference had taken place in the attitude of even such men of the world as Mr Greville, who was unable to resist succumbing to the excitement of travelling in this strange newfangled invention. "Tired of doing nothing," he wrote on July the 18th, "and of hearing about the Queen and the elections, I resolved to vary the scene and run down here to see the Birmingham railroad, Liverpool, and the Liverpool races. So I started out at 5 o'clock on Sunday evening, got to Birmingham at 5.30 on Monday morning, and got upon the railroad at 7.30. Nothing can be more comfortable than the vehicle in which I was put, a sort of chariot with two places, and there is nothing disagreeable about it but the sudden whiff of stinking air which it is impossible to exclude altogether. The first sensation is a slight degree of nervousness and a feeling of being run away with, but a sense of security soon supervenes, and the velocity is delightful. Town after town, one park and château after another, are left behind with the rapid variety of a moving panorama, and the continual bustle and animation of the changes and stoppages make the journey very entertaining. The train was very long, and heads were continually popping out of the several carriages attracted by well-known voices, and then came the greetings and exclamations of surprise, the 'Where are you going?' and 'How on earth came you here?' Considering the novelty of the establishment, there is very little embarrassment, and it certainly renders all other travelling irksome and tedious in comparison. It was peculiarly gay at this time, because there was so much going on."

Soon after this time, however, Mr Greville was to be involved in a moving panorama of quite a different kind, and one which he found by no means gay or agreeable. The panorama in question was that of her eighteen-year-old Majesty's Court at Windsor, where Mr Greville, clerk of the Privy Council, was a visitor. There was no room, it seems, in which the guests might assemble, where they could sit or lounge, remain silent or talk as they pleased and to whom they pleased. It was true that a billiard-table existed, but this was in such a distant and inaccessible part of the Castle that it was never discovered by a guest. Then again, there was a large library, and this was crowded with books, but no human being was ever to be found there excepting the librarian, the lighting was bad, and the room seemed to have none of the furniture of one that had ever been inhabited. There were two breakfast-rooms, one for the ladies of the Court and the guests, the other for the equerries, but these again were uncomfortable. In short, Windsor Castle was a wilderness of ennui, and comfortless ennui at that. It must be admitted that there was a certain relaxation of etiquette until it was time for luncheon and Her Majesty appeared (she breakfasted in her room, and transacted business throughout the morning), but after luncheon there was a long ride to be gone through, with the young Queen leading the procession, Lord Melbourne invariably riding beside her, and then, on the return of the cavalcade, Her Majesty would play the piano or the harp, sing, play battledore and shuttlecock, romp with children. It was all very tiresome, very boring for a middle-aged man of the world who was used to the conversation of Mr Macaulay, the brilliance of the society at Holland House. And then there were the evenings to be gone through, the interminable hours after dinner—for the gentlemen were not permitted to sit over their wine. Mr Greville sighed wearily. "When the company was reassembled in the drawing-room", says Mr Strachey, "the etiquette was stiff. For a few minutes the Queen spoke in turn to each one of her guests; and during these short uneasy colloquies the aridity of royalty was apt to become painfully evident.". . . On the night of his arrival, when Mr Greville's turn came, and "the middle-aged, hard-faced *viveur* was addressed by his young hostess:'Have you been riding today, Mr Greville?' asked the Queen. 'No, Madam, I have not,' replied Mr Greville. 'It was a fine day,' continued the Queen. 'Yes, Madam, a very fine day,' said Mr Greville. 'It was rather cold, though,' said the Queen. 'It *was* rather cold, Madam,' said Mr Greville. 'Your sister, Lady Frances Egerton, rides, I think, doesn't she?' said the Queen. 'She does ride sometimes, Madam,' said Mr Greville. There was a pause, after which Mr Greville ventured to take the lead, though he did not venture to change the subject. 'Has Your Majesty been riding today?' asked Mr Greville. 'Oh yes, a very long ride,' answered the Queen with animation. 'Has Your Majesty got a nice horse?' said Mr Greville. 'Oh, a very nice horse,' said the Queen. It was over. Her Majesty gave a smile and an inclination of the head, Mr Greville a profound bow, and the next conversation began with the next gentleman."[1]

Soon, reflected Her Majesty, these tiresome duties would be over, and she would be free to chatter to Lord Melbourne, and to elicit his opinions on all kinds of interesting subjects. And what a happy day it had been—full of excitements. That long gallop in the sparkling cold weather, with Lord Melbourne by her side—that wonderful two hours she had spent with her dearest, most lovely Cousin Victoire, showing her all the wonders of her house, her own house—oh yes, down to the very kitchens. How wonderful it was to have a household of one's own—kitchens, stillrooms, billiard-rooms, breakfast-rooms, libraries.

The days were too short for all the happiness they must contain; though there had been sorrow, too. There was, for instance, that sad day in April 1838, when the Queen was told that good old Mrs Louis, Princess Charlotte's devoted attendant, and one of the Queen's earliest friends, had died. She had written in her diary: "I felt very unhappy at dinner, in spite of my being gay when I spoke, and I could have cried almost at every moment; so much so, that when I got into bed, my nerves (which had been more shaken by the loss of *dearest* Louis than I can express, and by the struggle when in company to overcome *grief* which I felt so acutely) could resist no longer, and more than half-an-hour elapsed, in tears, before I fell asleep, and before I was asleep I saw her, in my imagination, before me, dressed in her neat white morning gown, setting out her breakfast in her room at Claremont, again, standing in my room of an evening, dressed in her best, holding herself so erect, as she always did, and making the low dignified curtsey so peculiar to herself; and lastly on her death-bed, pale and emaciated, but the expression the same, and the mind vigorous and firm as ever! These were

[1] Strachey, *op. cit.*, pp. 61–2. Greville, March 11, 1838 (unpublished).

the images I beheld as I lay in bed! Yet, mingled with my grief, were feelings of thankfulness that her end was so peaceful—so happy!"

The Queen could never think of her faithful old friend without a pang at her heart; but Mr Greville, as he encountered the equine conversation I have just chronicled, could not be blamed for not seeing into the real nature of this young creature, with her curious inability to express her thoughts.

She stopped before the next gentleman.

Then, when each gentleman in turn had undergone this experience, the Duchess of Kent sat down to her whist, the Queen looked at drawings in a portfolio and chattered to Lord Melbourne, who invariably sat beside her, and the rest of the company amused themselves as best they could—being rewarded with a haughty glare from Her Majesty's eyes if they relaxed from the slightest rule of etiquette—and so the long hours passed till half past eleven struck, and Her Majesty retired to bed.[1]

The Duchess of Kent enjoyed her whist with nearly her usual gusto, but there was yet a vaguely forlorn expression on her face as she looked at her daughter; and Sir John Conroy, her major-domo, though he still remained in that post, was not a visitor at Windsor. For on her accession to the throne, the Queen, with her innate generosity and justice, rewarded Sir John for his services to her mother with a baronetcy and a pension of £3000 a year; but she could not overcome her dislike of him, and she made it clear that these rewards marked the end of any personal relations with him. The hour of Lehzen's triumph had come, and Sir John Conroy's discomfiture was but another sign of this. "The person she" (the Queen) "loves best in the world", wrote Mr Greville, "is the Baroness Lehzen, and Lehzen and Conroy were enemies. There was formerly a Baroness Spaeth

[1] See Strachey, *op. cit.*, p. 62.

at Kensington, lady-in-waiting to the Duchess, and Lehzen and Spaeth were intimate friends. Conroy quarrelled with the latter and got her dismissed, and this Lehzen never forgave. She may have instilled into the Princess a dislike and bad opinion of Conroy, and the evidence of these sentiments, which probably escaped neither the Duchess nor him, may have influenced their conduct towards her, for strange as it is, there is good reason to believe that she thinks she has been ill-used by them both for some years past. Her manner to the Duchess is, however, irreproachable, and they appear to be on cordial and affectionate terms. Madame de Lehzen is the only person who is constantly with her" (the Queen). Her Majesty, it seemed as well, "never gives an immediate answer to applications. At first it was thought that this was because she wanted to consult Lord Melbourne, but he says this is her habit with him. The person consulted, therefore, is Lehzen."

It was the hour of Lehzen's triumph. The floods of caraway seeds, of conversation, became more copious; the watchfulness grew sharper, was less disguised. Lord Melbourne, that odd, rather eccentric, but urbane and experienced man of the world, recognized her influence, and set out to win her confidence and liking. He teased her flatteringly, until she relaxed a little from her natural stiffness. Her volubility never cast even a shadow of boredom over his frank countenance. He complimented her in a discreet manner. The Baroness pursed her lips, but secretly she was charmed, a faint flowering appeared in her cheeks, her gestures, though they could scarcely be called free, became less restricted, and a certain mature opulence of shoulders was no longer concealed.

Lord Melbourne, that odd, personally charming, whimsical, benighted and heartless, yet sentimental man—heartless because he feared his own sentimentality; sentimental because he knew his heart was dead, or, perhaps, had never been born—this mixture of contradictions soon won the little eighteen-year-old Queen's heart and confidence. Even dear precious Lehzen was, if not forgotten, at least not remembered when Her Majesty sat down to write her diary. The kindly, almost unpleasantly tolerant husband of Lady Caroline Lamb (whose lover, Lord Byron, found a confidante in the betrayed husband's own mother), the man who, whilst his wife was making public scenes and open declarations of her intrigue with Lord Byron, spent his time in making gentle jokes, turning over the pages of the Bible in an idle manner, reading Dr Lardner's *Observations upon the Jewish Errors with respect to the Conversion of Mary Magdalene*, the man who had said "You'd better try to do no good, and then you'll get into no scrapes," the co-respondent in the unsuccessful divorce cases brought by their husbands against Mrs Norton and Lady Brandon, the Prime Minister who, when receiving the delegates of the Society for the Abolition of Capital Punishment, disconcerted them by becoming suddenly absorbed in blowing a feather,[1] and who interrupted them with silly joke after silly joke, although he had spent the night before in studying the details of their case, the heartless condemner of the martyrs of Tolpuddle—this strange mixture no longer sprawled on sofas; he did not swear, his anecdotes became almost episcopal in their propriety. And all because of an enchanting little homely creature, of whom old Mr Creevey, seeing her when she was on a fleeting visit to Brighton, had said[2] "A more homely little being you never beheld, *when she is at her ease*, and she is evidently dying to be always more so. She laughs in real earnest, opening her mouth as wide as it can go, showing not very pretty gums. She eats quite as heartily as she laughs, I think I may say she gobbles.... She blushes and laughs every instant in so natural a way as to disarm anybody."

[1] See Strachey, *op. cit.*, p. 55.
[2] *The Creevey Papers*, Volume II, p. 326. Strachey, *op. cit.*, p. 58.

EARLY DAYS

This innocent little schoolgirl, who was to become one of the greatest of our sovereigns, looked up at him with large, blue, rather protruding eyes, drank in his every sentence, recorded the least look, the least gesture and remark, in her diary. This indeed, for some time, was full, to the exclusion of all else, of the sayings and doings of Lord M....Lord M. sitting beside her every evening after dinner....Lord M.'s opinion of books and plays, his knowledge of history, his wit—speaking of red-legged partridges, he had said to Lady Normanby, "Haven't you any of those red-legged fellows in Italy? I don't mean Cardinals," which made the Queen laugh very much and show her gums. Lord M. admiring the Queen's tight sleeves (Mama might frown at the compliment if she liked, but she could do nothing about the matter), and being pleased that she had discarded her curls, and that her lovely cousin Victoire, who would soon become the Duchesse de Nemours, and who was the friend of her heart, had discarded *her* curls, because they had a wicked look. Lord M. saying that girls who wore blue never got married—he could not *bear* blue—Lord M. riding through the dim blue January weather in a green coat, and asking the Queen if she thought it was a bad colour, to which she replied "Quite on the contrary", but she had never seen Lord M. wearing that colour before....Lord M. sitting for an equestrian portrait, and looking *so* funny as he bestraddled a plaster horse, without a head, wielding an umbrella instead of a sword. Lord M. made the Queen laugh very much with his opinions about public education: "The latter he don't like, and when I asked him if he did, he said 'I daren't say it in these times that I'm against it, but I *am* against it....The English would not submit to such thraldom,' and he went on to say that 'people of great genius were educated by circumstances', and that 'the education of circumstances was the best'." The Queen asked him if he didn't think Miss Murray's asylum for poor criminal children very good; but

[89]

he shook his head and said he doubted it. The Queen ventured to say "they would else commit every atrocity and wickedness"; but her minister replied "And they will yet, you'll see" (in which case they would be promptly dealt with; for, only two years before this time, we read in the *Observer* of March 15th 1835, "three prisoners under the age of fourteen were sentenced to death at the Old Bailey for burglary"). Then, as for child-labour, Lord M. said, apropos of children working for fourteen hours a day in factories, "Oh, if you'd only have the goodness to leave them alone." Yet this strange character had befriended Godwin, and, whilst telling Owen, genially, that he was one of the most foolish men he had ever met, saw no reason why "a gentleman should be prevented from entering his Sovereign's presence by reason of any opinions he happened to hold", and therefore presented the Duke of Kent's old acquaintance to what the *Quarterly Review* called "the unsuspecting innocence of a virgin Queen". Lord M.'s face wore often a smile half cynical, half tolerant; and how charming, how whimsical was that smile when he defended the Butcher of Cumberland in conversation with his sovereign. The Duke, it seems, was not cruel at all, or at least "only to a few rebels". For though tears were, according to the Queen, constantly springing to Lord M.'s eyes at appropriate moments, there were times when those eyes were tearless. "After the Agricultural Riots of 1830, Melbourne" (wrote Professor G. M. Trevelyan) "was allowed to stain the reputation of the Whigs by cruelties which History, now that she knows the facts, can pardon as little as Peterloo." There should, he decided, be a new Bloody Assize. This was no time for the government to show weakness. The death-sentences, therefore, were horribly numerous, but many of the men thus sentenced were transported instead, to a living hell ruled over by devils whose final blasphemy was that they called themselves Christians. The men who were actually sentenced to transportation, leaving aside those who were reprieved from a more merciful death, numbered between four and five hundred, and the anguish of the parting between them and their wives and children, their parents, their sisters, their brothers, blackens our History to this hour. Never again would the fate of these slaves of a damnable system be known to those who loved them, and never would they, flogged to the bone, kicked, starved, brutalized, robbed of their humanity, know what had happened to those they loved and from whom they had been torn: if they lived, if they died, or to what depths of starvation, misery, and utter destitution they had fallen.

Nor was this Lord Melbourne's only crime. Three years before the Queen's accession to the throne, six farm-labourers of the village of Tolpuddle in Dorsetshire, humble peasant saints of a beautiful and blameless life, George and James Loveless, Thomas Standfield and his son John, James Hammett and James Brine, had been arrested and committed for trial for the crime of "holding combinations of a dangerous and alarming character". These combinations were actually the result of Owen's theories, and, in the case of the men of Tolpuddle, were perfectly peaceable, for these labourers had only met together to discuss their intention of asking their employers to increase their weekly wage from seven to eight or nine shillings a week. But dear whimsical Lord Melbourne at once appointed a new judge, and we are told by Mr Owen Rattenbury, in his book *Flame of Freedom*, that it was decided that a new Dorchester Assize was to be held which should be a fitting sequel to some of the worst experiences of the West Country under Judge Jeffreys. Therefore Baron Williams, the judge who was appointed, was told that he was expected to find these men guilty and to sentence them to as severe a sentence as possible, so that their exemplary punishment might strike terror into the hearts of other trade-unionists in other parts of the country.

It may not be out of place, at this point, to follow the fate of these men, since they are amongst the noblest martyrs of our race. In answer to the Judge at the assize, one of the Loveless brothers replied: "We have injured no man's reputation, character, person or property; we were uniting to preserve ourselves, our wives and children from utter degradation and starvation."[1] Yet these saints of the people, these apostles of Christian love, were each condemned to seven years' transportation. George Loveless, as he was sentenced, wrote these words on a scrap of paper, and tried to throw it to the crowd, but was prevented from doing so by his handcuffs:

> *God is our guide! From field, from wave,*
> *From plough, from anvil, and from loom,*
> *We come, our country's rights to crave,*
> *And speak a tyrant's functions down;*
> *We raise the watchword Liberty!*
> *We will, we will, we will be free!*
>
> *God is our guide! No swords we draw,*
> *We kindle not war's battle fires,*
> *By reason, union, justice, law,*
> *We claim the birthright of our sires;*
> *We raise the watchword Liberty!*
> *We will, we will, we will be free!*[2]

There was a great agitation against this monstrous sentence, but Mr Greville, who was full of admiration for Lord Melbourne's behaviour, noted that he had, very sensibly, caused the men to be transported and out of sight before anything could be done about it.

They were transported to the penal settlements on May the 25th 1834, and in the hot and fetid hell, where they were

[1] *Flame of Freedom*, by Owen Rattenbury, J.P. (The Epworth Press).
[2] Rattenbury, *op. cit.*

confined in the ship, the berths measured five feet six inches for every six men, so that not one of these bundles of rags and bones enclosing a starved and aching soul could stretch himself to his full length, or lie at ease. On their arrival, they worked in chains. Some of their companions, if they turned faint under the heat of the sun, were beaten so horribly that "the flesh folded over in rolls, leaving the bare spot with no covering of either skin or shirt". After one man had been flogged (I quote from Mr Rattenbury[1]) "the man who had had these heavy strokes doggedly worked on, and Loveless like the others was much troubled by the flies buzzing round. He saw that it was the raw flesh that had attracted them, and one or two of them settled on this man. One of them laid its eggs in the wound and flew away. Loveless was near it and saw it and then forgot about it, until he saw the wound swelling one day." On seeing that this lost soul was about to faint, the overseer "lashed out with his whip again, and caught the open wound. This time, hardened as the man had been, he cried out with the pain of it, and then sank down on the road in a swoon. They unchained him and turned him over to examine the wound, and saw the opening-up which the lash had caused, and the maggots crawling about in the wound. It was a hospital case, and what happened to the man Loveless never knew."

Perhaps the Victorian age was right in its belief in an inexorable and eternal hell; there are moments, indeed, when, in spite of all my pity for suffering, I can find it in my heart to believe in it—but not for the starving creature, who has stolen that he may eat and be warm—not for the poor fallible being of flesh and blood who has fallen into temptation. I think, if it exists, it was built for the righteous creators of such an earthly hell as Botany Bay. There are times when I see dear, good, kind whimsical Lord M. wearing a devil's mask, and bearing a devil's grin.

[1] *Op. cit.*

When, as the result of agitations in England, that noble man George Loveless, respited with his companions from this iniquitous sentence, returned to England in 1836, he wrote:

"I can assure my Lord Stanley, who boasted a few years ago that he would make transportation worse than death, that his wicked and diabolical purpose is more than accomplished; for it would be doing such unfortunate men a kindness, a favour; it would be granting them an unspeakable privilege to hang them in England, and so prevent exposure to cruelties, miseries, and wretchedness connected with the present system of transportation.

"But I have been told that it is done for the good of Society and to uphold our most holy religion. Good God! What hypocrisy, and deceit is here manifested! The most cruel, the most unjust, the most atrocious deeds are committed and carried out under the cloak of religion! If I had not learned what religion meant, such practices would make me detest and abhor the very name.

"And yet, strange as it may appear, those hypocrites, who pretend to be so scrupulous, that rather than submit to have their most holy religion endangered, they would starve hard-working honest husbands and fathers, and who have solemnly pronounced 'What God hath joined together let no man put asunder,' are some of the first to separate man and wife, to send some to banishment and others to the Poor Law prisons; to oppress the fatherless and the widow. From all such religion as this good Lord deliver us!....

"Although I was sent out of the country and have been subjected to privations, to distress and wretchedness, transportation has not had the intended effect upon me, for after all, I am returned from my bondage with my views and principles strengthened. It is indelibly fixed in my mind that labour is ill-rewarded in consequence of the few tyrannizing over the millions; and that, through their oppression, thousands are now working in chains on the roads, abused by the overseers, sentenced by the commitants, and punished by flagellation; young and strong men, now emaciated and worn almost to skeletons. Is this the plan to reform men? I say, no; if they were bad before, they are tenfold more the children of Hell now!

"It has a tendency to harden the heart, stultify their feelings, make them careless and regardless of consequences, and they rush forward, plunging headlong into an abyss from which they are not able to extricate themselves. The groans and cries of the labourers ere long will bring down vengeance on the heads of those who have been, and are still, the authors of so much misery. I believe that nothing will ever be done to relieve the distress of the working classes unless they take it into their own hands; with these beliefs I left England, and with these views I am returned. Notwithstanding all that I have seen and felt, my sentiments on the subject are unchanged.

"Nothing but union can ever accomplish the great and important object: namely, the salvation of the world. Let the producers of wealth firmly and peaceably unite their energies, and what can withstand them? The power and influence of the non-producers would sink into insignificance, the conquest is won, the victory is certain."

It was the will of such men as these that dear whimsical Lord Melbourne tried to break by his cruelty. But no doubt he had forgotten both them and the hell to which he had condemned them, as he lounged against the mantelpiece in a room at Windsor Castle: for, according to him, "the Government's whole duty was to prevent crime and to preserve contracts". And really life was very pleasant! The Queen was delighted with him, with his anecdotes, and with his letters when he was absent. *How* interesting were these, though sometimes they contained alarming and sad news, such as that of the 6th January 1839: "Your Majesty will have seen Lord Norbury was shot at in his own grounds and dangerously wounded. He is since dead. This is a shocking event, and will, of course, create a strong sensation, much stronger than the death in the same manner of several persons of inferior degree."

Chapter VII

THE YOUNG QUEEN

"Thursday, June the 28th, 1838....I was awoke at 4 o'clock by the guns in the Park, and could not get much sleep afterwards on account of the noise of the people, bands, etc....Got up at 7. The Park presented a curious spectacle, with crowds of people up to Constitution Hill, soldiers, bands, etc."[1]

It was the day of the Queen's Coronation, and Her Majesty, jumping out of bed as if she were still a little girl, began to dress in state. All the ladies of her household were in readiness—the Duchess of Sutherland, her Mistress of the Robes, who was to become one of her dearest friends, Lady Lansdowne, the principal Lady of the Bedchamber, the other ladies of the bedchamber, Lady Tavistock, Lady Mulgrave, Lady Charlemont, Lady Portman, Lady Lyttelton, Lady Barham, and Lady Durham—with the bedchamber women, Lady Caroline Barrington, Lady Harriet Clive, Lady Copley, Lady Forbes, Mrs Brand, Lady Gardiner, Mrs Campbell, and the Resident Woman of the Bedchamber, Miss Davys. All seemed just as excited and as happy as the Queen herself; and downstairs the maids of honour, Miss Harriet Pitt, Miss Margaret Dillon, Miss Caroline Cocks, Miss Cavendish,

[1] Extract from Her Majesty's diary.

THE YOUNG QUEEN

Miss Matilda Paget, Miss Amelia Murray, Miss Harriet Lester, and Miss Mary Spring-Rice were chattering like birds.

When, at 9.30, the Queen went into the next room, she found her beloved sister Princess Feodore and her brother Prince Charles of Leiningen awaiting her, with her uncle the King of Hanover, his tall thin figure casting a strange cold black shadow on the bright sunlit carpet—a distorted shadow as of something not quite human.

Already the Procession had begun, and the cheers of the crowd, the sounds of the cannon, reverberated through the streets. The cheers grew to a roar as the great Duke of Wellington, the national hero, appeared, closely followed by his former adversary in the Spanish Peninsula and at Waterloo, Marshal Soult. Raikes, in his *Journal*,[1] says: "Soult was so much cheered, both in and out of the Abbey, that he was completely overcome. He has since publicly said 'C'est le plus beau jour de ma vie, il prouve que les anglais pensent que j'ai toujours fait la guerre en loyal homme.' When in the Abbey he seized the arm of his aide-de-camp, quite overpowered, and exclaimed, 'Ah! vraiment, c'est un brave peuple.'"

The huge procession with all the panoply of state, in all the splendour of the hot and brilliant June day, wound its way up Constitution Hill, down Piccadilly, through St James's Street, and across Trafalgar Square, amidst the lion-like roars of the crowds! The Queen, who had left Buckingham Palace in the state coach, accompanied by the Duchess of Sutherland and Lord Albemarle, reached the Abbey at 11.30 "amidst deafening cheers" as she noted in her diary, and went straight into the robing-room near the entrance, where she found her train-bearers, Lady Caroline Lennox, Lady Adelaide Paget, Lady Mary Talbot, Lady Fanny Cowper, Lady Wilhelmina Stanhope, Lady Anne Fitzwilliam, Lady

[1] Volume II, p. 107.

Mary Grimston, and Lady Louise Jenkinson, awaiting her, dressed in gowns of white satin and silver tissue, with wreaths of silver corn-ears on the front of their heads, and a small wreath of pink roses on the plait behind, whilst pink roses were strewn again, here and there on the dresses.

When the anthem began, the Queen retired to St Edward's Chapel, a small dark place immediately behind the altar, with her ladies and train-bearers, and there took off the robe and kirtle of crimson velvet, and the circlet of diamonds which she had worn in the procession, putting on, in their stead, a supertunica of cloth of gold, also in the shape of a kirtle, and over this "a singular sort of little gown of linen trimmed with lace". She then proceeded bare-headed into the Abbey.

As she entered, "with eight ladies all in white floating about her like a silvery cloud, she paused as if for breath, and clasped her hands",[1] then seated herself upon St Edward's Chair, where the dalmatic robe was clasped upon her by the Lord Chamberlain. Then came the moment for the Queen to receive the Crown, and for all the peers and peeresses to put on their coronets. As the Queen knelt for the Crown to be placed on her head, a ray of sunlight fell upon her, and the Duchess of Kent, overcome by the scene, overwrought by mingled emotions, burst into tears. The Queen's "excellent Lord Melbourne", too, was "completely overcome at this moment, and very much affected". The Queen added that the Enthronisation, and the Homage of the Bishops, followed by that of the Royal Dukes and then of the Peers, according to their rank, was very fine. One untoward incident, however, took place when Lord Rolle, who was nearly ninety years old and very feeble, fell down as he was getting up the steps of the Throne. Happily he was unhurt, but the Queen's first impulse was to rise, and afterwards, when he came again to do homage, she said "May I

[1] Prothero and Bradley's *Life of Dean Stanley*.

not get up and meet him?" and then rose from the Throne and advanced down one or two of the steps to prevent his coming up, an act of graciousness and kindness which made a great sensation. Among the spectators who were deeply touched at this incident was a young Member of Parliament, Mr Disraeli, whose brilliance was already beginning to be recognized, a young man of great beauty of an oriental cast, and extraordinary charm and personality. "Nothing could be more effective," he wrote afterwards. And he told his sister: "The Queen performed her part with great grace and completeness, which cannot in general be said of the other performers; they were always in doubt as to what came next, and you saw the want of rehearsal."

The Archbishop, for instance, was invariably at a loss; and the Queen noted that when he should have delivered the Orb to her, she had already got it, and he (as usual) was so confused and puzzled, and wandered away.

Before this incident, the Queen had made a descent from the Throne, leaning on Lord Melbourne's arm, and then entering St Edward's Chapel once more, with her ladies and train-bearers, she took off the dalmatic robe and the super-tunica, and put on, in their stead, a purple velvet kirtle, and mantle, after which she reascended the Throne. As she did so, she caught the eyes of another "dear Being" in the box immediately above the royal box, her dearly beloved Lehzen; they had, indeed, exchanged smiles when the Queen was on the Throne, and she and the dismissed, and now (I imagine, though I can find no actual record of it, save in this entry in the Queen's diary) reinstated Späth had seen the Queen leave the Palace, and arrive at the Abbey, had watched the ceremony, and would soon witness the Queen's departure from the Abbey and return to the Palace. The joy and ex-citement of the two friends, who had watched over the little Princess since she was five years old, petted her, scolded and loved her, quelled her impatience, reproved her temper, may be imagined.

The Queen once more descended the Throne, and followed by all the peers bearing the regalia, the ladies and train-bearers, walked to St Edward's Chapel; but, as Lord Melbourne said, "it was more unlike a Chapel than anything he had ever seen; for what was called an *Altar* was covered with sandwiches, bottles of wine, etc.... Lord Melbourne took a glass of wine, for he seemed completely tired." The little Queen had taken off her Crown, which was very heavy, but now she must replace it; and having done so, completely loaded, as she expressed it, with the regalia and her robes which almost weighed her down, she re-entered the Abbey, amidst wild cheering, and proceeding through it, went to the first robing-room, where the Duchess of Kent, deeply moved, and with the traces of tears still on her cheeks, the fidgety, crochety Duchess of Gloucester, quiet and amiable for once, and the Duchess of Cambridge were awaiting her, with their ladies. Here the Queen waited for at least an hour, part of which was spent in extricating her finger from the coronation ring which the Archbishop, in his flurry, had put on the wrong finger, and which hurt her considerably. Then at last, at half past four in the afternoon, with the Crown on her head and the Orb in her hand, she re-entered her carriage and was driven away, amidst even greater crowds than had witnessed her coming, and scenes of "enthusiasm, affection and loyalty which were really touching", as she wrote afterwards. The crowds were, indeed, moved by her youth, by her little childish figure, and by her look of pallor and tremulousness. Thomas Carlyle, who was one of the spectators, said "Poor little Queen! She is at an age at which a girl can hardly be trusted to choose a bonnet for herself; yet a task is laid upon her from which an archangel might shrink."

So she passed, amid the sea of faces, which to her tired eyes might indeed have been worlds or flowers or seas or stars, and at a little after six she was home again; and soon, when her splendid robes had been put away, she was giving Dash, her beloved spaniel, his evening bath, and laughing merrily and chattering to dear Lehzen and Späth, both of whom seemed very tired and on the point of tears, though they were just as voluble as ever. "Do you remember how naughty you were, that night at Claremont, when there was a great dinner-party and we could not find you anywhere—we looked for you in the nursery, we looked for you in the schoolroom, you were nowhere to be found, until old Mrs Louis[1] found you hiding downstairs in your little nightgown and dressing-gown, listening to the music?"... "Do you remember that day at Claremont when we, you and the Baroness and Princess Feodore and I, went picking cowslips, and there was a thunderstorm and our hands were so full of the cowslips we could not hold up an umbrella, and when we got home His Majesty said we looked like an Aviary after the Flood?"... "Do you remember?"....

At last it was time to dress for the quiet, family dinner-party, which was at 8 o'clock, and at which the Queen's uncles, her sister and brother, Späth and Lehzen, and all the Duke of Gloucester's gentlemen, as well as Lord Melbourne and Lord Surrey, were present. The Queen sat between her disagreeable uncle the King of Hanover, and Lord Melbourne, who had Princess Feodore on the other side of him. The Queen and Lord Melbourne chattered as usual, and talked to Prince Charles, and she told them the Crown hurt her a good deal. They talked of the young ladies' dresses, and Lord Melbourne thought that Lady Fanny Cowper did not make so much effect as the other girls—but this the Queen would not allow. Then Lord Melbourne said to her "You must be very tired," and added, with tears in his eyes, "and you did it beautifully—every part of it, with so much taste; it's a thing you can't give a person advice upon; it must be left to a

[1] The dresser of Princess Charlotte.

person." "To hear this", the Queen added, "from this kind and impartial friend, gave me great and real pleasure." Then the Duchess of York and Princess Feodore went on the balcony to see the illuminations, and the King of Hanover drove into the streets for the same purpose; and the little Queen, too, remained on her mama's balcony looking at the beautiful fireworks, until the night approached the dawn.

So the long, glorious, dreamlike day was over, and at last, in the Palace, the candles were extinguished.

All save one, which stood beside the bed of Baron Stockmar, who now, at the request of the King of the Belgians, had taken up his residence in the little Queen's household, in order to help her with his advice and his long experience—for was he not the King's shadow, his other self? and who could be a more fitting mentor, guide, and help, to the King's niece? If dear Uncle Leopold could not always be beside her, the Baron was undoubtedly the next-best person.

The Baron lay sleepless and staring past the light of the one candle. Why, on this night of all nights, should he remember that other radiant young girl, the gay and laughing creature who had been the bride of his greatest friend? Baron Stockmar had been a young doctor then, and attached to Prince Leopold's household; he had never been of a gay constitution, he suffered from melancholy and from indigestion, and from a variety of semi-imaginary diseases; but Princess Charlotte, though she was gay and always laughing, liked him at once and, as time went on, felt a hearty affection towards him. She romped with him—for she was more like a schoolboy than a girl—and chattered to him, in her loud ringing voice; she teased him, she called him Stocky. And he, glad to be part of such a happy household, wrote in his diary: "My master is the best of all husbands in all the five quarters of the globe; and his wife bears him an amount of love, the greatness of which can only be compared with the English national debt."[1]

It was at about this time that the foresight, the prudence, which were in after life to make young Doctor Stockmar so valuable an adviser, were shown. When, early in 1817, the Princess was expecting a child, and Doctor Stockmar was offered the post of one of her physicians-in-ordinary, he refused it, for he knew his English colleagues well enough to foresee that they would be jealous of a foreign doctor attending an English princess, that they would probably seize any opportunity not to follow his advice, and that, if anything went wrong, the blame would be placed on him.[2] It was not very long before he began to foresee that something was very likely to go wrong, for it was fashionable at the time to give women in this condition a low diet and frequent bleedings, and Stockmar saw that the Princess was looking ill, and utterly unlike herself. Taking the Prince on one side, he told him of his misgivings; but, when the other doctors heard this opinion, they paid no attention and continued the lowering treatment. At last, at 9 o'clock in the evening of November the 5th, after being in labour for over fifty hours, the unfortunate Princess was delivered of a dead boy. Then there was another terrible three hours in which the young mother, weakened by the treatment she had received, fought for life. It was in vain; and at midnight Stockmar was told that her last thread of strength had given way. He went into the dying girl's room, and found the doctors giving her wine; she put out her rough little hand and pressed his. "They have made me tipsy," she said, in a whisper that was very unlike her usual loud boyish voice. He was with her for a short time and then went into the next room, but he had hardly been there for a moment before he heard the loud voice to which he was accustomed call "Stocky, Stocky!" He rushed into her room, but even as he ran he heard the death-

---

[1] Strachey, *op. cit.*, p. 4.   [2] See Strachey, *op. cit.*, p. 4.

rattle—he saw her toss herself violently from side to side; then, with a sudden movement, she drew up her legs, and as she did so she died.[1]

Her husband, for the first time after all those terrible hours since the labour had begun, had gone to his room for a short rest; and now it fell to Stockmar to tell him his wife was dead. The Prince stared at him without any sign of understanding; here, then, was the dream into which he had really fallen when he was awakened by Stockmar's voice; it *was* a dream—for these things do not happen! Walking along the passages to his wife's room, suddenly he paused and sank down on a chair, while Stockmar knelt beside him. He stayed there for a moment, then, mechanically, rose again and walked into the dead girl's room. Falling beside her bed, he kissed her hands again and again.

When he rose, it was to throw himself into Stockmar's arms. "Now I am quite desolate," he said. "Promise never to leave me."[2]

Twenty-two years ago!...Why should Baron Stockmar think of it now, on this of all nights in the world? That little dead Princess would have been Queen now, if she had lived, and how different life would have been. Perhaps he and his dearest friend would not have stiffened into such a mould, they would have been less worldly, less cautious, less ambitious, if she had lived. For they were both changed— that he knew. Ageing men, ageing men!

But this, too, could be said: never was a man more faithfully served than was King Leopold by his friend. Leopold consulted Stockmar in all the moves, all the decisions of his life, and never was Stockmar at a loss. It was he who had advised the Prince to remain in England for the years that followed his wife's death; it was he who had smoothed over the difficulties resulting from the Prince first accepting, then refusing, the crown of Greece. It was owing to his

[1] See Strachey, *op. cit.*, p. 4.   [2] Strachey, *op. cit.*, p. 5.

[105]

advice that the Prince had, finally, decided to become the constitutional sovereign of Belgium. And, above all, it was owing to his unfailing tact, his diplomatic gifts, the respect in which his honesty was held, and his long and careful labours, that the neutrality of Belgium was guaranteed by the Great Powers.[1]

The next day, the Queen woke early, and her first thoughts were to write a note to Lord Rolle hoping that he had suffered no ill effects from his accident (she had, as well, inquired after him the evening before, on her return to the Palace), and to write a note to Lord Melbourne, inquiring if he had got home safely, and if he had slept well, and telling him how she herself had slept. Then all the excitements of the day began. The government had given permission for a Coronation Fair to be held for four days in Hyde Park; and the day after it was opened it was visited by the Queen. And, to conclude the festivities, Her Majesty held a review of five thousand men in Hyde Park on July the 9th, amidst enormous enthusiasm; and at this Marshal Soult, in whose honour the review was largely held, was once more acclaimed by the large crowds.

So the time passed, with business and gaiety, the prorogation of Parliament, and playing with Dash the spaniel. Neither the glowing summer days, nor the dark winter days and nights, seemed long enough for all the happiness, all the pleasure, they contained. Every day, every evening, there was some fresh experience, some new joy for the little Princess who had once worn a darned frock, and who now was the Queen of England.

[1] For the information in this paragraph I am indebted to Mr Strachey. See *Queen Victoria*, p. 49.

Chapter VIII

A BLACK CLOUD

But alas, in the midst of all the pleasure, in the midst of balls, and games of battledore and shuttlecock, a dark shadow overhung the Palace, a dark and menacing cloud, until, in that very same January, it spread over the whole sky.

For some time now, Lady Flora Hastings, the Duchess of Kent's lady-in-waiting, had presented a strange appearance. Her eyes were sunken and seemed filled with a haunting dread, her cheeks looked pinched as if by the cold, her manner was listless, and she crept humbly from room to room in the Palace as if she wished to hide. But, most strange of all, the shape of her body was changing, day by day. Lady Flora Hastings was devoted to, and loved by the Duchess of Kent, but there were other ladies with whom she was not so popular, and one of these ladies was dear, watchful Lehzen, who had not forgotten Lady Flora's sly jokes about the caraway seeds; another was Lady Tavistock, the Queen's Lady of the Bedchamber; these ladies put their heads together and whispered, and the more they whispered, the stronger became their certainty. Soon, the sound of this whispering could be heard all over the Palace, and it was remembered by everybody that a very short time before,

when the Duchess of Kent returned from Scotland, Lady
Flora had travelled in the same carriage with Sir John Conroy.
Under these circumstances, the ladies thought, Lady Flora's
appearance was only too easily explained: she was obviously
with child.

Lehzen held up her hands in horror, she pinched in her
lips until they almost disappeared altogether; but she was not
in the least surprised. There had always been something—
well—*peculiar* about Lady Flora...and she became more
voluble and more watchful than ever. Triumphant Lehzen,
contemplating from the height of her power her old enemy's
fall, and the relegation of the Duchess of Kent to a cupboard,
was insistent that the matter must not be allowed to rest.
Virtue was virtue, and her young ex-charge, sweet, innocent
girl-Queen, would be tarnished, oh yes, defiled, by being
brought into contact with such immorality as that of Lady
Flora.

At last Lady Tavistock took the extraordinary step of con-
sulting Lord Melbourne as to what should be done. Opinions
vary as to the part played by the Hero of Tolpuddle in the
affair—Mr Strachey believing that he merely allowed
matters to slide in his usual easy-going way, whilst other
authorities hold that it was he who suggested that the poor
lady should undergo the indignity of being examined by
Sir James Clark, who already, on his side, had been by no
means slow to voice his suspicions. It is hardly necessary to
say that by this time the sound of whispering had grown to
that of open talking, so loud, indeed, that at last it came to the
ears of the Queen. The Duchess of Kent, deeply wounded
already by the way in which she had been neatly packed
away in tissue paper, rushed to the support of her lady-in-
waiting—feathers flying in the wind, silks rustling gallantly
as in the good old days when she battled with King William.
But, in spite of all she could say, the examination—during
which Sir James, according to Lady Flora, behaved in a

brutally insulting manner though the other doctor present treated her with great politeness—took place; and, as a result, a certificate was signed by both the doctors establishing Lady Flora's complete innocence.

A few days later, we find this poor woman writing the following letter to her uncle:

"My dear Uncle,

"Knowing what a very good-natured place Brussels is, I have not a hope that you have not already heard a story with which I am told London is ringing; but you shall, at all events, have from my own pen the account of the diabolical conspiracy from which it has pleased God to preserve the Duchess of Kent and myself; for that it was intended to ruin the whole concern, though I was to be the first victim, I have no more doubt than, *that a certain foreign lady, whose hatred to the Duchess is no secret, pulled the strings,* though it has not been brought home to her yet. I told you I was ill when I came to town, having been suffering some time from bilious derangement, with its agreeable accompaniments, pain in the side and swelling of the stomach. I placed myself immediately under the care of Sir James Clark, who, being physician to the Duchess as well as to the Queen, was the natural person to consult. Unfortunately, he either did not pay much attention to my ailments, or did not quite understand them, for in spite of medicines, the bile did not take its departure. However, by dint of walking and porter I gained a little strength, and, as I did so, the swelling subsided in a very remarkable degree. You may guess, therefore, my indignant surprise when, about a fortnight since, Sir James Clark came into my room and announced to me the conviction of the Ladies of the Palace that I must be privately married or at least ought to be—a conviction into which I found him completely talked over. In answer to all his exhortations to 'confession' 'as the only means of saving my character', I returned, as you may believe, an indignant but steady denial that there was anything to confess. Upon which he told me that nothing but my submitting to medical examination would ever satisfy them, and remove the stigma from my name. I found the subject had been brought before the Queen's notice, and all this had been discussed, and arranged, and *denounced* to me without *one word* having been said to my own mistress, one suspicion hinted, or her sanction obtained for their proposing such a thing to me. From me Sir James went to the Duchess, and announced his conviction that I was in the family way, and was followed by Lady Portman, who conveyed a message from her Majesty to her mother to say that the Queen would not permit me to appear till the examination had decided matters. Lady Portman (who with, you will grieve to hear, Lady Tavistock, are those whose names are mentioned as most active against me) took the opportunity of distinctly expressing her conviction of my guilt. My beloved mistress, who never for one moment *doubted* me, told them she knew me and my principles, and my family, too well to listen to such a charge. However, the edict was given. The next day, having obtained the Duchess's very reluctant consent, for she could not bear the idea of my being exposed to such a humiliation (but I felt it right to her, and to my family and myself, that a point-blank refutation should be instantly given to the lie), I submitted myself to the most rigid examination, and I have the satisfaction of possessing a certificate, signed by my accuser, Sir James Clark, and also by Sir Charles Clarke, stating, as strongly as language can state it, that 'there are no grounds for believing pregnancy does exist, or ever has existed'. I wrote to my brother who, though suffering from influenza, came up instantly.

"It would be too long to detail all his proceedings, but nothing can be more manly, spirited, and judicious than his conduct. He exacted and obtained from Lord Melbourne a distinct disavowal of his participation in the plot, and would not leave town till he had obtained an audience of the Queen, at which, while disclaiming his belief of any wish on the part of her Majesty to injure me, he very plainly, but respectfully stated his opinion of those who had counselled her, and his resolution to find out the originator of the slander, and bring him or her to punishment. I am quite sure the Queen does not understand what they have betrayed her into. She has endeavoured to show her regret by her civility to me, and expressed it most handsomely with tears in her eyes. The Duchess was perfect. A mother could not have been kinder, and she took up the insult as a personal one, directed as it was at a person attached to her service, and devoted to her. She immediately dismissed Sir James Clark, and refused to see Lady Portman, and would neither re-appear, or suffer me to re-appear at the Queen's table for many days. She has crowned her goodness by a most beautiful letter she has written to poor Mama, whom the accounts, kept from her while there was a hope that matters might not become public, would reach to-day. I am told there is but one feeling as respects me—sympathy for the insult offered to one whose very name should be a protection to her, and that in many places the feeling is loudly expressed that public reparation should have been offered me by the dismissal of the slanderers. This does not, however, appear to be the view of the Ministers; and as personally I wish for no revenge on those who have insulted me, I cannot say I much regret it, though I doubt whether they are quite judicious as respects the general feeling. And poor Clark who has been the women's tool, can hardly be sacrificed alone. The Duchess has stood by me gallantly, and I love her better than ever. She is the most generous-souled woman possible, and such a heart! This business made her very ill. It shattered me, too, very much, and I am wretchedly thin; but, under Dr Chambers' good management, I am getting round, and hope soon to be well. Hastings says he has not done with the business, nor ever will while there is anything left to sift.

"Good-bye, my dear Uncle. I blush to send you so revolting a tale, but I wished you to know the truth, the whole truth, and nothing but the truth—and you are welcome to tell it right and left.

Your affectionate niece,
Flora Eliz. Hastings."[1]

Nor did the matter stop there. The indignant Lady Hastings, Lady Flora's mother, wrote to the Queen, also demanding that Sir James Clark should be dismissed. To this letter Her Majesty did not even reply. The Hero of Tolpuddle, however, wrote to Lady Hastings stating that the Queen had taken the first opportunity of personally acknowledging her regret to Lady Flora, and that it was not intended to take any other step.[2] But by this time the daily papers had taken up the affair, the *Morning Post*, the organ of the political party to which the Hastings family belonged, rushed into the fray, the scandal grew, and Lady Flora was claimed to be "the victim of a depraved Court".

Lady Hastings published all her correspondence with the Queen and with Lord Melbourne in the newspapers; Sir James Clark published, also in the papers, a defence of his own conduct, and the general indignation grew every day, spread from London to the provinces. But it was to grow still deeper when the end of the story was reached; for this poor slandered woman was dying of a terrible internal disease, enlargement of the liver; hence her changed figure, hence those humbled movements, the haunting dread in her eyes.

On July the 4th, it was known that she was dying at

[1] *Sober Truth*, by Osbert Sitwell and Margaret Barton (Gerald Duckworth and Co., Ltd.).
[2] See Lee, *op. cit.*, p. 94.

A BLACK CLOUD

Buckingham Palace, and the royal banquet which was to have taken place that evening was countermanded hastily. Once again the sound of whispering could be heard in the Palace, but the whispers were of a very different nature from those which had floated from room to room, down the corridors, into the servants' quarters, through the windows and away, far away, till they reached all the great houses of the town, were heard in the city, and were blown even to the distant provinces; now, once again, these very different whispers spread over the whole country.

On the next day Lady Flora Hastings died, and the entire nation was shocked; there were angry rumours against the Court on all sides, the masses were indignant that an innocent woman, and one who was soon to die, had been so slandered and had suffered such ill treatment; society in its narrower sense was shocked at the lack of delicacy and reticence that had been shown by the Court. And the anger was deepest towards the Queen and Lord Melbourne; indeed, of the glamour which surrounded the Queen, the affection felt by the whole people towards the young and innocent girl who had been called upon to reign over them, nothing remained. "Nobody cares for the Queen, her popularity is sunk to Zero, and loyalty is a dead letter," wrote Mr Greville; and that was in March, four months before Lady Flora died; and now the indignation felt had increased a hundredfold. So great, indeed, was the anger felt against her that, when she appeared at Ascot, the Duchess of Montrose and Lady Sarah Ingestre hissed her as she passed. But, shocking and painful as was the whole incident, the blame, I think, rests principally with Lord Melbourne. It is true that two, or three, malicious, self-righteous, and petty-minded women, eager for any excitement, had indulged in vulgar and cruel gossip; but of these women one had little worldly experience; whereas Lord Melbourne was an accomplished and experienced man of the world, and he should have understood the ugliness of these women's behaviour; he should, as well, have foreseen the effect it would have upon the minds of the people, and the light in which the Queen would be shown, once the scandal became known.

He foresaw nothing, but with his usual carelessness and laziness simply allowed matters to drift. It was, indeed, just another case of "Oh, if you'd only have the goodness to let them alone".

The Queen, on her side, was less to blame, because of her youth and the fact that she can never have had any experience of a case of the sort, and because of the influence exerted by Lehzen over her mind. She was probably over-persuaded, both by the Baroness and by Lady Tavistock, and, however strong her will, the warring factions in the Palace must have been difficult to control; but it would have shown more generosity and a greater spirit had she apologized publicly to the victim of these ladies' malignity, once her innocence became known; and, in any case, her behaviour with regard to Sir James Clark is difficult to understand. Mr Strachey cites an unpublished writing of Greville, dated August 15 1839, which tells us that "the Duke of Wellington, upon whom it was customary to fall back, in cases of great difficulty in high places, had been consulted upon this question, and he had given it as his opinion that, as it would be impossible to remove Sir James without a public enquiry, Sir James must certainly stay where he was. Probably", added Mr Strachey, "the Duke was right; but the fact that the peccant doctor continued in the Queen's service made the Hastings family irreconcilable and produced an unpleasant impression of unrepentant error upon the public mind."[1] So the presence of Sir James was not removed from the Palace. Alas! could the Queen but have foreseen the unspeakable tragedy which in twenty-two years' time would befall her, owing to that continued presence, blotting out all the

[1] Strachey, *op. cit.*, p. 72.

happiness of her life, casting the shadow of death upon the forty long years that yet remained to her!

But this tragedy could be foreseen by none, and Sir James remained at Court.

Until the death of Lady Flora brought dismay to everyone concerned, the life at the Palace and at Windsor continued much as usual, in spite of the scandal that had been raised. In May 1839, the Hereditary Grand Duke of Russia, afterwards the Czar Alexander the Second, paid a visit to the Queen at Windsor, and a ball was given in his honour. The Queen, who had written playfully in her diary "I am really quite in love with the Grand Duke; he is a dear, delightful young man," danced a mazurka with him and noted that "he is very strong, and in running round you must follow quickly, and after that you are whisked round like in that rather shocking new dance the Valse, which was very pleasant". When the time came for the Grand Duke to take his leave of the Queen, she recorded that "he took my hand and pressed it warmly; he looked pale, and his voice faltered, as he said 'Les paroles me manquent pour expresser tout ce que je sens'". He then pressed and kissed the Queen's hand, and she kissed his cheek, whereupon he kissed hers in a very warm, affectionate manner. And the Queen felt very sad taking leave of "the dear amiable young man, whom I really think (talking jokingly) I was a little in love with". And when, next night, the band played the Queen's and the Grand Duke's favourite quadrille, "Le Gai Loisir", the Queen felt quite melancholy.[1]

So the days passed, but there were troubles in the Queen's life, as well as youthful pleasures, and the greatest of these was the resignation, long dreaded by Her Majesty, of Lord Melbourne and his ministers, in May 1839. How great this trouble loomed in the mind of the Queen may be gauged by the fact that she had been in constant communication with him, not only every day, but several times a day, ever since

[1] See the Queen's *Journal*, May 1839.

her accession to the throne. She relied upon his advice and judgment in everything, and, six months after she became Queen, had written in her diary: "I shall be sorry to lose him even for one night"; and now she saw herself faced with losing him altogether. Something would have gone out of her life, she told herself, which could never be replaced. Then, too, she was a Whig by inheritance, and the ladies of her household were of this political party, and she had a strong prejudice against the Tory faction. This was bad enough; but her dread of losing Lord Melbourne's presence, his invariable guidance and help—this was the worst of all. And that dread had been with her now for some time. "I cannot say", she had written in her diary when a critical division in Parliament was about to take place, "(though I feel *confident* of *our success*) how *low,* HOW sad I feel, when I think of the POSSIBILITY of this excellent and truly kind man not *remaining* my Minister! Yet I trust fervently that *He* who has so wonderfully protected me through such manifold difficulties will not *now* desert me. I should have liked to have expressed to Lord M. my anxiety, but the tears were nearer than words, throughout the time I saw him, and I felt I should have choked, had I attempted to say anything."[1]

And now the Queen's dread had been fulfilled, and Lord Melbourne was about to leave her. The reason for the resignation of the Ministry was this: during the Parliamentary session of 1839, the Whig government was faced with putting into action the great measures for abolishing slavery in the British Colonies, which had been passed in 1833—and the freeing of the slaves in the Crown Colony of Jamaica caused the planters, their owners, to rebel. The government was, in consequence, forced to ask Parliament to suspend the constitution of the island. This was done, on May 7th, but the motion was carried by a majority of only five, and the natural result was that Lord Melbourne felt obliged to lay the

[1] *The Girlhood of Queen Victoria,* Volume I, p. 324.

resignation of himself and his ministers in the Queen's hands. Her grief was too great to be restrained, and when Lord John Russell, the leader of the House of Commons, was shown into her presence she burst into tears.

She did, however, calm herself sufficiently to send for the Duke of Wellington and ask him to form a ministry, which he declined to do on the score of his great age, and because he believed the Prime Minister should be a member of the House of Commons. It would be better, he told Her Majesty, if she sent for Sir Robert Peel.

Terrible thought! She had always detested the man. He had the manners of a dancing-master—Greville said of him that he was "unable to resist", in his interview with the Queen, "putting himself into his accustomed attitude of a dancing-master giving a lesson. The Queen would like him better if he would keep his legs still"—and he had, according to his enemy O'Connell, a smile like the silver fittings of a coffin. His supporters, too, were just as bad; "and as for Sir James Graham, she could not bear the sight of him; he was exactly like Sir John Conroy."[1]

The Queen was in despair. Her farewell to her dear faithful Lord M. was long and touching, and next morning she wrote to him: "The Queen...couldn't touch a morsel of food last night, nor can she this morning." And in another letter, written later the same day, she exclaimed: "Peel is such a cold odd man she can't make out what he means.... The Queen don't like his manner. After—oh! How different, how dreadfully different to that frank, open, natural, and most kind warm manner of Lord M."[2]

The interview between Her Majesty and Sir Robert had, indeed, been a painful one, although the Queen's hostility was at no moment put into words. Sir Robert was anxious to be conciliatory, but the cold eyes, the distant bearing of the royal lady made this difficult; and he was hampered too

[1] Strachey, *op. cit.*, p. 74.   [2] *Letters*, Volume I, p. 159.

by his natural shyness, whilst the very fact that he wished
to please, added to this, exaggerated the dancing-master
manners, enhanced the gloom of the coffin's silver fittings.
For Sir Robert was conscious that his manners lacked charm;
the slightest thing—a word, a gesture—could embarrass him,
and his very consciousness of these facts made his manner,
at such moments when he was embarrassed, more stiff and
formal, less pleasing than ever. The Queen did nothing to
help him; though she noted—not, I imagine, without satisfaction—that he seemed both unhappy and "put out", she
did nothing to ease the unhappiness. Still, the interview
passed without any outward break—the nearest approach to
this being when Peel requested that there should be a change
in the Queen's household, since it was no longer fitting that
she should be entirely surrounded by Whig ladies, who could
be trusted to do their utmost to influence the Queen against
the new government. The Queen at once said, with an added
firmness in her look and manner, that she intended no alteration to take place in her household. Sir Robert, seeing that it
was useless, at the moment, to attempt to change her on this
point, said that the matter could be settled later, and left
the Palace to arrange the composition of his Cabinet. The
Queen, during his presence, had shown no signs of emotion,
she had remained, as she herself said, "very much collected;
civil and high, and betrayed no agitation"; but, when he had
gone, she burst once more into floods of tears. How could
she *ever* find anything to say to this hard, formal man, with
his absurd positions and pointing of the toe, and that ever-
lasting, cold smile. Then again, she knew what he meant
when he asked that the composition of her household should
be changed. They had taken Lord M. away from her—and
now they were going to take Lehzen.

She sobbed until she was exhausted, and then, drying her
eyes, sat down to write the story of her experience and her
unhappiness to Lord M. "She feels", ran the letter, "Lord

Melbourne will understand it, amongst enemies to those she most relied on and most esteemed, but what is the worst of all is the being deprived of seeing Lord Melbourne as she used to do."[1]

In vain did Lord Melbourne try to pacify her, in vain did he speak well and generously of the Tory leaders, and assure Her Majesty that, when she came to know Sir Robert better, she would perceive his many good qualities; the Queen would not be soothed. She was not a child to have the ladies of her household chosen for her; she was the Queen of England, and Sir Robert should know it. Why, he would be wanting to choose her housemaids and her dressers soon.

It must be said at this point, however, that Sir Robert was not quite so much at fault as the Queen believed, for according to constitutional practice the Queen Regnant must follow the wishes of her Prime Minister as to the personnel of the female part of her household. But the Queen would not be moved; she would not listen even to Lord M.; and when, next morning, Sir Robert appeared again, he found the Queen even more haughty in her manner than she had been the day before. Pointing his toe nervously, he spoke of the Cabinet appointments, and then, after an awkward pause, began, "Now, Ma'am, about the ladies"—but went no farther, for the Queen cut him short: "I cannot give up *any* of my ladies," she said with great asperity. There was another pause. "What, Ma'am," exclaimed Sir Robert, "does Your Majesty mean to retain them *all*?" "*All*," said the Queen, and looked at him. Sir Robert's face showed an almost uncontrollable dismay, he seemed momentarily incapable of speech. "The Mistress of the Robes, and the ladies of the bedchamber?" he managed to say at last. "*All*," repeated Her Majesty.[2]

Sir Robert, in a low voice, with the silver fittings of the coffin shining more and more gloomily as his discomfort in-

[1] *Letters*, Volume I, p. 159.   [2] See Strachey, *op. cit.*, p. 76.

creased, mentioned the British Constitution, he recalled to
Her Majesty's memory the customs which were expected
of the Queen Regnant. In vain. Her Majesty's look did not
waver, her eyes held his commandingly; and when at last
Sir Robert, having executed several most intricate *pas seuls* in
his embarrassment, left her, nothing had been decided. The
Queen flew to her writing-table, and sent a hurried letter to
Lord Melbourne. "Sir Robert has behaved very ill," she
declared; "he insisted on my giving up my ladies, to which I
replied that I never would consent, and I never saw a man so
frightened....I was calm but very decided, and I think you
would have been pleased to see my composure and great
firmness; the Queen of England will not submit to such
trickery. Keep yourself in readiness, for you may soon be
wanted"[1]—for Her Majesty had already some inkling of
what would be the ultimate, highly desirable result of her un-
yielding attitude. No sooner was the letter finished than the
Duke of Wellington was ushered into her presence, saying, as
he bent over her hand, "Well, Ma'am, I am very sorry to
find there is a difficulty." "Oh," replied the Queen, clearly
and distinctly, "*he* began it, not me!"[2]

Will clashed with will, and the Duke of Wellington knew
that he had found one which at least equalled his—a calm
and a resolution which were by no means less than his own.
He was unable, as Mr Strachey says, to move the Queen one
inch. At last, "Is Sir Robert so weak", she asked, "that even
the ladies must be of his opinion?" This showed that there
was nothing to be done, and the Duke, after a final expostula-
tion, made his obeisance and departed.[3]

The Queen was triumphant; there could only, she felt, be
one end to the affair, and she was right; for Sir Robert Peel
returned within a short time and told Her Majesty that, if
she insisted upon holding to her decision, he could not form
a ministry, to which Her Majesty replied coldly that she

[1] *Letters*, Volume I, p. 162.   [2] See Strachey, *op. cit.*, p. 77.   [3] *Ibid.*

would give him his final answer in writing. Next morning, Lord Melbourne and the ministers of the last Cabinet met together. The Queen's letters were read, amidst extraordinary enthusiasm, and, heedless of logic or of caution, unregarding of the fact that as far as the nation was concerned there was no reason why they should give up their decision to resign, they declared, one and all, that "it was impossible to abandon such a Queen and such a woman", and, ignoring the fact that they were no longer the Queen's ministers, they actually went to the length of advising Her Majesty to cut off all negotiations with Sir Robert Peel.[1]

The Queen saw no reason to hesitate for a moment, and the second victory of her reign was won.

That night, at the state ball at Buckingham Palace, it was noticed that the Queen was looking particularly radiant, and this radiance was reflected in the face of dear Lord M., who was once more in his accustomed place. But, the Queen said, "Peel and the Duke of Wellington came by looking very much put out."

Such was the state of affairs before the death of Lady Flora Hastings threw the Court into a dismay that spread over the whole country. The victory over Sir Robert Peel was followed by an interval of peace during which the Duke of Wellington, who was inevitably called in as adviser in every delicate matter, had, with a view to smoothing over the difficulties existing between the two royal households, actually succeeded in inducing Sir John Conroy to resign his post and to leave the Palace, and, this done, had prevailed upon the Queen to write an affectionate letter to her mother. But the Duchess, reading the letter, was unappeased. Her daughter had not written it, that was clear to the Duchess. She never used those terms, that was not her handwriting; and she sent for the Duke of Wellington to tell him of this fresh intrigue, this fresh slight that had been put upon her. At last,

[1] See Strachey, *op. cit.*, p. 78.

however, after much volubility of a stormy kind from the Duchess, the Duke of Wellington was able to make himself heard: the letter was, he assured Her Royal Highness, from the Queen; it was a genuine effort at reconciliation. Would not the Duchess try to forget the mistakes of the past, help to smooth over the difficulties? But when the Duchess thought of the slights to which she had been subjected, the way in which she had been kept out of everything—yes, everything—the way in which she had *never* been consulted, and her daughter had shown her—oh yes! that had hurt her more than all the rest put together—that she wished to be *alone*—when the Duchess thought of the shameful way in which Lady Flora had been treated, she felt it was not so easy to be conciliatory. There were too many difficulties in the way. "What am I to do", she asked the Duke, "if Lord Melbourne comes up to me?" "Do, ma'am? Why, receive him with civility." The Duchess said she would do her best, but that it would be a considerable effort....'"But what am I to do if Victoria asks me to shake hands with Lehzen?" "Do, ma'am? Why, take her in your arms and kiss her." The Duchess turned scarlet with rage; every feather, all her silks, seemed flying on a wind of war. Then, suddenly, she burst out laughing. "No, ma'am, no," said the Duke, laughing too. "I don't mean you are to take Lehzen in your arms and kiss *her*, but the Queen."[1]

But now Lady Flora lay dead, and all the Duke's hopes of making a reconciliation between the Queen and her mother were shattered. The break between them was now definite and, whilst it lasted, complete.

[1] See Greville, June 7, June 10, June 15, August 15, 1839 (unpublished). Strachey, *op. cit.*, p. 79.

Chapter IX

TROUBLES AND INDECISIONS

The undisguised breach between the Queen and the Duchess of Kent, the gloom into which the Court had been thrown by the death of Lady Flora Hastings —these were by no means the only troubles which encompassed the Queen at this time. There was in addition the shadow, ever deepening, cast by the very odd behaviour of her beloved uncle Leopold. Since the accession of the Queen, the tone of his letters had undoubtedly altered; and although at first the change had been almost imperceptible, yet before very long the Queen realized that another attempt was being made "to lead her as if she were a child".

The King of the Belgians, leaning back in his chair with half-closed eyes and that rather peculiar smile by which he was distinguished, felt as he reread, before despatching it, one of the earlier letters to his dearly loved niece, now the Queen of England, that the tact of that letter was unassailable—that it paved the way to his intervention in graver matters. So far, he had confined himself to "recommending" the Church of England, and to advising her to say little on any subject of importance: "You cannot," he wrote, "without *pledging* yourself to anything *particular, say too much on the subject.*"[1]

[1] *Letters*, Volume I, p. 70.

But then came a slightly menacing note, for His Majesty added that he would be glad if his niece consulted him before coming to any decision. Yes, decidedly a tactful letter, His Majesty thought, as he folded it up. His niece had invariably followed his advice, before she came to the throne; she had been only too anxious to know his views on every subject; and now, at last, had come the great opportunity in the life of one who only existed in order to serve the good: to assure the well-being of Europe, to make his influence felt on the foreign policy of England, gently and imperceptibly, through the person of his niece and unknown to her ministers.

His niece, in reply to this letter, wrote a hurried but affectionate note: "Your advice is always of the greatest importance," she declared.[1] But somehow that advice, though always read, was never invited. His Majesty felt that the time had now come for a little caution; it would not do to be too precipitous. Besides, a queer change had come over the child since her accession; always the same warm-heartedness, the same filial affection, appeared in her correspondence with him; but there was, too, a strange undertone which he could not quite understand—and the subjects discussed in these letters were more domestic than political. The King would have imagined that his niece would have turned to him for advice in every matter concerning the ruling of England, the foreign policy of her ministers. He folded his hands and pondered. Better, he told himself, to delay political instruction for a while, and instil a little good advice as to the ordinary conduct of everyday life, and how to deal with the Princess de Lieven, who, the King of the Belgians felt, was a dangerous woman, whom his niece must keep at a distance—otherwise it was certain that she would make impertinent efforts to interfere in matters which were none of her business. A sense of humour had never been one of His Majesty's most

[1] *Letters*, Volume I, p. 79.

striking characteristics, and he added: "A rule which I cannot sufficiently recommend is *never to permit* people to speak on subjects concerning yourself and your affairs without you having yourself desired them to do so. Should such an impertinence be attempted, change the conversation, and make the individual feel that he has made a mistake." "People", he told his niece, "must come to the opinion that *it is of no use intriguing, because when her mind is once made up and she thinks a thing right, no earthly power will make her change.*" And His Majesty concluded with the prayer that his niece would allow nobody, not even her Prime Minister, to broach subjects that concerned her personally, without her permission.

Alas, as regards this advice, his niece benefited only too clearly by it; for, although the Princess de Lieven, on the occasion of her making a visit to the Queen, was undoubtedly "made to feel she had made a mistake",[1] eventually the advice was to be applied in an even more marked degree, to His Majesty himself.

The correspondence continued, with long homilies from King Leopold to his niece, affectionate if rather vague replies from the recipient of the sermons. And the Queen, thinking over these letters, wondered why the letters, the homilies, which in the past had seemed so wonderful that she could never have enough of them, appeared to have lost their interest. And then Lord Melbourne appeared, with his breezy manner and his charm and his jokes, and the sermons were forgotten.

For it was, indeed, Lord Melbourne's delightful companionship, his unending and wonderful flow of information, his charming and easy way of teaching the Queen the business of being a queen, of instructing her in the history and constitution of her country, that had thrown a shadow over that earlier companionship. The Queen was faithful in her

[1] *Letters*, Volume I, pp. 85–6.

affections, but it is undoubted that she loved a new face, a new sensation, and that the better-known face, the older sensation, became a little dulled by contrast. Uncle Leopold's image grew dim beside Lord Melbourne's; Lord Melbourne's and Lehzen's faded out altogether when she saw the light of the Prince Consort's countenance—although of course Lord Melbourne was still her poor good old friend Lord M., and Lehzen was still her dear good Lehzen; Sir Robert Peel, who had once been "that cold, odd man, how unlike Lord Melbourne", became in the end "almost a father to us". Then, too, King Louis Philippe and his Queen, although she still remained friendly with them and did all in her power to relieve their misfortunes, were like pale ghosts in the glory, the splendour of the Emperor Napoleon the Third, of whom she had once had such a dread. She remained attached to her uncle Leopold throughout her life, but by now she, who had never found a single blemish in him, was undoubtedly aware of his faults. Where, for instance, was that hatred of deception, which had once seemed to be so much a part of his character? Why, to take an example, should he have written her this very curious letter?[1] "I have told Stockmar to try to settle something for *regular* safe communication.... You know now that all letters are read, and that should not *always* be the case with ours." Still, the letter insinuated, this peculiar fact might be made use of, if the opportunities were understood. ...And His Majesty explained that it would be possible, because of this habit, to convey a subject to the knowledge of the persons concerned without the writer being in any way compromised. For instance: "We are still plagued by Prussia concerning those fortresses; now, to tell the Prussian Government many things which we *should not like* to tell them *officially,* the Minister is going to write a despatch to our man at Berlin, sending it *by post*; the Prussians *are sure* to read it, and to learn in this way what we wish them to hear."

[1] On October 9th 1837.

TROUBLES AND INDECISIONS

...His Majesty added that the same kind of thing—he felt it only right to warn his niece—might happen in England; diplomats, anxious, perhaps, to injure *some people they may fear* in the Queen's eyes, might resort to the same methods. "I tell you the trick," wrote King Leopold, half closing his eyes, and smiling his peculiar smile, "that you should be able to guard against it."[1] Could this letter really be from the same hand that, only two years before, had written her such long homilies about political honesty, and the lamentable decay of this quality?...It was hardly to be believed.

Then followed a rather guarded correspondence about foreign affairs, conducted on both sides with caution, until at last the King, remembering how easily in the past his niece had been led by him, felt it necessary to put matters a little more openly. In a letter dated the 2nd of June 1838 he told the Queen that he knew it would be very wrong in him, after so many proofs of her affection for him, to feel that in so short a time, without any cause, those feelings which were so precious to him could have changed. And it was this knowledge that made him appeal to the feelings in question. After reminding the Queen of England how deeply important the independent existence of Belgium—or the provinces which form that kingdom—had always been to England, the surest proof of that was, he assured her, that for centuries England had made the greatest sacrifices of blood and treasure for that object. The late King of England, for instance, had assured the King of the Belgians, on the occasion of their last meeting, that if ever France or any other power invaded Belgium it would be a question of immediate war for England. The King read over this part of the letter and added: "All I want from your kind Majesty is that you will *occasionally* express to your Ministers...that as far as it is *compatible* with the interests of your own dominions, you do *not* wish that the Government should take the *lead* in such

[1] *Letters*, Volume I, p. 93.

measures as might in a short time bring on the *destruction* of this country, as well as that of your uncle and his family,"[1] and the letter ended in the usual grumbling, self-pitying note: all, it seemed, that the King of the Belgians had wished was *to be left alone*; and it must not be forgotten that during the last seven years all the dangers, all the trouble, were piled upon his shoulders. He, alone, bore all the burdens.

The letter was sent, and a strange and chilly silence fell which lasted for more than a week. When, at last, the Queen did reply, it was in a letter which seemed curiously vague when we consider the will which inspired it. Her dearest uncle, she told him, in her usual affectionate way, would be very wrong if he thought that her feelings of warm and devoted attachment for him could ever be changed. *Nothing* could ever change them. Her beloved uncle must be aware, too, that the ancient policy of the country made the Queen most anxious that the government should do nothing prejudicial to Belgium, and should do everything that did not conflict with the interests and engagements of England to promote the prosperity of King Leopold's country....Nobody, she assured him, could feel more for the difficult situation of the King of the Belgians, than his devoted niece.

But of definite promises and commitments there were none.

In return, the King assured his dearest and most beloved Victoria that she had written him a *very dear* and long letter, which had given him great satisfaction, since *all* he had wanted was to be assured of her affection, and of this he could no longer have any doubt. He felt it only right to tell her honestly that he had previously felt some misgivings. He did not think exactly that the Queen had forgotten him, but he thought he had been put aside as one does a piece of furniture which is no longer wanted. He did not complain,

[1] *Letters*, Volume I, p. 116.

however, "because I fear that if affection is on the decline, reproaches only diminish it further; I therefore said nothing; but in a life full of grief and disappointments like mine, the loss of your affection would have been one of the most severe." It was because of this, added the King, that Lord Palmerston's declaration to the Prussian government (giving Prussia unmistakable evidence of England's disposition to support Holland against Belgium) had grieved him so much. It looked as if the British government were saying: "You imagine, perhaps, that we mean to have *égards* for the Uncle of the Queen; these, you see, we shall make even shorter work with, than we did under our late master." This had hurt him, even more in his *English* capacity than in his Belgian, for he came to Belgium from England and was chosen for that reason. Besides, the King was happy to say that he had never yet been in the position to ask for any act of kindness from the Queen, so that whatever little service he had rendered her remained on a basis of perfect disinterestedness. Therefore, as the first act of the Queen's government had seemed to be directed against him, this had naturally created a great sensation throughout Europe. He would never ask any favours of his niece that could in the least be regarded as *incompatible* with the interests of England. But his niece could readily understand that there was a great difference between asking a favour, and asking not to be treated as an enemy.[1] And in a further letter he reminded the Queen that she knew from experience that he never made any demands upon her kindness, preferring, indeed, to remain in the position of having rendered great services with no reward save her affection. Still, if everybody was not very careful, he continued, they might see serious consequences which would affect more or less everybody.[2] In answer to this, Her Majesty, after a consultation with

[1] See *Letters*, Volume 1, pp. 117–20.
[2] See *Letters*, Volume 1, p. 134.

Lord M., told her beloved uncle that it seemed to her that these affairs could only be settled by the agreement of the four powers, and that it was absolutely necessary that France should be in accord as well as the others. She only, she assured her uncle, refrained from mentioning political matters in her letters, lest these should lose their delightful and familiar tone, and become too formal. To which His Majesty replied, with remote dignity, that his dearest Victoria's extremely kind and dear letters had made him *very* happy, and that he was glad to think that she had enjoyed Brighton, which might undoubtedly be said to be agreeable till the east winds set in. It was there, he remembered, that he had first met Princess Charlotte, at a now very distant date. Distant, thought His Majesty, as he folded up the letter, but not more distant than the behaviour of his niece since her accession. Yet, even now, he was unwilling to admit to himself the uselessness of any attempt to rule Victoria's actions; and not so long afterwards we find him expressing his satisfaction at having "extracted some sparks of politics from your dear Majesty, very kindly and nicely expressed". To which Her Majesty, casting aside every vestige of vagueness, replied: "Though you seem not to dislike my political sparks, I think it is better not to increase them, as they might finally take fire, especially as I see with regret that upon this subject we cannot agree."

She was firm, but the letters, the constant requests and hints, were worrying. And through all this nagging irritation of her beloved uncle's attempts to interfere, like an incessantly sounding note, or slow water-dropping, came the thought, ever present at the back of the Queen's mind, that soon she would be faced with the "odious" ordeal of seeing Albert again—Albert whom her uncle had determined she should marry. The meeting would be very awkward, for she knew that Albert was also aware of the destiny his uncle had prepared for him. She could not bear the idea of marriage; she liked Albert, but what was to happen if she did not come to love him? She had a strong distaste for the whole affair, and the thought of it poisoned all her pleasure, and made everything seem too much trouble. Her uncle wanted her to entertain King Louis Philippe and his Queen, his parents-in-law, in the Pavilion at Brighton. She really did not feel well enough to receive them; but dear Uncle Leopold, who could never take "no" for an answer, was determined that she should, so that in the end she was obliged to refuse point blank. The note at the back of her brain persisted with its maddening reiteration; so that at last, in July 1839, she wrote to her uncle and told him, point plank, that he, and Prince Albert, must understand there was no definite engagement. Even if she should feel it possible to marry Albert, she could make *no final promise this year,* for, at the *very earliest,* any such event could not take place till *two or three years hence!* She had a *great* repugnance to change her present position; and above all, it must be understood that if she settled not to marry him, it would be no breach of promise, for she *never gave any!*

But in spite of all indecisions, in spite of her dislike of the situation, the time for the visit of Albert came nearer and nearer. The tour in Italy on which he had been sent with Baron Stockmar as his cicerone—watchful, prudent, shrewd Stockmar, who must pronounce on his suitability as Consort to the Queen of England—was over. Before this journey, the Baron would express no definite opinion as to the qualifications possessed by the Prince; it was true that he was intelligent, and that he was discreet; but this was not enough. "The young man", he added, "ought to have not merely great ability, but a *right* ambition, and great force of will as well. To pursue for a lifetime a political career so arduous demands more than energy and inclination—it demands also that earnest frame of mind which is ready of its own accord to sacrifice mere pleasure to real usefulness. If he is not satisfied hereafter with the consciousness of having achieved one of the most influential positions in Europe, how often will he feel tempted to repent his adventure! If he does not from the very outset accept it as a vocation of grave responsibility, on the efficient performance of which his honour and happiness depend, there is small likelihood of his succeeding."[1]

With the visit to Italy, many of Baron Stockmar's doubts were set at rest. The young Prince, it seemed, was earnest-minded, he was devoted to duty, his principles were high. Whilst at Bonn he had spent much of his time, when not walking with his friend Prince William of Löwenstein, in thoroughly discussing "juridical principles or philosophical doctrines"; he had written an essay on the "Mode of Thought of the Germans", and a sketch of the "History of German Civilisation", "making use," as he explained, "in the general outlines, of the divisions which the treatment of the subject itself demands", and ending with "a retrospect of the short-comings of our time, with an appeal to everyone to correct those shortcomings in his own case, and thus set a good example to others". But there were also disadvantages; there was decidedly room for improvement. The Prince, for instance, seemed unwilling to exert himself to any great extent, he took no interest whatever in politics, and, as well, was "too indifferent and retiring" in the presence of women. When he attended a ball in Florence, he spent the whole evening discussing learned matters with the distin-guished scholar Signor Capponi, and though the Grand Duke of Tuscany was so much struck with this conduct that he exclaimed: "Voilà un prince dont nous pouvons être fiers! La belle danseuse l'attend, le savant l'occupe," Baron Stockmar was not so certain that this was a matter for pride.[2]

Still, it was decided to send Albert to England, and Sep-tember the 30th 1839 was originally fixed as the day of his

[1] Strachey, *op. cit.*, pp. 89–90.   [2] See Strachey, *op. cit.*, p. 90.

arrival with his brother Prince Ernest; there was, however, a Council at Windsor on that day, and the Queen, anxious to delay her meeting with Albert as long as possible, and unwilling to let the Council think that an engagement was impending, wrote to put her cousins off for a few days. But she was distinctly annoyed when Prince Albert wrote to her from the Winter Palace in Belgium saying he intended to delay his visit still further. Was it possible, she wondered, that Albert's unwillingness matched her own? If so, in what an odious position the Queen of England had been put! ...However, ten days after the date first fixed for this visit,[1] they arrived, after a terrible crossing from Antwerp and several mishaps—one being the loss of Prince Albert's luggage, so that, being unable to change his clothes, he was obliged to dine upstairs. The Queen sent carriages to meet her cousins at the Tower of London, and they drove through the misty blue October evening to Windsor. Standing at the top of the staircase in the Castle the Queen of England was waiting to receive them. As she looked at Albert, the whole of her past melted away as if it had been a palace made of snow built for an unreal monarch who had yet to find her kingdom. That kingdom was now at hand. "It was with some emotion", she wrote in her diary, "that I beheld Albert—who is *beautiful*."

[1] On October 10th.

Chapter X

THE QUEEN'S ENGAGEMENT

Victoria of England was conceived, born, and bred to be a queen. Long before the marriage of her parents, before she was conceived, that queenship had been preparing. Her destiny was to mount to the summits of greatness, but not in youth or in her middle years. Only as an old and desolate woman, alone in those mountain peaks to which she had risen by such long and difficult ways, would she see the future of the world and of her people with the clear eyes of the eagle. In old age, the wisdom of the serpent, the heart of the lion, were hers, but not in youth, though her heart was always great. "You call me the little Queen," she told her uncle the King of the Belgians; "my body is little, but my heart is not."

Now she was a young girl, in love, and the terrible solitude of greatness had not yet fallen upon her. It would come only when she was old, and the shadows of those mountain peaks were reflected upon her face.

The Queen of England, even in youth, had no beauty as the world knows it. She was a little homely being without loveliness of colouring or features, but she had a speaking voice like that of a bird in spring, an enchanting and gay laugh, and such an amazing grace both in movement and in stillness, such an expressiveness of gesture, that these have never been exceeded. She had, indeed, an extraordinary power of expressing any state of being, any emotion, by her very walk, which had now the beauty of a swan floating upon its native lake, now the melancholy grace and splendour of a cloud in transit, now the pride and pomp of a wave marching. When silent and thoughtful, she seemed a statue, her attitude evoking all the greatness of the past, so that it seemed a shadow about her; when she emerged from this stillness, all the banners and the brave music of the world seemed to have gone to make the walk of the Queen of England. But her face was not beautiful, and she knew it. On the other hand how great, how transcendent was the beauty of Albert. Every day the Queen noticed fresh causes for admiration, that "lovely mouth", the "delicate moustachios and slight but *very* slight whiskers", the "exquisite nose", the "beautiful figure, broad in the shoulders and a fine waist". She fell headlong in love with him, and could not understand how she could have had these past reluctances and hesitations. Was it possible? Could she be the same girl who had, such a short time ago, written that irritable letter to her uncle making it clear that she had entered into no engagement? The day after the arrival of the Princes, the Queen told Lord Melbourne that her mind was made up: she intended to marry her cousin; and he discussed with her what honours should be conferred on the Prince—for it never entered her head that Albert might refuse her hand, although, much hurt by her former hesitation, he had come to Windsor with the intention of telling her that if she still delayed making up her mind he must regard the plan as at an end....She wished her future husband, she told Lord Melbourne, to be made a Field-Marshal, and a Royal Highness; and Parliament would be required to provide for him. But all this could be settled definitely at a later time.

THE QUEEN'S ENGAGEMENT

For three days the cousins danced together, sang duets, and played games of Tactics and Fox and Geese[1]; they rode together in the Forest, and chattered; and whilst she was at work she could hear her cousins playing Haydn's duets downstairs. Then, on the fourth day, at half past twelve, she sent him a message asking him to come to her. He came, and she said he must be aware of why she had sent for him, and it would make her "too happy" if he would consent to what she wished. "I told him", she wrote in her diary, "I was quite unworthy of him. He said he would be very happy to spend his life with me. I *love* him more than I can say, and I shall do everything in my power to render the sacrifice he has made, (for sacrifice in my opinion it is,) as small as I can."

She did love him—her letter to the King of the Belgians was full of rapture—but a significant sentence appeared in her letter to her aunt, the Duchess of Gloucester. She had been obliged, she said, to make the proposal, for Albert would "never have presumed to take such a liberty as to propose to the Queen of England".

The bridegroom thus chosen accepted the offer of the Queen's hand, not because he was in love with her—love was to come only after some years of marriage—but because the position which would be his would enable him, as he explained to his stepmother, to do good. "Life has its thorns", he added, "in every position, and the consciousness of having used one's powers and endeavours for an object so great as that of promoting the good of so many, will surely be sufficient to support me."[2] In a letter of a singularly melancholy tone, he assured Stockmar that "I will not let my courage fail. With firm resolution and true zeal on my part, I cannot fail to continue noble, manly, and princely in

[1] See E. F. Benson: *Queen Victoria* (Longmans, Green and Co., Ltd.).

[2] Grey, *op. cit.*, p. 238. Benson, *op. cit.*, p. 89.

all things."[1] And he told his beloved grandmother the Dowager Duchess of Coburg: "She '(Victoria)' is really most good and amiable, and I am quite sure heaven has not given me into evil hands, and that we shall be happy together.

"Since that moment Victoria does whatever she fancies I should wish or like, and we talk together about our future life, which she promises to make as happy as possible. Oh, the future, does it not bring with it the moment when I shall have to take leave of my dear, dear home, and of you! I cannot think of that without deep melancholy taking possession of me.

"The period of our marriage is already close at hand. The Queen and her Ministers wish that it should take place in the first days of February, in which I acquiesced after learning their reasons for it."[2]

Although these letters can scarcely be said to express rapture, this quality was present, in the most striking degree, in those of King Leopold. In answer to a letter from his niece announcing the date of the marriage, the astute monarch replied that he experienced "the feelings of Zacharias: 'Now lettest Thou Thy servant depart in peace'". He added that the position of Albert might indeed be a difficult one, but that "*all* will depend on your affection for him. If you love him and are kind to him, he will easily bear the burthen of the position, and there is a steadfastness and at the same time cheerfulness in his character which will facilitate this."[3]

The triumph of King Leopold was indeed complete. Baulked in his wish to rule England through his wife, whom, notwithstanding his ambitious character, he had married for love, he had succeeded in placing his sister, a widow of no fortune, in the position of the mother of the Queen of England, and now his brother's younger son, a youth for whom

[1] Grey, *op. cit.*, p. 232. Benson, *op. cit.*, pp. 89–90.
[2] Grey, *op. cit.*, pp. 239–40. Benson, *op. cit.*, p. 90.
[3] *Letters*, Volume I, p. 190.

destiny, under other circumstances, would have held little, was to become the Consort of that Queen.

As for the boy, he was dutiful, he was quiet and studious, and, thought His Majesty, he would accept this fate as he would accept any other that had been chosen for him.

The situation was, however, as the King of the Belgians had foreseen, a difficult one. To begin with, Parliament behaved most impertinently. Shortly after Her Majesty, wearing a bracelet on her arm containing the miniature of the Prince set in diamonds, and gazed at from afar by Lord M. with tears in his eyes, made the announcement of her engagement at a meeting of the Privy Council at Buckingham Palace, questions were asked about the religion of Albert. Could it be possible, Parliament would like to know, that Albert was a Papist? Then the Tories, furious, according to the Queen, at the failure of the Bedchamber Plot, succeeded in reducing the proposed allowance to the Prince of £50,000 a year to £30,000, and in this they were supported by the Radicals, the amendment being carried by a majority of over a hundred. It is difficult to know who was more indignant at this disrespect, the Queen or King Leopold. The latter, indeed, in one of his usual grumbling letters, proclaimed this behaviour to be both disgraceful and vulgar. Prince Albert, who was by now in Brussels, had to be smoothed down by the King, with whom his niece was once more displeased because of his incurable habit of interfering or trying to interfere. "Dear Uncle", she told Albert, "is given to believe that he must rule the roast everywhere. However, that is not a necessity."[1] The King wrote a long letter to the Queen of England explaining how, by some miracle of tact and diplomacy, he had succeeded in soothing the ruffled feelings of Albert. But it had been a difficult matter, and was undertaken without any hope of any reward except the affection of his niece.

[1] *Letters*, Volume I, p. 201. Strachey, *op. cit.*, pp. 93–4.

THE QUEEN'S ENGAGEMENT

Irritated by her uncle's constant statements of devotion, his interference, and his advice, all the doubts and hesitations of Victoria returned. It was true that Albert's lovely mouth, his delicate moustachios, and slight, but *very* slight whiskers, were *beautiful*—but what if he had inherited Uncle Leopold's passion and genius for interference, his masculine longing to command? He must be shown that she was the Queen of England—he must understand their relative positions. For, since the evening when her bed had been removed from dear Mama's room, no voice had been raised to check her; youthful she might be, and inexperienced; but every sentence that fell from her lips was treated as if it were the pronouncement of the Sphinx, awaited through ages of silence. Every wish was fulfilled, it was unthinkable that it should not be. There was no higher power, excepting the God whom she worshipped, but regarded as a beneficent Father, ready to give, but not to take away. "You have written to me...about our stay at Windsor" (their honeymoon), she wrote to her prospective husband; "but, dear Albert, you have not at all understood the matter. You forget, my dearest Love, that I am the Sovereign, therefore two or three days is already a long time to be absent....Everybody, including all my Aunts, say I must come out after the second day, for, as I must be surrounded by my Court, I cannot keep alone. This is also my wish in every way. Now as to the Arms; as an English Prince you have no right, and Uncle Leopold had no right to quarter the Royal Arms, but the Sovereign has the power to allow it by Royal Command. This was done for Uncle Leopold by the Prince Regent, and I will do it again for you. But it can only be done by Royal Command."[1]

Then again, the Prince, who would have liked to have a German private secretary, was told by the Queen that this would not do, for it would offend the susceptibilities of the English; nor could he be allowed to choose his gentlemen-

[1] *Letters*, Volume I, p. 213.

in-waiting; these must be the choice of the Queen, and Mr
Anson, who was to become in after years one of the Prince's
most intimate friends, but who was, as yet, unknown to him,
was appointed as his secretary, whether the Prince liked it
or not.

It was with a heavy heart that he contemplated the future;
it was true that his wife-to-be loved him; but she had a will
of iron; and he was entering a foreign country where he
would rarely be alone—the Prince loved solitude. The
Queen assured him that her good old Prime Minister would
dine with them at least two or three times a week, and always
on Sundays, and that on Sundays no one else would be
present, "as it is not reckoned right here for me to give
dinners on Sundays!" The Sabbath, reflected Prince Albert,
was regarded by the English almost as if it were a day of
national mourning; the prospect was melancholy. The
Queen apologized for writing to him on "picture note-
paper", in spite of the fact that she was in deep mourning,
adding that, for the day of the wedding and two or three
days following, the Court would not wear black.[1]

At last the day came when he must leave his home and his
beloved Germany for ever. His biographer, Mr Hector
Bolitho,[2] describes how "Coburg and Gotha waved wet
handkerchiefs to him. Little boys climbed the trees and
called out to him, and old women cried at the doors and
windows." As he entered the carriage which was to bear him
far away a terrible scream rang through the castle: "Albert—
Albert!" It was the voice of his grandmother, the Dowager
Duchess, and as the sound died away she fell back in a faint
into the arms of her ladies.

[1] *Letters*, Volume I, p. 212.
[2] See *Albert the Good*, p. 66.

Chapter XI

VICTORIA AND ALBERT

An aged ghost that would soon fade in the light of a long summer day (first the eyes, then the smile, then the features, then the whole presence—crumbling away into a little dust in the happy sunlight), Lord Melbourne stood amid the throng of royalties, courtiers, and statesmen in the open doorway of Buckingham Palace. "God bless you, Ma'am," he said to the tiny figure in white silk pelisse edged with swan's-down, and a white bonnet with a little bunch of orange-blossom under the brim, as she stopped to talk with him for ten minutes before it was time for her to enter her carriage, accompanied by Albert, and set out on her wedding journey to Windsor. During ten minutes the Queen had teased Lord M. about his smart coat, and had reminded him that he was to dine at Windsor in two days' time—but the ghost would soon fade, and perhaps he knew it.

Near him stood another ghost, more sharply outlined, more like a Jack-in-the-box in her movements, shriller than he in her fading—dear Lehzen, for whom the hour would come when she too must crumble; for the reign of unreality was over.

Together the ghosts watched the Queen and her husband as they passed through the doors of the Palace.

The February day had passed like a dream, had melted away like the pale frail mist. In the early morning, Prince Albert had been handed a little folded note without an envelope, which the Queen had sent to his bedroom in Buckingham Palace:

"Dearest,

"How are you today, and have you slept well? I have rested very well and feel very comfortable today. What weather! I believe, however, the rain will cease. Send one word when you, my most dearly loved bridegroom, will be ready.

Thy ever faithful

Victoria R."[1]

As the twenty-year-old Prince, dressed as a British Field-Marshal, with the Ribbon of the Garter across his breast, the Order in diamonds and other precious stones on his coat, and the Garter also in diamonds below his knee, appeared in the doorway of Buckingham Palace, accompanied by his father and brother in their dark-green uniforms, there was the sound of many thousands of people cheering, a blare of trumpets, colours were lowered, and the Prince received the salute which is usually reserved for the monarch.

The air seemed to be alive with flags, and the lion-like roars from the welcoming crowds bewildered the young Prince as he drove to the Chapel at St James's Palace to await his bride. Then a fresh tumult of cheering, a new blare of trumpets arose, and with the consummate amazing grace and majesty of movement, which with her amounted to genius, the Queen of England appeared in the doorway of the Palace. The pale mists of spring among the violet forests, the faint and delicate spring rain, were not whiter than her dress. With her was the Duchess of Kent, and as they drove through the thousands of happy, laughing, cheering people, between the lines of soldiers, through the streets whose

[1] *Letters*, Volume I, p. 217.

banners and whose sound seemed indivisible, the bride thought of that day, not so long ago, when she had driven through the streets to Westminster Abbey, there to be crowned Queen of England.

The glories of the day melted one into another like those of a dream. The ceremony was performed in the jewelled gloom, amidst pomp and splendour; then the young Queen as she left the Chapel gave the Queen Dowager, a touching and impressive figure in purple velvet with ermine, a farewell kiss, and, her hand in that of her bridegroom, walked through the Chapel once more and out into the white February day. Again there was the blare of trumpets, the sound of drums, the leonine sea-like roar of thousands of voices, and the young couple drove through the streets to Buckingham Palace.

A long and rather stiff banquet followed—it seemed interminable—then the Queen was divested of her white satin wedding-gown, with the deep flounce of Honiton lace, and her magnificent diamonds; dressed like any other young bride setting out on her wedding journey, she kissed her mother, said good-bye to her other relations, her Court and her ministers, and with Albert beside her set off on her journey to Windsor.[1]

At the end of three days the whole Court made its appearance; dear Lord M., the Queen's "good old Primus", came to dine, Lehzen's incessant chatter and birdlike swooping and rustlings were heard in the land, and Prince Albert's life as the Consort of the Queen of England began in good earnest.

It was a life, at first, of intense mental loneliness, and the solitude grew deeper still when the day came for his brother Ernest, his beloved and inseparable friend, to return to Coburg. "Pale as a sheet and his eyes full of tears", the Prince tried to restrain his emotion: "Such things", he said to his wife,

---

[1] See Bolitho, *op. cit.*, pp. 68–71.

"are hard to bear." And, indeed, he felt that his youth was ended. Henceforth, his must be a life given up to duty alone; and one of the principal parts of that duty was to train his young, headstrong, but loving wife to curb that will which, if put to proper use, would be so great a strength. But this, he found, was to be a difficult task, for he had not only the Queen's will but Lehzen's to contend with. He was faced with—if I may so express it—endless avenues of Lehzen: every door opened on to Lehzen, every sound was an echo of her voice. Hers had been the supreme influence in Victoria's life since she was five years old, and she intended that influence to remain, undiminished and unchanged; and the fact that she managed all the Queen's private correspondence, and was by now the superintendent of the royal establishment and the Privy Purse, gave her an increased power. Lehzen's permission must be obtained before anything could be done, she was consulted in every matter. In the May following their marriage, Albert told his friend Löwenstein: "In my whole life I am happy and contented, but the difficulty in filling my place with proper dignity is that I am only the husband and not the master of the house."

Then, too, the Prince complained that the Queen showed him "a want of confidence in trivial matters, and in all matters connected with the policy of the country", although when Lord Melbourne spoke of this she declared it was the result of indolence; perhaps it was wrong, but when she was with the Prince she preferred talking of other matters. Melbourne, repeating this conversation to Anson and Stockmar, added: "My impression is that she fears a difference of opinion....I do not think the Baroness is the cause of this want of openness." Stockmar, however, was of a very different opinion, and said: "The Queen has not started upon a right principle. She should by degrees impart everything to him, but there is danger in his wishing it all at once. A case may be laid before him, he may give a crude and unformed opinion; the opinion may be taken and the result be disastrous, and a forcible argument is thus raised against advice being asked for the future. The Queen is influenced more than she is aware by the Baroness. In consequence of that influence, she is not as ingenuous as she was two years ago."[1]

It is an undoubted fact that Albert's loneliness and unhappiness during the first few months of his marriage must have been very deep, in spite of the Queen's passionate adoration; for he was deprived of all mental companionship, save that of Anson (who was already his intimate friend, and was regarded by the Prince, to use his own words, almost as a brother), he was not allowed to do the work for which he had been trained from his earliest childhood, the conversations to which he was accustomed—those happy talks about juridical principles and philosophical doctrines—were denied him, nor was he allowed to gather persons of interest about him. Lord Melbourne[2] declared: "The Prince is bored with the sameness of his chess every evening. He would like to bring literary and scientific people about the Court, vary the society, and impose a more useful tendency into it. The Queen, however, has no fancy to encourage such people. This arises from a feeling on her part that her education has not fitted her to take part in such conversation; she would not like conversation to be going on in which she could not take her fair share, and she is far too open and candid in her nature to pretend to an atom more knowledge than she really possesses."

Deprived of the company of literary and scientific people, condemned to interminable evenings of chess, the Prince found no comfort in another kind of society. It was, indeed, impossible that English society, to use the word in its narrower sense, should appreciate this young German Prince

---

[1] *Letters*, Volume I, 224.
[2] See Anson's *Memorandum*; Windsor, 15 January 1841.

on first acquaintance. The lovely mouth with the slight, very slight whiskers, those large blue eyes, and that perfect profile did not tally with the English idea of manly beauty. His manner was frigid and formal, and, too, he behaved as if sport were a matter to be undertaken lightly, and not as life's most serious occupation; whilst womanly pursuits, such as playing the piano and singing, he regarded, as Mr Benson has pointed out, as "high and ennobling".[1]

But the Queen worshipped him. To her, he was perfection, and although she allowed Lehzen to rule the household, yet her husband could do no wrong. He was her "dearest angel", the "most beloved being". And little by little, but very slowly, the mass of the people, who had begun by distrusting the influence a German prince might exert over their Queen, and society in the narrower sense, came to know and to admire, though not to love, his qualities of sense and discretion, his strong and noble sense of duty.

One of the first appearances made by the Prince, as husband of the Queen, was as President of the Society for the Abolition of Slavery and the Civilisation of Africa; "I got through the speech very well", he told his brother, "and had much applause." And he began to mingle in the life of the people—accompanying the Queen to the Derby—an action which, according to his biographer Mr Bolitho, was a democratic gesture, for no sovereign had ever mingled with the Derby crowds before.

A few days after this, on June the 10th 1840, the whole nation was roused to fury by a murderous attack on the Queen. Her husband, in a letter to Prince Ernest, wrote: "You will not yet know that you have nearly lost your brother and sister. I will hurry to tell you how.

"The day before yesterday, Wednesday, we drove as usual at six o'clock in our small carriage, with four horses and two postillions. I sat to the right, Victoria to the left. We

[1] See Benson, *op. cit.*, p. 203.

had hardly got a hundred and fifty paces from Buckingham Palace, between the wall of Buckingham Palace and the Green Park, when I saw a small, disagreeable-looking man, leaning against the railing of the Green Park, only six paces from us, holding something towards us. Before I could see what it was, a shot cracked and so dreadfully loud that we were both quite stunned. Victoria, who had been looking to the left, towards the rider, did not know the cause of the noise. My first thought was that in her present state the fright might harm her. I put both arms around her and asked her how she felt, but she only laughed. Then I turned around to look at the man (the horses were frightened and the carriage stopped). The man stood there in a theatrical position, a pistol in each hand. It seemed ridiculous. Suddenly he stopped, put the pistol on his arm, aimed at us and fired; the bullet must have gone over our heads, judging by the hole where it hit the garden wall. Now the many onlookers came forward. They had been almost petrified before, and cried 'Kill him, kill him.' I called out to the postillion to drive on, we went to see our aunt, and then we drove through the parks, where we were most enthusiastically cheered."[1]

The little Queen, with her lion-like courage, was undismayed, and this although she was to give birth to a child in November; and the people, who since the affair of Lady Flora Hastings had lost some of the enthusiasm with which they had greeted her at her accession, felt a return of loyalty, as they contemplated that bravery and dignity.

In the following month, the Prince, in a letter to his brother, wrote: "A Bill of especial importance for me, was brought into the House, and accepted without any debate, after many intrigues had been tried against it. This was the Regency Bill. In case of Victoria's death and her successor being under eighteen years of age, I am to be Regent—*alone*—

[1] Bolitho, *op. cit.*, pp. 77–8.

Regent without a Council. You will understand the importance of this matter and that it gives my position here in the country a fresh significance. Sussex was against it and declared it an affront against the legal family. He intended to bring a protest into the House, but when his friends abandoned him, seeing the superior power of the Ministers, Whigs, and the whole Tory party, he let the matter pass without intervention. Without Stockmar, the Ministers would probably have retired on account of the risk and trouble. But he (this only between us) won those people over and they are willing to undertake it. Victoria is most satisfied with the arrangement."[1]

On the 21st November 1840, the Queen gave birth to her first child, a daughter, at Buckingham Palace; and amongst the sponsors at the christening, which took place on February the 10th, was the Duke of Wellington, "that old rebel", whom the Queen had not wished to invite to her marriage because of his attitude towards the Prince's alliance—but who was now reinstated in favour. "He is", she wrote in her diary, "the best friend we have."

[1] Bolitho, *op. cit.*, p. 79.

Chapter XII

SOME PHENOMENA

"How lucky you are", Her Majesty wrote to the King of the Belgians,[1] "to have seen the Comet. It is distinctly to be seen here, and has been seen by many people." But not, it seemed, by members of the English royal family.

Far away in a dingy room in Paris, a shabby young man, one year older than the Queen of England, decided after many qualms about the extravagance to spend some of the small sum left in his pocket on a cup of coffee, for he felt ill and weak. So, overcoatless, since his threadbare overcoat was in pawn, he went out into the rainy streets in search of a café. The noise of the rain, as he moved along, was like that of the marching of crowds, menacing multitudes, blown forward in an irresistible hurricane on the wind of their wrongs.

Two years later, Karl Marx, for it was he, expelled from France at the request of Prussia, was in Belgium, where he founded a society of German workers. Five years from that time, he accepted the invitation of a secret society of German working-class revolutionaries, "The League of the Just", and joined them at their headquarters in London; making his

[1] 28th March 1843.

home in England, there he eked out the rest of his half-starved existence—half-starved until his generous and beloved friend, Friedrich Engels, came to his rescue by making him an allowance of £350 a year.

It was as the result of a congress in London in November 1847 (shortly after the title "League of the Just" had been changed to "Communist League") that the views of Marx and Engels, the leaders of the meeting, were printed in all possible languages, as many, at least, as could be afforded by the funds of the League. This paper was to be known afterwards as the *Communist Manifesto*, and is claimed to be "a document more influential in human history than any other, except the French Declaration of the Rights of Man". So he worked, so he organized the belief of his fellow revolutionaries, side by side with his friend Engels. But the Queen of England never heard of him, or, if she heard of him, she forgot him again immediately.

The last few years had been by no means devoid of trouble for the Queen. In 1835, two years before she came to the throne, a committee of the General Working-Men's Association of London, with William Lovett at the head, had drawn up what is known as the People's Charter. For this, there were six points: the Charter claimed universal suffrage for every man who was of age, sane, and unconvicted of crime; annual Parliaments; salaries for Members of Parliament in order that poor men should be enabled to stand for election; voting by ballot so as to put a stop to bribery and to intimidation by the propertied classes; equal electoral districts, so that equal representation should be secured; and the abolition of the merely nominal property qualification of £300 in order that every voter, irrespective of property, should become eligible.

Naturally, as it was remarked at the time, no sensible government would take any notice of such nonsensical demands; and this led to the Chartist riots of 1839, with crowds like destructive whirlwinds of fire, the sound of their voices rising like the roaring of flames. What, it was wondered, could the people, formerly so docile, so manageable, want with such foolish luxuries as the ballot, universal male suffrage, annual Parliaments, the payment of members, the abolition of a property qualification for voters, and equal electoral districts? Yet, for such luxuries as these, they would break the law against rioting, they would defy law and order. The most disgraceful behaviour occurred even from people who should have known better.

At Newport, for instance, a linen-draper named Frost, who had been appointed a magistrate by Lord John Russell, actually headed a riot—a violent course of conduct which is both dangerous and, as a rule, wrong—but it is a little difficult to know how otherwise those brave and high-principled martyrs to their convictions—for they knew what was the fate in store for them—could have brought the wrongs of the people before the authorities, since both Tories and Whigs refused to listen to them.

Frost was betrayed and captured with his companions, and, after they had been condemned to death, their sentences were commuted to transportation for life by the indefatigable Hero of Tolpuddle.

So to the Hell of the penal settlements, hallowed by the memory of the men of Tolpuddle, went Frost the linen-draper who, with his companions, had braved death for the sake of those who lie in darkness.

At the time when the Queen came to the throne,[1] there were roughly thirty thousand convicts in Australia (since 1787, when the first shiploads of these doomed creatures were despatched, seventy-five thousand had been sent to this hell), and they were sent at the rate of about four

[1] See the very interesting essay: "Expansion and Emigration", by Douglas Woodruff, in Early Victorian England, edited by G. M. Young (Oxford University Press).

thousand a year. They were mostly starvation-haunted men, boys, and children, who had fallen into this death-trap through thefts brought about by despair, or had come to it through some poor and childish vanity. We have seen already, in a previous chapter, many of the horrors that they endured; but though these must have been, to some degree, known, it was the noble Bishop Ullathorne's book *The Catholic Mission in Australia*, published in 1837, which was, according to Mr Woodruff, "the first popular denunciation of the convict system", and this gives an anguished description of the suffering endured by these helpless creatures, their dread of being sent to Norfolk Island—the most terrible of all the penal settlements—their prayers to God that they might undergo the pains of execution rather than face the worse and more lingering horrors of that place of damnation. The scenes which Bishop Ullathorne witnessed when certain of these unhappy creatures who had been condemned to death were informed of their reprieve were, he said, the most heartrending he had ever experienced:

"The prison was in the form of a square, on one side of which stood a row of low cells, covered with a roof of shingle. The turnkey unlocked the first door and said: 'Stand aside, Sir.' There came forth a yellow exhalation, the produce of the bodies of the men confined therein. The exhalation cleared off, and I entered and found five men chained to a traversing bar. I spoke to them from my heart, and after preparing them and obtaining their names, I announced to them who were reprieved from death, and which of them were to die after five days had passed. I thus went from cell to cell until I had seen them all. It is a literal fact that each man who heard of his condemnation to death went down on his knees, with dry eyes, and thanked God. Among the thirteen who were condemned to execution three only were Catholics, but four of the others put

themselves under my care. I arranged to begin my duties
with them at six o'clock the next morning, and got an
intelligent Catholic overseer appointed to read at certain
times under my direction for those who could not read,
whilst I was engaged with the others. Night had now fallen,
and I proceeded to Government House, where I found a
brilliant assembly, in strange contrast with the human
miseries in which my soul had just been steeped. It may
seem strange to the inexperienced that so many men should
prefer death to life in that dreadful penal settlement. Let me,
then, say that all the criminals who were executed in New
South Wales were imbued with a like feeling. I have heard
it from several in their last moments, and Father McEncroe,
in a letter to me, which I quoted to Sir William Molesworth's
Committee on Transportation, affirmed that he had attended
seventy-four executions in the course of four years, and that
the greater number of criminals had, on their way to the
scaffold, thanked God that they were not going to Norfolk
Island.

"There were two thousand convicts on the island, all of
them men, all retransported for new crimes, after having
been first transported to New South Wales. Many of them
had, at one time or other, received sentence of death. They
were a desperate body of men, made more desperate by their
isolation from the outer world; by being deprived of access
to all stimulants; by the absence of hope; by the habitual
prospect of the encircling sea that isolated them from other
lands by the distance of a thousand miles; and by the absence
of all religious or other instruction or consolation."

Great, however, as was the sensation created by such
revelations as these, yet, to quote Mr Woodruff again, "the
evidence given to the Parliamentary Commission by the
officials themselves who had to work the system, was the
evidence that finally brought home to everyone what was
going on. 'When the veil was lifted by Sir William Moles-

worth's Commission,' said the *Edinburgh Review*, 'the people of England stood aghast at the sight of the monster they had created; and for very shame the system was abandoned.'"

But not, however, in spite of this shame, until the year 1853.

The attitude towards the penal system was, however, changing for the better; and, six years after Frost and his companions were sent to Australia, Sir James Graham informed Her Majesty[1] that the proceedings at Newgate on the occasion of the last condemned sermon and on the morning of the execution had been fully investigated, and that the report established the necessity for legislative interference in order to prevent any recurrence of scenes so disgraceful and so demoralizing. He would, he said, in obedience to Her Majesty's desire, bring the subject under the notice of his colleagues. He was inclined to think that executions might be carried out in the presence of a jury, and the great body of the spectators might be excluded without diminishing in any way the salutary terror and awful warning. At the same time he would consider any cause inexpedient which was likely to lead the public to desire the remission of capital executions in all cases without exception. It was not until twenty-three years had passed that public executions were abandoned (in the year 1863).

The Chartist riots continued, ever increasing in fierceness, and three years after the Newport outbreak Lord Melbourne, no longer Prime Minister, told the Queen that "there is a great mass of discontented feeling in the country, arising from the actual state of society. It arises from the distress and destitution which will fall at times upon a great manufacturing population, and from the wild and extravagant opinions which are naturally generated in an advanced state of society. However, it seems from the reports of the Ministers that 'a

[1] In a letter headed "Whitehall. 13 May, 1845".

bolder and firmer spirit is rising among classes possessing property, in defence of their rights'."[1]

Starvation and the new conditions which had been brought about through the use of machinery—these were doing their work. Yet, even at this time, Sir Robert Peel, that great-hearted man whose love of the people was hidden under such an unattractive and hard exterior, Lord Ashley, Sir James Graham, and such men as Richard Oastler were bringing about, slowly but surely, the reforms that were, in the end—but only after long struggles—to change the life of the poor.

Before the Queen came to the throne, the factory act of 1831 prevented any young person under the age of twenty-one from working between 7.30 at night and 5.30 in the morning. Then, in 1833, the factory act of that date made it compulsory, in all textile factories, for the working-hours or a young person under eighteen to be limited to twelve a day or sixty-nine a week; whilst for children under eleven the maximum was nine hours a day or forty-eight a week, and children must attend a school for two hours a day. But this act disappointed the workers, and only led to a deeper discontent, whilst the laws were disregarded as often as possible, as we shall see from the following chapter. No worker dared, for fear of dismissal, inform against his employer, in the cases when they were forced to work overtime, and so the abuses continued. Now, however, in 1840, there were further reforms. That year saw an act passed which protected the child chimney-sweepers, and the setting up of the Employment of Children Enquiry, registered in the mines act of 1842. Next year, Peel and his government attempted to improve upon the act of 1833, but they were defeated by a union of manufacturers and dissenters. Four years later, Sir James Graham reintroduced his bill, leaving out the clauses about education that had angered the dissenters, and reducing the hours children's labour to six and a half, those of men and women to

---

[1] *Letters*, Volume I, p. 425.

twelve. Lord Ashley went still further, and wished the twelve hours to be reduced to ten. Peel, on his side, pointed out that *the bill only protected textile workers, whilst the condition of many other workers was more terrible still.* "Will you legislate for all?" he cried. A shout of "Yes!" arose from the whole House. "Without meaning it," says Mr G. M. Young, from whose interesting essay, "Portrait of an Age", the foregoing passage is a transcription, "the House of Commons had undertaken to regulate the factory system throughout the land, and a few nights later they recalled their decision. But the tide was running fast...." Richard Oastler—the "good old king of the factory children, the man who, because of his opposition to the New Poor Law, was imprisoned for debt by his employer, a Mr Thornley— had recently been released by a collection raised amongst the workers and his personal friends. The Whigs had repeatedly offered to set him at liberty by paying his debts, if, in return, he would cease his agitation against the Poor Law. His answer was to remain in prison (from whence he published his Fleet Papers against the factory system and the Poor Law)."[1] Now at last he was free, and the strength of will, the passion that had sustained him in prison, were thrown into the various agitations for the reform of working conditions.

Unhappily, side by side with this increasing enlightenment on the part of the governing classes, grew a wish to interfere with all nations possessing a different pigmentation of the skin—purely, of course, for their good, and because Britain had been appointed to this work by Heaven. Mr Roebuck, ten years after this time, even went so far as to say that it would be better if all dusky-complexioned persons were wiped off the face of the earth altogether. "We have no business in Kaffraria", he explained, "except on the understanding that we are going to plant there a people of higher

[1] Engels, *op. cit.*

intelligence, and this can only be done by the gradual annihilation of the native population.

"It is an utter pretence to talk of humanity, and the principles of the Christian religion, and the Decalogue; the black man must vanish in the face of the white."[1]

But at the time of which I write it was the yellow race, and not the black, which was occupying the attention of Britain, and the yellow men had brought this state of affairs on themselves by refusing to allow opium to be imported into China by the British. Yet, as the *Saturday Review* pointed out, when, forty years later, fresh trouble arose on the same subject, "there is indubitable testimony to the wholesome effect of an occasional or regular opium pipe. It soothes the nerves, lessens coughs and consumptive tendencies; and can be used medicinally in all kinds of unpleasant and hidden disorders.

"If there is one thing clear in the whole controversy, it is that the authorities have no wish to put the cultivation down. Occasional requests for a high prohibition duty on sea-borne opium are obviously dictated by the mere spirit of protection."[2]

It was this regrettable spirit which led to the war between Britain and China with the renewal of the East India Company's charter in 1834; the Chinese ports were thrown open, and British private traders soon found the traffic in opium a huge source of wealth. Suddenly, to their wrath, the benighted barbarians upon whom they intended to force their wares forbade the importation of the drug. But the British Ministry, secure in their Christian rectitude, connived at the trade, and the traffickers took it for granted that in forcing the drug upon the Chinese they had the British government behind them. When the government proclaimed that they found it their duty to maintain the laws of

[1] *Victoriana*, by Osbert Sitwell and Margaret Barton (Gerald Duckworth and Co., Ltd.).   [2] *Ibid.*

China, Captain Elliot, the head superintendent of the trade, not believing in the sincerity of this announcement, asked that warships should be sent to China to protect the lives and property of the British. This was done; but the barbarians were obdurate in their refusal to countenance the drug, and their obduracy led to a war. However it is gratifying to know that in the end all was for the best in the best of all possible worlds, that the barbarians got a thorough beating, and the Queen got the island of Hong Kong, though at first all the circumstances were not entirely happy. We find her assuring the King of the Belgians[1] that *all* the government had wanted might have been got, if it had not been for the unaccountably strange conduct of Charles Elliot, who completely disobeyed his instructions and *tried* to get the *lowest* terms he could. . . . Finally, in 1842, the war was brought to a glorious conclusion, and we find Lord Stanley writing to Her Majesty, on the 23rd of November: "It is difficult to estimate the moral effect which these victories may produce, not in Asia merely, but throughout Europe also. . . . In China a termination has been put to the effusion of blood by the signature of a treaty which has placed Your Majesty's dominions on a footing never recognized in favour of any foreign Power—a footing of perfect equality with the Chinese Empire; which has obtained large indemnity for the past, and ample security for the future, and which has opened to British enterprise the commerce of China to an extent which it is almost impossible to anticipate."

Encouraged by the moral effect of this victory, England at once began a dispute with the United States of America, claiming (quite properly though a little illogically) the right to search ships suspected of carrying cargoes of slaves.

It is sad to think that not everyone shared Lord Stanley's enthusiasm about the moral victory. On the 8th April 1840 a young man of thirty-two years of age, whose career as a

[1] On 13th April 1841.

statesman was already held to be promising, Mr William Gladstone, spoke against it with indignation in the House of Commons.

"I do not know", ran the speech, "how it can be urged against the Chinese that they refused provisions to those who refused obedience to their laws whilst residing within their territory. I am not competent to judge how long this war may last, nor how protracted may be the operations, but this I can say, that a war more unjust in its origin, a war more calculated in its progress to cover this country with disgrace, I do not know and I have not read of. Mr Macaulay spoke last night in eloquent terms of the British flag waving in glory at Canton, and of the animating effect produced upon the minds of our sailors by the knowledge that in no country under heaven was it permitted to be insulted. But how comes it to pass that the sight of that flag always raises the spirits of Englishmen? Is it because it has always been associated with the cause of justice, with opposition of oppression, with respect for national rights, with honourable commercial enterprise? But now under the auspices of the noble lord (Palmerston) that flag is hoisted to protect an infamous contraband traffic, and if it were never to be hoisted except as it is now hoisted on the coast of China, we should recoil from the sight with horror, and should never again feel our hearts thrill with emotion when it floats magnificently and in pride upon the breeze.... Although the Chinese were undoubtedly guilty of much absurd phraseology, of no little ostentatious pride, and of some excess, justice in my opinion is with them, and whilst they the pagans and semi-civilised barbarians have it, we the enlightened and civilised Christians are pursuing objects both at variance with justice and religion."

In spite of all Mr Gladstone could say, however, the war was carried to its glorious conclusion, and there was nothing he could do about it.

SOME PHENOMENA

Meanwhile, at the Palace, domestic life had continued much as usual, with the games of ball and battledore and shuttlecock, the conversations after dinner, and dear woolly Islay, whom Lord Melbourne had called a dull dog, much to the Queen's indignation, sitting up and begging for Lord M.'s spectacles—though what he hoped to see through them I do not know, unless it was the happy condition of convicts in Australia, or of the factory children ("Oh, if you'd only have the goodness to leave them alone"). And sometimes the Queen, who was particularly attached to animals, would witness the performance of a wild-beast tamer. There was one particularly striking show of the kind, some months before the Queen's marriage, and this is best described in Her Majesty's own words. "Van Amburgh surpassed even himself, and was miraculous....In the second cage, as usual, the little lamb was brought in while he (Van Amburgh) was reclining on the Lion's body and head, and put before the Lion's nose, which he, as usual, bore with indifference; when one of the Leopards, the smallest of all the animals and a sneaking little thing, came, seized the lamb and ran off with it, all the others, except the Lion, and all those in the other cage making a rush to help in the slaughter; it was an awful moment and we thought all was over, when Van Amburgh rushed to the Leopard, which he beat severely—took the lamb in his arms—and only looked at all the others, and not one moved, though in the act of devouring the lamb. It was beautiful and wonderful....They had *not* been *fed since* early the *preceding day* and consequently were wilder than usual....

"Van Amburgh, who was in plain clothes, is a tall but not very powerful looking man; young, very modest, quiet and unassuming; with a mild expression, a receding forehead and very peculiar eyes, which don't exactly squint, but have a cast in them. I asked him if that had ever happened before with the lamb; he replied 'Sometimes it does, it did the first time I took one in' but the lamb was unhurt; they then fed

SOME PHENOMENA

them and they roared and fought with one another terrifically; but it was very fine....He scarcely ever uses an iron bar to them, but only a stick made of Rhinoceros hide, which he showed me."

Sometimes, however, Her Majesty was brought face to face with a saddening spectacle, as when, for instance, on the 8th September 1842, she was at the house of Lord Glenlyon (afterwards the 6th Duke of Atholl) who had become blind, and she told the King of the Belgians, "It was very melancholy, to see him do the *honours, not* seeing anything."

Chapter XIII

MARCH PAST

════════

J ust behind the cannibal mart, where all day long, under the Bedlam daylight's murderous roar, the shambles for souls are set in the street, are the Rookeries of St Giles. These thin canvas-bellying slums consist of tall three or four storied houses, so thin one would think that only Nothingness lay behind, as indeed was the case with many of them—Nothingness, and in the midst of that nothingness human meat, carcases piled away one on top of each other, old and young, those who are sick with all known diseases, with the fresh and fair and still untainted, men, women and children, piled on top of each other mounds deep, in all degrees of nakedness, or with rags so unutterably dyed in woe and in all the filth of the world that not even the waters of Lethe could wash them clean or make them forgetful of their stains. Here they lie until, with the first dawn light, they must find their way to the cannibal mart once more.

To some of these houses there are no doors, for, as Engels says, why should there be doors when there is only Nothingness, and nought else to steal?[1]

Here comes the tramp of a hundred thousand feet, ac-

[1] See Engels, *op. cit.*, p. 27.

companied by the fluttering of rags whose darkness would put out the lights of heaven. "In London", said Engels, "fifty thousand persons get up every morning not knowing where to lay their heads at night."[1] For some there will be the lodging-houses where they will be packed one on top of each other. To the foul Refuge for the Homeless in Upper Ogle Street, for example, a shelter meant to house three hundred persons, come nightly two thousand, seven hundred and forty living beings (to take an average),[2] with their train of sweat, stink, drunken illuminations and ravings, blows, apelike thefts, or, as they lie piled five or six deep in the darkness, worse than all these, sins against the sun.[3]

For others again, there is the twopenny lean-over.... "Poor devil couldn't afford price of a bed. Tuk him all his time, t' find for a tupp'ny leanover!...Y' should go an' have a look at it. Its for t' real down and outs as can't afford price of a bed. They charge y' tuppence t' leán o'r a rope all night. Hell! y' should see 'em! about forty blokes sittin' on forms in a line and leanin' o'er a rope...elbow t' elbow all swayin' fast asleep, except the old bastards who're dyin' and can't sleep for spittin' and coughin' their guts away...ay, and Sam wouldn't ha' been able t' afford that if he hadna gone buskin'. Jesus! That's work for y' if y' like....Trapesin' streets, singin' in t' perishin' cold, an' sometimes nobody'd give him a stiver!"[4]

Here, in "the port of poverty, the enormous city with its sky stained with fire and blood, (oh, the stinking rags, the bread soaked in rain)", under the railway arches, huddled together like dead bodies, stretched out among unknown men, without age, without feeling, lies many a youthful adventurer, whose heart had once held the world. "On the roads, during the winter nights," wrote one who had endured

[1] Engels, *op. cit.*, p. 31. [2] See Engels, *op. cit.*, p. 32.
[3] See Engels, *op. cit.*, p. 31.
[4] Walter Greenwood: *Love on the Dole* (Jonathan Cape, Ltd.).

all the rigours of starvation, "...a vow gripped my frozen heart:...Thou wilt no more be killed than if thou wert a corpse. In the morning my eyes were so blank, and my look so dead, that perhaps those I met *saw me not*." [1]

Here they lie, here they wander, and round them creeps a civilization of the mud, a circle of hell peopled by beings who have been able to make a capital and a fresh civilization, like that of Hell, out of their destitution.... Unbelievable horrors of prostitution, "simpletons, hyenas, Molochs, old insanities", all these welter together in the slum overhanging that last gulf which is the death from starvation.

Upstairs on the floor of a windowless room at 3 Lion Court, Bermondsey, lies a thin huddled drift of feathers, so thin and dirty that it might be a cobweb. It does not cover the body of Ann Galway, aged forty-five, who is lying dead beside the starved but living body of her nineteen-year-old son. In this room, there is not one stick that had once been part of a table, a chair, a bedstead. There is no cup, no knife, no plate, no utensil of any sort. It is a room for the dead, who have no necessities. There is only the small drift of feathers, scattered over this ghost of a ghost, lying dead beside the living ghost of her nineteen-year-old son. No coverlet, no sheet, hides her nakedness, but the feathers have stuck so fast she must be plucked like a fowl before the cause of death can be known and proclaimed at the inquest—hunger and cold. So here she lies in that room in which she had eked out her misery with her husband and child, and in which the only sign, that these three beings had human needs, is that part of the floor has been torn up, and the bare hole used as a privy. [2]

The torrent of the homeless sweeps past the empty place where Ann Galway waits for the majesty of the law to pronounce on her death...a million footsteps are heard in all

[1] Arthur Rimbaud: *Une Saison en Enfer*, translated by Helen Rootham.
[2] Inquest, November 14th 1843. Engels, *op. cit.*, pp. 29–30.

the cities, as they are joined by the multitudinous army of the Workers, those legions of the Dead who have been resurrected for the purpose of the cannibal market, and who now listlessly seek the holes where they may lie down under the sheets of the darkness.

In Edinburgh, built upon the slopes of the great hill, tumbling down into Hell, are multitudes of narrow, crooked alleys called wynds. "These streets", says *The Artisan* (October 1842), "are often so narrow that a person can step from the window of one house into that of its opposite neighbour, while the houses are piled so high, storey upon storey, that the light can scarcely penetrate into the court or alley that lies between. In this part of the city there are neither sewers nor other drains, not even privies belonging to the houses. In consequence all refuse, garbage, and the excrements of at least 50,000 persons are thrown into the gutters every night;"[1] and from this dried filth, from these hellish slums, huge clouds of vapour arise. Here, and in other slums that equal them, will be the first breeding-place of those appalling epidemics of typhus (that result of starvation, anxiety, and filth) and cholera, which will sweep away, first the myriad unnamed poor, and then the shivering rich from their hiding-places.

Far away in Manchester, under the shadow of the Iron Man, "in several" (houses), says Engels, "I found absolutely nothing, while the door stood open, and the inhabitants leaned against it".[2] These unspeakable slums which were visited by Engels are cities of the Dead. We see the rocking, bellying houses, we see the privies without doors, the long blackened covered passages leading from one horrible slum courtyard to another (in some courtyards, pork butchers had put pens for swine, which grew fat on the foulness of these places), our feet sink into the defilement that covers the desecrated soil with inches of mudlike substance; the various

[1] Engels, *op. cit.*, p. 35. [2] *Ibid.*, p. 51.

poisonous reeks and exhalations that rise from the conglomeration of hovels, from factory debris, and from contaminated putrefying water—these fill our throats and choke us; but so full are these slums of foulness of every description, of stenches and sickening refuse-heaps, that there seems no room for any human being except the writer. We read that in certain small rooms there are people who sleep in layers, but it conveys no effect of life, and makes much the same impression on us as when we read, in descriptions of the Plague, that there were so many dead that they had to be buried pell-mell, in common pits. So did these unfortunates seek their nightly respite from life in these common pits of sleep.

Only in one place visited by Engels do we get the impression of movement on the part of any inhabitants, and that was in the phrase quoted above. What solemn march of armies can compare with the doomed tread of those destitutes who, when day knocked at the hovels, rose from the bare floors on which they had passed the hours of night, opened the doors which had made their misery secure, and, turning their backs upon the empty shells, looked across the filthy refuse which was theirs, to a world of light and movement.

And, over all, broods the giant shadow of the Iron Man.

During a strike, wrote Dr Ure, in his *Philosophy of Manufactures*, a certain inventor "produced in the course of a few months a machine apparently instinct with the thought, feeling, and tact of the experienced workman—which even in its infancy displayed a new principle of regulation ready in its mature state to fulfil the functions of a finished spinner. Thus the Iron Man, as the operatives fitly called it, sprang out of the hands of a modern Prometheus at the bidding of Minerva—a creation destined to restore order among the industrial classes and to confirm to Great Britain the empire of art. The news of this Herculean prodigy spread thorough dismay through the Union, and even long before it left its cradle, so to speak, it strangled the Hydra of misrule."[1]

Under this shadow, the huge procession sweeps onward.

These gaunt towers of rags and bones that come first in the endless procession are the Hand-Loom Weavers, earning sometimes as much as eight or nine shillings a week, which must suffice for the needs of their families. They are crawling home to the damp cellars in which they live, for woven goods require a damp weaving-room. Sometimes, Engels tells us, "six hand-loom weavers, several of them married, live together in a cottage, with one large sleeping-room and several work-rooms. Their food consists entirely of potatoes, with occasionally a little porridge, rarely milk, and scarcely, if ever, meat."[2]

Next come the Stocking Weavers, of whom it might be said that even their bones seem as if they were crumbling, from lack of nourishment. The *Morning Chronicle* published letters from a stocking weaver in Hinkley, stating that, of fifty families in that place (three hundred and twenty-one persons), each family earned on an average eleven shillings and fourpence weekly. Out of this the house rent, the frame rent, fuel, light, soap, and needles cost five shillings and ten-pence weekly, so that only a penny halfpenny per head remained for the daily food. "No eye", wrote this stocking weaver, "has seen, no ear heard, and no heart felt, the half of the sufferings these poor people endure." Beds were in most cases wanting, and the people were forced by starvation to work on Sundays. "Last Monday", said one man, "I got up at two in the morning and worked until near midnight, the other days from six in the morning to between eleven and twelve at night. I've had enough of it. I shan't kill myself, and so now I go to bed at ten, and make up the lost time on Sundays."[3]

[1] Ure, *op. cit.*, pp. 366 *et seq.* Engels, *op. cit.*, p. 223.
[2] Engels, *op. cit.*, p. 140.   [3] Engels, *op. cit.*, pp. 189–90.

Now come the Nail Workers of Sedgeley....They are
herded together for their work in filthy stable-like huts, girls
and boys together from the tenth or twelfth year, and they
are only considered fully qualified workers when they can
make a thousand nails a day. For twelve hundred nails the
pay is fivepence three farthings. "Each nail", says Engels,
"receives twelve blows, and the hammer weighs one and
a quarter pounds. The nailer therefore is obliged to lift
eighteen thousand pounds in succession before he can earn
his pay." They are fed, for the most part, on "meat from
diseased animals, or pork from swine smothered in transportation".[1]

What is this terrible sound, as of multitudinous wooden
shuttles, or air being driven through thousands of wooden
tubes? What is this cloud of black dust, expectorated from
dying lungs? It is the sound and symptom of the industrial
disease from which the Grinders die.

"In Sheffield", wrote Dr Knight of that city, "there are
some two thousand five hundred grinders at work. About
one hundred and fifty (eighty men and seventy boys) are
fork grinders; these die between the twenty-eighth and thirty-
second year. The razor grinders, who grind wet as well as
dry, die between forty and forty-five years; and the table
cutlery grinders, who grind wet, die between the forty-fifth
and fiftieth year."[2] This comes from "the sharp-edged
metal dust particles freed in the cutting, which fill the air and
are thus inhaled", and, too, from the bent position in which
they must work, and in which the chest and stomach are
cramped. Here they come, with their yellow faces, their
"features expressing anxiety",[3] their rough hoarse voices,
and that loud cough "whose sound is as if air were driven
through a wooden tube". Dr Knight adds that he has often

[1] Engels, *op. cit.*, pp. 201–2.
[2] Report of Dr Knight of Sheffield. Engels, *op. cit.*, p. 203.
[3] Evidence of Dr Knight of Sheffield. Engels, *op. cit.*, p. 204.

told grinders with the first symptoms of this disease that if they returned to work they would die. It was useless, for "he who is once a grinder falls into despair, as if he had sold his soul to the devil".[1]

What is this feeble sound, this hopeless whispering of multitudes, so faint it seems the despairing prayer of those about to die? It is the voice of the Pottery Workers in the grip too of their industrial disease. Here they come, twitching and writhing as if they were being agitated by some vast machine, some Moloch which folds them in its grasp. Their work is to dip the finished pottery into fluid containing great quantities of lead or arsenic. The hands, the clothing of these men, women, and children, are perpetually wet with this fluid, the skin softens and is scraped away by the contact with hard or rough objects, and their fate has them in its grasp, for into these wounds, these soft places, the lead, the arsenic is absorbed. Violent pain, serious disease of the stomach and intestines, tuberculosis, but most often epilepsy, are the results. Amongst men, partial paralysis of the hand muscles, or paralysis of whole limbs, is frequent.[2] One witness[3] swore that two children who worked with him died of convulsions at their work; whilst another witness, who had been used for dipping work for two years as a boy, told how this disease had started with violent pains in the bowels, then convulsions had followed, so that he was bedridden for two months, and how since then the convulsions had increased in frequency, so that each day he was subjected to from ten to twenty epileptic fits, his right arm was completely paralysed, and it was a medical certainty that he would never recover the use of the limb In one factory, according to the same commission, four men, all epileptic and affected with severe colic, and eleven boys, several of them epileptic, were found in the dipping-house. In those rooms of the potteries in which the

[1] Engels, *op. cit.*, p. 204. [2] See Engels, *op. cit.*, p. 206.
[3] According to the Scriven Report and Evidence.

stone-work is scoured, the air is filled with the dust of ground flint which has the same result as the steel dust on the Sheffield grinders. Breathlessness, inability to lie down, sore throat, and a terrible cough—these are the result.... Until at last they come to have so feeble a voice they can scarcely be heard. They, too, all die of tuberculosis.[1]

Here come the Runners for the Lacemakers—children of seven years, or even four or five. Commissioner Granger, indeed, actually found one child of two in this slavery. Their work consists in following a thread which is to be withdrawn by a needle from an elaborate design, and the hours are generally fourteen or sixteen a day. Incurable blindness is the usual result.[2] The bobbin-lacemakers, who are for the most part very young girls, are obliged to sit almost bent double over their lace cushions; and, to support them in this deadly fatigue, they wear stays with a wooden busk, which "at their tender age," as Engels says, "while their bones are still very soft, wholly displace their ribs. They usually die of consumption, after suffering the severest forms of digestive disorders. They are almost wholly without education or moral training. They love finery, and prostitution is almost an epidemic among them."[3]

These thinnest rags of all, these fluttering banners, which now pass before us, contain the souls of the Sewers of Neckties, who are contracted to work sixteen hours a day for the sum of four shillings and sixpence a week—and, more wretched still, the Shirtmakers, whose weekly wage is from two shillings and sixpence a week to three shillings, for work continued from the earliest dawn to late into the night. Crowded together in little airless rooms so close together that not another being could find a place, the warmth that

[1] According to the Scriven Report and Evidence.
[2] See Engels, *op. cit.*, pp. 191–2.
[3] Burns: Children's Employment Commission's Report. Engels, *op. cit.*, p. 193.

TREMENDOUS SACRIFICE!

THE EXPLOITATION OF THE SEAMSTRESSES

From a caricature by George Cruikshank

British Museum

comes from those bodies packed so closely together is their only heating. Here they sit from four or five till midnight, and in a year or two they are dead.[1]

Now comes the trailing sound of thirty thousand weary feet, as the Seamstresses who work for the dressmakers creep past. There are not less than fifteen thousand of them in London; and during the season their working-hours are anything from fifteen to eighteen hours a day; the result is, that these young girls, sometimes scarcely more than children, never have more than six, frequently not more than three or four, and often only two hours out of the twenty-four in which to rest, sleep, and eat. It is not unusual indeed for these girls not to undress for nine consecutive days and nights, during which time they throw themselves "for a moment or two upon a mattress, and are given food, ready cut up in order to require the least possible time for swallowing".[2] Incurable blindness and tuberculosis are often the fate of these girls; even if they leave this work whilst still very young, their health is ruined, and, should they marry, they bear feeble and sickly children on whom the marks foretelling an early death are visible from the moment they are born.

The vast procession sweeps forward, and the sound of their multitudinous footsteps is echoed far away in the Black Country, amongst the grassless desolation of the slag-heaps. This land looks as if it had been torn by an earthquake, and through it another interminable army drags its way. Here come the coal-miners, who must die between the ages of forty and fifty. For twelve or fourteen hours a day or even more, buried beneath the earth as if they were already dead, they yet make the frantic movements of the living. In the mines, the doors which separate the divisions of the mine and regulate its ventilation are watched by the smallest

---

[1] See Engels, *op. cit.*, p. 211.
[2] Engels, *op. cit.*, p. 209.

children available, "who thus pass twelve hours daily in the dark, alone", without any occupation but this.[1] The transport of coal and iron-stone is very heavy and exhausting work, for it must be pushed in large tubs without wheels over the uneven floor of the mine, or sometimes, worse still, through wet clay or through wide pools of water, up steep inclines, and under roofs so low that those who are pushing the tubs must creep on their hands and knees. For this heavy and terrible work the older children and young girls are employed, and they work from eleven to twelve hours a day, sometimes even longer, whilst in Scotland fourteen hours is the usual working-day, and they must often submit to double time, when all workers, men, women, and children, down to the very smallest, are in the mines from twenty-four to thirty-six hours at a stretch, and when food must be snatched at odd moments, as best it can.

Here, in an endless, shambling army, come the Factory Workers, the makers of our new and prosperous England; and the Report of Factory Inspector L. Horner, given in October 1844, states that there are hundreds of young men between twenty and thirty, employed as piecers, etc., who do not get more than eight or nine shillings a week, whilst children under thirteen earn five shillings, and young girls of sixteen to twenty from ten to twelve shillings. It was of these poor creatures that sleek, complacent, rosy-faced Dr Andrew Ure, in his *Philosophy of Manufactures*, wrote: "It was their high wages which enabled them to maintain a stipendiary committee in affluence, and to pamper themselves into nervous ailments by a diet too rich and exciting for their indoor employment."[2] These swollen hulks, shambling along, so bowed that their arms almost touch the earth and they seem like some hopeless and outcast animals, are the women who within two or three hours will bear a

---

[1] See Engels, *op. cit.*, p. 244.
[2] Ure, *op. cit.*, p. 298. Engels, *op. cit.*, p. 168.

child, and who for twelve or fourteen hours, without a moment's rest, have stood at the loom for the sum of one penny an hour. Frequently they must stoop, and they must lift heavy burdens. If they dared to sit down for an instant, they would be fined sixpence, and if they left their work they would leave it for ever—there are plenty of other workers to take their place. In eight, or even three or four days' time, starvation will have driven them back to their places at the loom, where they will work all day from five in the morning, with their breasts dripping with milk so that their clothing is saturated with it,[1] and the baby, if it has been born alive, will be looked after by another baby a few years older than itself. Often these babies will be without food until night has fallen.

What are these tiny bundles of rags that, from time to time, we see lying in the road? They are the unhappy little children (sometimes only five years of age) who are condemned to the slavery of the mills, and who have fallen exhausted on the roads on the way home, and presently will be found by their parents, asleep where they have fallen. If they manage to reach their homes unaided, they will throw themselves down on the floor as soon as they have crawled through the door, and, falling asleep without having touched a single morsel of food, they must be washed and put to bed in their sleep. Dr Ure, however, gives a roseate picture of the delights which fall to the lot of the little children working in the factories. "I have visited", he says, "many factories, both in Manchester and in the surrounding districts, during a period of several months, entering the spinning-rooms unexpectedly, and often alone, at different times of the day, and I never saw a single instance of corporal chastisement inflicted on a child, nor, indeed, did I ever see children in ill-humour. They seemed to be always cheerful and alert;

[1] See Evidence before Ashley Commission, 1844. Engels, *op. cit.*, p. 143.

taking pleasure in the light play of their muscles, enjoying the mobility natural to their age. The scene of industry, so far from exciting sad emotions in my mind, was always exhilarating. It was delightful to observe the nimbleness with which they pieced broken ends, as the mule carriages began to recede from the fixed roller beam, and to see them at leisure, after a few seconds' exercise of their tiny fingers, to amuse themselves in any attitude they chose, till the stretch and winding on are once more completed. The work of these lively elves seemed to resemble a sport, in which habit gave them a pleasing dexterity. Conscious of their skill, they were delighted to show it off to any stranger. As to exhaustion by the day's work, they evinced no trace of it on emerging from the mill in the evening; for they immediately began to skip about any neighbouring playground, and to commence their little games with the same alacrity as boys issuing from a school." [1]

It is sad to think that the Stuart Evidence, to take only one case, did not agree with optimistic Dr Ure; [2] for in this we read how children are seized naked in bed by the over-lookers, and driven with blows and kicks to the factory, their clothing over their arms; how their sleepiness is driven off with blows, how they fall asleep over their work nevertheless; how one poor child sprang up, still asleep, at the call of the overlooker, and mechanically went through the operations of its work after the machine was stopped; one reads how children, too tired to go home, hide away in the wool in the dyeing-room to sleep there, and can only be driven out of the factory with straps; how many hundreds come home so tired every night, that they can eat no supper for sleepiness and want of appetite, and their parents find them kneeling by the bedside, where they have fallen asleep

[1] Ure, *op. cit.*, p. 301. Engels, *op. cit.*, p. 168.
[2] See Engels, *op. cit.*, p. 167.

during their childish supplication to the God Who looks down on this man-made horror.

The huge procession wends on its way, darkening the earth with its misery, destroying the natural rhythm of life with the sound of its weary footsteps, putting out the lights of heaven with its fluttering, stained, and blackened rags.

Chapter XIV

HOME LIFE

"Sir Robert", wrote the Prince,[1] "has an immense scheme in view; he thinks he shall be able to remove the contest entirely from the dangerous ground upon which it has got—that of a war between the manufacturers, the hungry and the poor against the landed proprietors, the aristocracy, which can only end in the ruin of the latter; he will not bring forward a measure upon the Corn Laws, but a much more comprehensive one. He will deal with the whole commercial system of the country"...and he added: "Part of the maintenance of the poor, according to the Poor Law, might be undertaken by the State. A great calamity must be foreseen, when the immeasurable railroads, now in progress, shall be terminated, which will be the case in a few years. This will throw an enormous labouring population out of employment. There might be a law passed which would provide employment for them, and improve the agriculture and productions of the country, by enabling the State to advance money to the great proprietors for the improvements of their estates, which they could not obtain otherwise without charging their estates beyond what they already have to bear."

[1] 25th December 1845. *Letters*, Volume I, p. 78.

Lord Melbourne was fading away, and that once dreaded ogre, Sir Robert Peel, had taken his place in the Queen's regard. His dancing-master manners were forgotten, the silver fittings of the coffin no longer alarmed—he had, in short, become one of the Queen's greatest friends, for, on closer acquaintance, the Queen came to appreciate his loyalty, his patriotism, and his chivalrous conduct towards herself. And, above all—supreme virtue—did he not appreciate her husband at his true worth?

The Queen's alarm, when, in January 1843, her friend and minister's secretary, Mr Edward Drummond, was murdered in mistake for him—her anger when the murderer Mac Nagton was pronounced "guilty but insane"—could not be exaggerated. "The proof of the wretch Mac Nagton's madness", she wrote to Peel, "seems to the Queen very slight, and indeed there is and should be a difference between that madness which is such that a man knows not what he does, and madness which does not prevent a man from purposely buying pistols, and then with determined purpose watching and shooting a person."[1]

That her good Sir Robert should have been in an instant's danger—that his faithful secretary should have been murdered in his place—this was unthinkable. Thank God, reflected the Queen, this loyal friend and trustworthy minister remained to them, working side by side with the Prince for the good of her people, to banish poverty, to increase education, to bring the arts into the national life—for the Queen was, by now, as keenly interested in the arts as was the Prince, and to this new point of view she had been won largely by her love of music. For, if one art was so safe, could the others really be dangerous and subversive?

The influence of Albert was, by now, supreme; the Queen, who had always adored him, had become completely at one with him, her ideas were moulded by him, her aspirations

[1] *Letters*, Volume I, p. 457.

were his. Albert, her duty to her country, and her ever increasing family, filled her whole mind. The Prince of Wales had been born just a year after the Princess Royal, then, less than eighteen months later, came Princess Alice, a year elapsed and Prince Alfred was born, then Princess Helena, and then, some two years afterwards, Princess Louise. And there were still more children to come. And all must, as far as possible, resemble their beloved papa. Oh, *how* fervently she prayed that the Prince of Wales would resemble his angelic, dearest father in *every, every* respect, both in body and mind. Life was one long romance, in which every incident, both great and small, was invested with glamour. The Prince leading dearest little Pussy (the Princess Royal) into her mother's room, dressed in a very smart dress of white merino trimmed with blue, given her by her grandmother the Duchess of Kent, lifting her up and placing her on the Queen's bed, and then seating himself between his wife and child [1]—could anything be more full of happiness? It seemed that moments such as this could never fade.

There was indeed, by now, no room for any other influence but Albert's; and one day in 1842, six years before the final fading of Lord Melbourne, another ghost, an elderly woman with a parrot-sharp face, her eyes reddened by weeping, left the Castle and, in the midst of a perfect city of luggage, set off for her home at Bückeburg, where for the rest of her life she lived with her sister in a tall and narrow house, the walls of whose rooms were entirely covered with portraits of the Queen. Her Majesty for many years wrote to her regularly once a week until, at the Baroness' request, the interval between the letters was increased to once a month; and when the Queen and the Prince were in Germany they passed through Bückeburg, and once again saw her dear old Lehzen, now an old woman. But she had faded

[1] See Sir Theodore Martin: *The Life of His Royal Highness the Prince Consort* (John Murray). Strachey, *op. cit.*, p. 108.

QUEEN VICTORIA AND THE PRINCE CONSORT WITH
THEIR FIVE ELDEST CHILDREN, 1847
From an engraving by S. Cousins after a painting by F. Winterhalter
British Museum

into a far distance, and when, in September 1870, this friend, so faithful and devoted in spite of all her faults, died, the Queen, usually so meticulous in noting everything in her diary, did not mention the death till three days after it had occurred, and when she did, wrote: "Forgot to mention that my dearest, kindest friend, dear old Lehzen, expired quite quietly and peacefully on the 9th. For two years she had been quite bedridden as a result of breaking her hip. Though latterly her mind had not been clear, still there were days when she constantly spoke of me, whom she had known from the age of six months. She had devoted her life to me, from my fifth to my eighteenth year, with the most wonderful self-abnegation, never even taking one day's leave. After I came to the throne she got to be rather trying, and especially so after my marriage, but never from any evil intention, only from a mistaken idea of duty and affection for me....I feel much too that she is gone."

Other friends were fading fast, meanwhile, fading away in the sunlight. Nothing remained of Lord Melbourne now excepting an empty voice, for ever chattering. He was, by now, out of office, and his place, as we have seen, was filled by the formerly dreaded Sir Robert Peel.

The Queen, contemplating the fading figure of Lord M. when it appeared, as it still did from time to time, wrote: "the dream is *past*."

At first, however, Lord Melbourne did not realize that he was only a ghost; the dust into which he was crumbling seemed still to have the bright living glitter of the sun-motes. When he ceased to be Prime Minister, he still continued to keep up a correspondence on political subjects with the young Queen, who for three years or more had been the centre of his life and of all his thoughts, and for whom he had felt a parental devotion, and Stockmar, horrified at this indiscretion, and at the fact that the garrulous Mrs Norton was aware of it, remonstrated with him vigorously. Lord Melbourne, must, he declared, be aware of the impropriety of such a proceeding. Lord Melbourne replied that he thought it unnecessary to keep Baron Stockmar's messenger waiting, and that he would send an answer at a later time; but the Baron waited in vain. No answer came, and the flood of letters to the Queen continued. At last, however, they began to die away, until in the end they ceased altogether. And only the void shell that had contained Lord Melbourne, the empty voice, remained, floating miserably from dinner-party to dinner-party, drifting down to Windsor, where he was still the Queen's "good old friend", but where his former place was occupied. For the Court seemed full of new interests. In the first place, there were the royal babies (the Queen's second child, a son, had been born on November the 9th 1841), and these occupied most of the royal attention; and then the Queen's political outlook had changed. Once she had been an ardent Whig—but Prince Albert was an equally enthusiastic Free Trader—so of course the Queen was a Free Trader too. It was very awkward when, dining at Windsor at the time when the corn laws were being repealed,[1] Lord Melbourne, whose conversation had by now become noticeably disjointed, ejaculated, apropos of nothing: "Ma'am, it's a damned dishonest act!..." "Her Majesty laughed", wrote Mr Strachey, "and tried to change the conversation, but without avail"; Lord Melbourne clung to it in spite of all her attempts to dislodge him, repeating the phrase again and again, until the Queen exclaimed, "'Lord Melbourne, I must beg you not to say anything more on this subject now'; and then", said Mr Strachey, "he held his tongue."

A year after the time when he had ceased to be Prime Minister, he had a paralytic stroke, and although he seemed by now to have recovered his health, something within him was broken. The three years in which he had sat by the

[1] See Strachey, *op. cit.*, p. 121.

HOME LIFE

Queen's side, listening to her chatter, and telling her of all the marvels he had seen, of all the wonders of history—these had been a romantic dream, and now it was over. The Queen had an affection for him, it was true, but her enthusiasm had faded away. Nothing interested Lord M. now—neither reading Cicero on Old Age, nor his own reflections on the dinner-parties he had once enjoyed. The conversations were empty—and, as for the books, he knew them all. Small but terrible delusions fretted away what remained of his mind. He had lost all his money, he declared, he could not afford to be Knight of the Garter. But surely there was even yet some chance of his return to power? There was none. When Peel went out of office, the Whigs passed him by, and it was Lord John Russell, and not Lord Melbourne, who was asked to form a Cabinet. He lived, now, only in expectation of a letter from the Queen, and when those letters came they were kind, and they were long; but they were changed. "It was kindness at a distance," said Mr Strachey, "and he knew it. He had become 'poor Lord Melbourne'."[1] But still the ghost that once had been whimsical, good Lord Melbourne haunted, from time to time, the world that had once known him, for a few long empty years during which his mind crumbled and sank into dust, then into unconsciousness, until, at the end of these few years, he died.

The Queen, some days before his death, though pitying that sad and empty ghost, yet could not wish the days back again, when he was in power and stood at her side.

One ghost from the past, however, remained, and that was the Duchess of Kent, who had suddenly, in the light of Albert's presence, become real. Albert it was who had taken her out from the cupboard to which she had been relegated, dusted her down, and restored her to the family circle. Her advice was asked, she was consulted about everything, and the past few years seemed to have been

[1] Strachey, *op. cit.*, p. 121.

nothing but a bad dream. Her happiness was complete, and, as for the Queen, how was it possible, she wondered, that she could ever have become alienated from her dearest mama?

Life had become a round of simple pleasures and domestic delights—walks and rides and Mendelssohn's melodies played by the Prince upon the organ, "the first of instruments",[1] games with the children and talks about their upbringing with dearest Mama. But there were excitements and new experiences, too. There was, for instance, the first journey undertaken by the Queen and the Prince in a train—on the new Great Western line from Windsor to Paddington —and this was no light matter, since according to Court etiquette the Master of the Horse and the coachmen under him were responsible for the Queen's travels by land, and how was this possible under these new circumstances, considering that neither the Master of the Horse nor the coachmen had ever driven a train in their lives?

Somehow the difficulty was disposed of, and the journey, which took half an hour, was, to the Queen's delight, quite free from any dust, and was neither hot nor crowded. Prince Albert, however, was slightly alarmed by the speed, and said, on reaching London: "Not quite so fast next time, Mr Conductor, if you please."[2]

It was in the autumn of the same year that the Queen and the Prince visited Scotland for the first time, and this was one of the most wonderful experiences of all, for the Queen was proud of her Stuart blood, and Mr Benson tells us that Prince Albert was enraptured by the wildness of the scenery, and by Arthur's Seat, which he declared must be as fine as the Acropolis at Athens, a city which he had never visited; and, as for Perth, it resembled Basle to a striking degree, and near Birnam Wood he would really have believed himself

[1] See Strachey, *op. cit.*, pp. 107–8.
[2] See Mona Wilson: "Travel and Holidays", in *Early Victorian England*.

to be once again in Thuringia. The people, too, had a German
look, and this again made him feel at home. The royal pair
were delighted with Lord Breadalbane's house—"a kind of
Castle built of granite"—and with the oatmeal porridge and
the finnan haddock, the tartan, the kilts, the bagpipes, and
the sword-dances and reels;[1] in short, the delights were in-
exhaustible, and the Queen and the Prince were sorry when
it was time to return to Windsor.

So fresh joys, new excitements and experiences, succeeded
each other, though there were flying shadows, too. The year
had not been free from cares. There had been, for instance,
the perpetual demands on the part of the Prince's father, who,
since his son's marriage, had developed tendencies that were
strongly characteristic of his brother, dear Uncle Leopold—
but with this difference, that the Duke never hesitated to
make anything clear, so that the answer to the demand must
be a straight "yes" or "no". He had, for instance, written
a letter to Prince Ernest, from whom his brother had so lately
parted with tears, suggesting that, as Prince Albert had
married a rich wife, it was his duty to give Ernest, poor as he
was, an allowance. Prince Ernest forwarded this letter to his
brother, and received, as a reply: "Always money and always
money. The principles" (Papa) "reveals really sting me to the
heart. God help you and your affairs." And Albert made it
quite clear that *he* would not. The heart, indeed, however
stung, remained singularly untouched, although Albert had a
large allowance, was married to the Queen of England,
whilst his brother was poor. But then we must remember
that Prince Ernest had offended against Albert's sense of
morality. I do not know in what, exactly, the offence
consisted, but he had undoubtedly been involved in some
scandal, his health was affected, and Prince Albert in a letter
that seems strangely cruel, coming as it did from a man whose
heart was warm and compassionate, told him that, though

[1] See Benson, *op. cit.*, p. 121.

he would never curse him or take away the love he owed him as a brother, he found it necessary to "leave him to perish in immorality". Nor, he added, could he allow Prince Ernest to visit England at present. The invitation sent he regarded as cancelled. "Nothing", he added, "would be more disagreeable at present than your visit." The only thing left for Prince Ernest to do—and this was made plain—was for him to marry a virtuous wife—in which case he would be put right in the eyes of the world, and his misdemeanours would be forgotten.

In a short time Prince Ernest married Princess Alexandrina of Baden, and his brother and sister-in-law, forgetting the requests for money, and the necessity of leaving him to perish in immorality, invited him to spend his honeymoon at Claremont.

Chapter XV

VISITS AND VISITORS

===========

The year 1844 began sadly enough; for Duke Ernest, whose principles, some time before, had cut Prince Albert to the heart, died in January, and the Queen, who had met him for a short while in 1836, and again at the time of the marriage, was dissolved in tears. She was, she assured the King of the Belgians, crushed, overwhelmed, bowed down, and to describe to her dearly beloved uncle, who must now be the father to those two broken-hearted bereaved children, herself and her husband, all that the children in question had suffered, would be difficult. The violence of their grief might be over; but, she added, the desolation which now invaded them was worse, and tears were undoubtedly a relief.

As for the Duke's younger son, writing to the new Duke Ernest, who so lately had been in such deep disgrace, he exclaimed: "We have no home any more, and this is a terrible idea....I am far away from you, but the whole love of a brother fills my heart, and I shall always stand by you with advice and deed....Our poor little children do not know why we cry, and they ask us why we are in black.

"...Victoria weeps with me, for me, and for all of you. This is a great comfort for me, and your dear Alexandrina will weep with you. Let us take great care of these two jewels; let us love and protect them, as in them we shall find happiness again....Victoria...sends you a pin with a curl of dear Father's hair."[1]

Still worse was to come, for Prince Albert must go to Coburg, and the Queen had never been separated from him for even one night. She did not know, she could not imagine, how she would be able to bear it. Could not her beloved uncle allow her aunt Louise to come and stay with her for that one unbearable fortnight, so that she might have the comfort of her companionship? For, "if I were to remain *quite* alone," she told her uncle, "I do not think I *could* bear it quietly. I may be indiscreet, but think of what the separation from my *all and all* even for only a fortnight will be to me."

Meanwhile, from Dover Harbour, Prince Albert wrote the first love-letter of his life.[2] "My own darling," he began, "I have been here about an hour, and regret the lost time which I might have spent with you....Poor child! You will, while I write, be getting ready for luncheon, and you will find a place vacant where I sat yesterday. In your heart, however, I hope my place will not be vacant...you are even now half a day nearer to seeing me again; by the time you get this letter, you will be a whole one—thirteen more, and I am again within your arms.... Your most devoted Albert." He added: "I cannot go to bed without writing two words more. I occupy your old room....We had a rather unpleasant voyage. I kept my seat on one spot all the way with my eyes shut, but I was far from easy in my mind." Two days afterwards, writing from Gotha, he exclaimed: "Remembrance, sorrow, joy, all these together produce a peculiar sadness....Farewell, my darling, and fortify yourself with the thought of my speedy return. God's blessing rest upon you and the dear children....I enclose an

[1] Bolitho, *op. cit.*, p. 127.   [2] See Bolitho, *op. cit.*, pp. 128-9.

auricula and a pansy, which I gathered at Reinhardtsbrun.... I have got toys for the children, and porcelain views for you...."[1]

A few days afterwards, he returned to Windsor, amidst, as he wrote in his diary, "great joy".

Happiness had returned to the heart of Victoria, and the days passed so quickly that they seemed like shining birds whose lovely plumage is seen for a moment, flashing through the wide dark summer leaves. Sometimes a royal visitor would arrive with his suite, and all would be excitement and expectation; there would be balls and reviews and dinner-parties, and the visitor would be gone again before the Queen had time to realize all the pleasures there had been. A year before this time, however, there was one visit which did not cause an unmitigated joy, and that was of the Queen's dreaded uncle, the King of Hanover, who had been invited to be godfather to her third child, Princess Alice, who was born on April the 25th 1843.

This sinister old gentleman caused a good deal of consternation by arriving at Buckingham Palace in a four-wheeler, and too late for the christening.[2] Indeed, he was not even in time for the luncheon that followed that ceremony, but appeared when all was over, and in a state of extreme bad temper because the Queen had not waited for him. However, he was smoothed down, and the visit bid fair to be an uneventful one, until, a few weeks later, he was a guest at the marriage of his niece, Princess Augusta of Cambridge, to the Grand Duke of Mecklenburg-Strelitz. At this ceremony he arrived with the most praiseworthy punctuality, but proceeded to behave in a manner which could only be described as odd. For, as the royal procession moved forward, the King of Hanover made a sudden rush, and

[1] Bolitho, *op. cit.*, p. 130.
[2] See Benson, *op. cit.*, p. 126.

pushing Prince Albert, whom he was in the habit of describing as "a paper Highness", out of the way, he took his place next to the Queen. A remarkable scene ensued, for the Prince, on recovering himself, "was forced to give him a strong punch, and drive him down a few steps", and His Majesty was then led out of the chapel by the Master of the Ceremonies. But the matter did not end there, for the King waited patiently in the vestry until the register was to be signed, and then tried to repeat the performance in order to sign it immediately after the Queen, and before her husband. But the Queen was too quick for him, and flew round to the other side of the table, the book was passed to her, and Prince Albert was able to sign it before His Majesty, slower of movement, was able to reach the spot.

A short time after this remarkable series of events, the Prince was able to tell his brother: "Happily he" (the King) "fell over some stones at Kew, and damaged some ribs."[1] And that was the end of the visit.

In the late summer of that year, the Queen and her husband were the guests of King Louis Philippe, who, with his wife, was staying at the Château d'Eu near Le Tréport. Arriving in their yacht, they were met by the King on his barge, and the glittering gold-spangled days and moon-haunted nights were one long round of entertainments. On the 2nd of September there was a great banquet in the Château, and on the 4th a *fête champêtre* in the forest. The old King had been in "the seventh heaven of rapture" at receiving them, and so anxious was he to please, that he had ordered immense quantities of cheese and bottled beer in order to conform to their odd English tastes. The Queen was particularly glad to find among the King's guests Monsieur Auber, the composer, to whose work she was much attached; and, indeed, the pleasures and delights were so many that she hardly had time to count them all before they were gone again, and she must

[1] Benson, *op. cit.*, p. 126.

leave her kind hosts and sail away to Brighton, where her children were staying in the Pavilion.

In June of next year, three months after the death of Duke Ernest, the Czar of Russia paid Her Majesty a state visit, and the Queen fluttered like a small bird at the thought of this great and alarming potentate sleeping under her roof. "It seemed like a dream", she noted in her diary, "to breakfast and walk out with this greatest of all earthly Potentates, as quietly as if we walked with Charles or any one." The Czar had not visited England since his earliest youth, and then he had caused great astonishment by refusing to sleep in a bed, preferring a sack of straw. But now he caused no surprise, and, although the Queen said that the expression of his eyes was formidable, he aroused but little awe. He won the Queen's heart completely by his appreciation of the Prince, who, he declared, had "l'air si noble et si bon", and by his admiration of the children, who were not at all shy with him. Indeed Princess Alice allowed the Czar to take her in his arms, and gave him a kiss of her own accord. The nights and days were full of delight, and the Queen could not help feeling proud of the beauty of Windsor, and of the Waterloo Room, which, at night, seemed lit by the service of gold as if a million suns were shining reflected in water. One early morning after breakfast, the Queen and the Emperor and the good King of Saxony, who was so different from the Emperor, and so homely, visited the Adelaide Cottage, walking over the grass which was yellow and dry from the sun; and on another day there was a great review in Windsor Park in honour of the Emperor; and he and the King of Saxony paid a visit to the races with their host and hostess; then that visit, too, came to an end.

So the days passed; and in October 1844 the Court was thrown into a flutter by the approaching visit of King Louis Philippe. This visit was, it appears, fraught with danger to the King, because of his incurable habit of forgetting that he was no longer twenty years old, and the peril that, in the excitement of finding himself in such new and strange sur-roundings, he might eat too much. The Queen of the Belgians, indeed, was obliged to write to her mother, the Queen of the French, *everything* that her dearest and most be-loved Victoria told her of the King's visit, in order to quiet her. And, before his arrival, all possible instructions were given as to how the dangers I have mentioned were to be circumvented. The King would, it seems, give no trouble; he was *most* easy to accommodate; but it was important to remember that he must not be allowed to come down early in the morning, and especially must he be prevented from attending breakfast. He had shown every sign of wishing to do so, and it would be fatal. Luncheon and dinner should, for him, be the only meals allowed. On the other hand, a bowl of *chicken broth* would be a necessity in the morning. He was, it seems, naturally so imprudent and so little ac-customed to caution and care that he must be watched all the time, and prevented, at all costs, from catching cold. As for his rooms, the arrangement of these would be quite simple: a large table, for his papers, and a hard bed were all that were required. As a rule, he slept on a horse-hair mattress with a plank of wood under it, but really any bed would do providing it were not soft.[1]

In a second letter,[2] the Queen of the Belgians assured her beloved friend that her mother *knew* the King would be in safe hands. But still the great fear remained, to tell the truth, that he would *eat too much*. Indeed, such had been his wife's distress at this thought, that he had been obliged, in order to reassure her, to promise not to attend breakfast. And Queen Louise added that she begged her beloved Victoria, if possible, to prevent his riding at all, and, if expeditions were made, that these might be undertaken in carriages. And, speaking of expeditions, she hoped that two at least would

[1] See *Letters*, Volume II, pp. 21–2.   [2] See *Letters*, Volume II, p. 27.

be arranged for the King, one to London, and one to Wool-
wich. The last would interest him enormously, since he was
a cavalry officer.

A day later, the Queen told the King of the Belgians that
his father-in-law had just arrived, at 2 o'clock that day,
accompanied by his son, and that their arrival seemed like a
dream, and a very pleasant one.

Indeed, the visit was a success from beginning to end, and
the dear King, with his hair so elaborately curled that it
looked like a picture of the sea by Korin, was enthusiastically
and affectionately received on all sides. The Queen of
England was charmed with him, thought him *such* an extraordinary man, with such a wonderful memory—"and how
lively, how sagacious". Then too he had been so charming
with Albert, had called him "mon frère", and treated him
completely as his equal, saying "Le Prince Albert, c'est pour
moi le Roi." He was very sad at parting, but expressed the
determination to see Her Majesty every year.

Little did he foresee the way in which that determination
was to be fulfilled, and how, only three and a half years later,
he, flying with his family on the outbreak of the revolution
in France, with his whiskers shaved off, a sort of *casquette* on
his head, a coarse overcoat, and immense goggles over his
eyes, would find in England a permanent refuge and home.

His daughter, contemplating the fate which had overtaken
him, lamented his policy of inaction; for if only,[1] she sighed,
he would have granted in time some trifling reforms, the
public would have been content, and he would still be King
of France.

But now he was an exile in England, and sometimes had
barely enough to eat, and the King of Prussia, though he was
cut to the heart by the downfall of the poor old ex-King of
France, was yet forced to recognize in his fate "the avenging
hand of the King of Kings".[2]

[1] See *Letters*, Volume II, p. 153.   [2] *Letters*, Volume II, p. 152.

Chapter XVI

THE NEW HOME

"All right human song", said Mr Ruskin, "is the finished expression, by art, of the joy or grief of noble persons for right causes. And accurately in proportion to the rightness of the cause, and purity of the emotion, is the possibility of the fine art.... And with absolute precision from highest to lowest, the fineness of the possible art is an index to the moral purity and majesty of the emotion it expresses....

"You must be good men, before you can either paint or sing, and then the colour and sound will complete in you all that is best."

On the 19th of July 1842, a man in whom sound had completed all that was best stood amid the shadows of a large shuttered room in Buckingham Palace, listening to a young and simple-mannered man and his little homely wife playing upon the organ and singing. Outside the Palace, the nasturtium-coloured July sun was high, but in this room the shadows were so tall and grey that they might almost have been the romantic English-Gothic imitation ruins that had lately come into fashion. The sleek-looking Herr Felix Mendelssohn, for it was he, whose appearance was like that of some strange thin oriental bird with dark and glistening plumage, stood listening to the music with his head held slightly on one side, and a faint smile on his dark face. The summer-coloured, smooth, and too honeyed melodies floated through the shutters, down and down to the sentries below, as if they had been petals of homely flowers, velvety dark calceolarias or sharp bright fiery nasturtiums, flickering through their flat green leaves, for in music, though in none of the other arts, it was allowable to omit both moral grandeur and a moral lesson. Prince Albert, however, with his usual seriousness, had—urged to this course by Herr Mendelssohn, who wished to hear him play "in order to boast about it in Germany"—begun his performance with a chorale which, under his fingers, took on a strong likeness to Mr Gilbert Scott's admired English Gothic architecture, with the join in the bricks clearly discernible. Herr Mendelssohn had then, at the Queen's request, performed the chorus "How lovely are the Messengers", from his oratorio "St Paul", to which, before the composer reached the end of the first verse, Her Majesty and His Royal Highness added their voices—but afterwards the proceedings took on a lighter quality. The Queen sang the "Pilgerspruch", "Lass dich nur", "really quite faultlessly," the composer told his mother, "and with charming feeling and expression"; but he thought that one should not pay too many compliments on such an occasion, so he merely thanked her a great many times, upon which she said: "Oh, if only I had not been so frightened! Generally I have such long breath." Then the Prince sang "Es ist ein Schnitter", and when he had finished the song it struck him that Herr Mendelssohn must really be asked to improvise something before he left the Palace; so the composer sat down to the organ and improvised, and the Queen clapped her hands, her eyes sparkled, and she said he must come to England again soon and pay them a visit. Soon afterwards Herr Mendelssohn took his leave, and after a quarter of an hour or so had passed Her Majesty and His Royal Highness got into the "splendid carriage with the scarlet outriders" that Herr Mendelssohn had seen waiting outside, and were whirled away to Claremont; the flag was lowered, and the *Court Circular* announced that "Her Majesty left the Palace at twenty minutes past three".[1]

Before this time, concerts were frequently given in the Palace, although Herr Mendelssohn was the first eminent composer to be received by the Queen. Two years before this time, on June the 12th 1840, a magnificent concert was given under the direction of Signor Costa, and as usual the royal pair took a large share in the performance. This opened with a duet, "Non funestar Crudele", from Signor Ricci's *Il Disertore*, sung by Her Majesty and Prince Albert, the simple drooping melody, clear and liquid as a waterfall, sounding refreshing in the hot June night. This was followed by a great set piece from Signor Costa's own pen—"Coro Pastorale"—in which Her Majesty, Lady Sandwich, Lady Williamson, Signor Rubini and Signor Costa, Prince Albert, Lord Charles Paget, and Signor Lablache took part. After that, the Queen with Signors Lablache and Rubini sang the trio "Dunque il mio bene", from *The Magic Flute*, and then came the final triumph performed by Her Majesty, Lady Williamson, Lady Sandwich, Lady Norreys, Lady Normanby, Miss Liddall, and Miss Anson.[2]

It must not be supposed for a moment, however, that the arts, with the exception of music, had yet attained to the high position in the domestic lives of the people which they afterwards held—a position midway between that of the Voice of Conscience and that of a pet dog. At first, as we have seen in a previous chapter, the Queen was averse to admitting them into her home life. At last, however, she was won round to Prince Albert's point of view; the arts seemed to her just as friendly and no more dangerous than dear Dashy, and in the end the whole nation felt that they might safely be petted and even fed with sugar.

[1] See Lee, *op. cit.*, pp. 190 *et seq.*   [2] See Lee, *op. cit.*, pp. 124–5.

THE NEW HOME

This feeling became even more assured when it became known that the Prince was to preside over the commission that had been formed with a view to encouraging the growth of the fine arts in England. The Prince, it was felt by the nation, would never have undertaken such a task were he not certain of the propriety of his protégés; and the nation was right. For there was another side to these household pets; and that was the suddenness with which, from these dear woolly companions of our leisure, the Voice of Conscience would trumpet forth; yet it never seemed in any way to disconcert their masters. Therefore, when the question was broached of decorating the walls of the rebuilt Houses of Parliament with frescoes, and the Prince was asked by the committee whether these paintings should, or should not, inculcate a moral lesson, His Royal Highness replied, with the greatest firmness, that they should. The committee was much relieved at this conclusion, and the moral lesson was produced. Alas, in a short time the frescoes had faded completely away, and the lesson might just as well never have been given.[1]

Frescoes, however, remained a passion with the Prince, and he went so far as to draw plans for a pavilion to be erected in the garden of Buckingham Palace and, when the pavilion had been built, to have it painted with frescoes by great living artists, Mr Landseer and Mr Uwins among others. And oh, the moral lessons to be learned from those frescoes, the delight to be gained from them! The Prince enjoyed his conversations with these great men, who, on their side, were much impressed by the solidity of his knowledge of the arts and by his domestic virtues. He and the Queen were, Mr Uwins declared, "an example to the age"; every morning before half past nine o'clock they had breakfasted, heard morning prayers, and might be seen walking in the garden and approaching the beloved pavilion,

[1] See Martin, *op. cit.*, Volume I, pp. 119–25, 167. Strachey, *op. cit.*, p. 115.

to watch Mr Uwins at his task. Mr Uwins might have gone still further in his praise: he might have said that not only were the royal pair an example to the age, they were its epitome.

Some time after the Prince had evoked the admiration of Mr Uwins, the Queen, delighted with the results brought about in the Garden Pavilion by her husband's taste for interior decoration, decided that a still larger scope must be found for the exercise of this gift. For some time she had longed for a more intimate, more private home than Buckingham Palace or Windsor Castle—a home where she could be "free from all Woods and Forest and other charming Departments, who really are the plague of one's life", and where Albert could feel far away "from all the bitterness people create for themselves in London". And, in the Isle of Wight, such a place was found.

The Queen, as a little girl, had twice paid a visit to Norris Castle near Osborne Cottage, the home of her bugbear Sir John Conroy, and remembered the beauty of the island.

In 1845, therefore, she bought the two thousand acres which surrounded Osborne House; the latter not being large enough for the royal family, a new house must be built in its stead, and, in the designing of this, and the planning of the garden, the Prince's gifts were fully displayed.

The Prince, who was immediately reminded of Naples, because the garden ended with the Solent (for him, every place inevitably resembled some other place—some home of culture), set about designing terraces, walks, gardens, and summer-houses, and beautifying the interior of the house. In the long corridors, the alcoves were painted Garter blue, and were framed in a design of highly gilded plaster shells, forming an admirable background to the very classical bronze busts of the Queen's German uncles. Whilst these were being arranged, the English sculptors Thornycroft, Theed, and Edgar Boehm, in a state of feverish activity, produced the multitudinous Albert Marbles, which began with the group of the Prince and the Queen as Edward the Third and Philippa, and continued with a statue of the Prince in Roman armour. Nor were these the only decorations brought about by the sculptors' art: for there were reproductions, in marble, of the hands and feet of the Queen's children, and statuettes of dogs and ponies and of loyal Highland gillies, and to these were added, says Mr Benson, from whose book I have culled this description, "porcelain views".[1] "This remarkable form of reminiscent art", he continues, "was introduced by Prince Albert from Germany; famous or familiar views were painted below glaze on plates and teapots, glimpses of Rosenau or the Thuringian Forest. He adopted this form to domestic memorial pieces, and Eos and the Queen's dogs with their names for identification lived again, in china. Etchings were executed by the Royal pair, and there were stacks of lithographs of the family pictures." There were, as well—again I quote from Mr Benson—"two chairs hewn out of solid blocks of coal, for mining was the greatest of English industries, and, later, there were other chairs of which the legs and framework consisted of the horns of stags which the Prince had shot in the deer-forests of Balmoral."

How happy and quiet was life in this paradise, with the children playing happily in the woods, hunting for the wild strawberries, the wild violets beneath their swan-skin leaves, picking the green-hooded "lords and ladies", the marsh-marigolds, the sweet rubied cowslips, the bluebells, and making them into bunches to bring home to their mama. It is ninety years ago that these flowers faded, but to those children it seemed they would never die. They ran, they laughed, amongst the woods, and about a mile from the house Prince Albert built a Swiss chalet for them, where they could play and live over again his life as a child at Rosenau.

[1] See Benson, *op. cit.*, pp. 139-41.

Meanwhile, the children grew, their characters became marked, and that of "Fat Pussette", as the Queen called the little Princess Royal, was, from the Prince Consort's point of view, perfection. In the Queen's eyes, too, she could do no wrong. She was so clever, and recited Lamartine so beautifully, and understood him so well that, when out for a ride on her pony, she, looking at the cows and sheep, turned to Mademoiselle Charier and said "Voilà le tableau qui se déroule à nos pieds." Was not that extraordinary for a little child of three years old? The Queen thought it was more like what a person of twenty would say. And, too, as she told the King of the Belgians, "you have no notion *what* a knowing, and I am sorry to say, sly little rogue she is and *so obstinate*". And how she loved her dearest papa. She never tired of trying to please him, her voice, childish as it was, echoed his opinions, she was never untidy, she had no odd ideas—nor had she a superabundant vitality and friendliness. How disappointingly different was her little brother, Albert Edward, who one day would be King of England, and must be trained for this task.

This lonely little child, with his longing to give and to receive affection, his warm-hearted gaiety, and "his manners very dear and not shy" (as one of his earliest friends, young Mrs Gladstone, noticed), his diminutiveness, and his unbecoming "long trousers tied below the ankles and very full", would have won the hearts of most people, but the Prince Consort did not understand this little boy's longing for companionship, his lack of interest in German philosophy.

And the Queen, though of course she believed herself to be equally devoted to all her children, was moulded by her husband to his point of view. For in her eyes he could do no wrong.

The little Prince, therefore, in the years of earliest childhood, had for friends only his governess Lady Lyttelton—

who loved his "politeness of manner", and, in after
years, remembered how at three years old "he bowed and
offered his hand beautifully, besides saluting à la militaire—
all unbidden"—and Mrs Gladstone and her husband, the
rising young politician. The latter's little boy, William
Henry, was, indeed, the only child of the Prince's age
with whom he was allowed to play; and, with that warm-
hearted faithfulness which was part of the Prince's nature, he
cherished for his childhood's friend a lifelong devotion.
Affection for their parents was taught in the royal nursery,
side by side with reverence for their God. Each birthday,
each Christmas, brought carefully prepared presents, well-
thought-out notes of congratulation, early morning visits....
But, in spite of this carefully fostered affection, a cold damp
mist separated Prince Albert from his son. The child was a
disappointment, and the child knew it. For this reason, he
clung all the more to his first friend, Lady Lyttelton, and to
his first tutor, the Reverend Mr Birch, whom he came to
love as he might have loved his father. But Mr Birch, too,
was unsatisfactory. Instead of reporting to Prince Albert, as
was obviously his duty, every slight fault of temper or dis-
obedience on the part of his pupil, every failure to learn his
lessons, he omitted to do so, and the Prince looked upon him
with increasing disapproval. Mr Birch's religious views, too,
were a disappointment, and these, and his too ready, almost
parental affection for the lonely little Prince of Wales, led
to Mr Birch's dismissal. Henceforward, the Prince of Wales
would be alone with his duty.

Every night till the time when he went away, Mr Birch
found sad little childish notes and little presents inscribed in a
child's handwriting, under his pillow. But he went, and his
place was taken by the "prim and correct" Mr Wayworth
Gibbs, who could be relied on to repeat every fault, report
on every failing, to Prince Albert. Why *could* not the boy
take an interest in theology and German philosophy? He

seemed to have no proper sense of the seriousness of life. Why, some years after this time, when he was taken to see the Great Exhibition, it being part of his duty to write letters to Baron Stockmar, in order that that conscientious person should superintend his education as he had done that of his father, the boy had actually told him that he was much excited by some waxwork models of the murderous Indian thugs. In reply, the Baron very properly reminded him that he was "born in a Christian and enlightened age in which such atrocious acts are not even dreamt of".

It was evident that the boy must be, if possible, repressed even more closely, drilled with an even greater rigour. And his companions, when he was allowed these, must be carefully chosen.

Before the little Prince was old enough to be drilled, the reforms necessary in the royal household had occupied much of Prince Albert's time, and in these tasks he found Baron Stockmar a willing collaborator. It was obvious that something must be done to stop the endless waste, and put some degree of order into the muddle which existed in every department. As a result of his investigations, the Baron, in a fit of despair, announced that if the Queen wanted a fire lit in the dining-room this could not be done without two departments being called in for the purpose. Every day hundreds of fresh candles were put in the drawing-rooms and dining-rooms, but, whether they were used or not, next day they disappeared, having become the perquisite of the footmen, and were replaced by others; on the other hand, it was a rule that not more than two candles should be put in any bedroom. Then there was the absurd state of affairs which existed about housemaids; there were forty of these at Windsor, and forty at Buckingham Palace, with the result that, for only six months' work, each housemaid received her board and lodging and £45. There was a perfect army of footmen, of which only one-third was fully employed at a time, whilst another third was placed on half duty, and the rest did nothing at all.[1]

To reform the household, reduce the waste, and restore order took time; but the Prince, with Stockmar's aid, accomplished his aim, and in this showed the great capacity for business which in after years was shown so incomparably in matters of state.

[1] See Benson, *op. cit.*, p. 123.

Chapter XVII

LORD PALMERSTON AND
THE QUEEN

O n June the 29th 1846, to Her Majesty's despair, Sir
Robert Peel resigned from his post as Prime
Minister, and his place was taken by Lord John
Russell, with, as Foreign Minister, that terrible man old
Lord Palmerston, with his Pandora's box full of embroil-
ments and wars and menaces and undesirable *rapprochements*,
his extraordinary obstinacy alternating with equally astonishing *volte-faces*, his strong common sense and his love of
liberty, his loud, mockingly jay-like laugh, his clothes that
were as brilliantly coloured as a jay's feathers, his jaunty
manner and his dyed whiskers.

The whole attitude of Lord Palmerston was summed up
by a story told by Mr Strachey: "One day, returning from
Osborne, he found that he had missed the train to London;
he ordered a special, but the station-master told him that to
put a special train upon the line at that time of day would be
dangerous, and he could not allow it. Palmerston insisted,
declaring that he had important business in London, which
could not wait. The station-master, supported by all the
officials, continued to demur; the company, he said, could
not possibly take the responsibility. 'On *my* responsibility,

then!' said Palmerston, in his off-hand, peremptory way; whereupon the station-master ordered up the train, and the Foreign Secretary reached London in time for his work, without an accident."[1]

The Queen was horrified, and so was the Prince, that Lord Palmerston should become Foreign Minister; for they knew that, the moment he came into power, he would try to convert them from living, working intelligences into dummies and figureheads.

He began this work at the earliest possible opportunity. In the same year, at the time of the question of the Spanish marriages, he aroused the Queen's wrath by a paragraph which the Prince had insisted should be deleted, and, as a result of ordering the reactionary Spanish government in a peremptory manner to become more liberal, he not only brought about the immediate expulsion of our ambassador from Madrid, but, by appearing to support the Progressive Party in Spain, of which the Queen Mother was thoroughly frightened, he succeeded in throwing that lady into the arms of France, with the result that in a short time Louis Philippe could announce the engagement of the young Queen of Spain to that sinister semi-idiot, Don Francisco d'Assisi, and of the Queen's sister to his own son. This was the very last thing that was wanted, and Victoria and Albert were naturally highly indignant.

But this was not all. Three years before this time, the Queen of Portugal, wife of Victoria's first cousin, and the friend of her childhood, was threatened with the loss of her throne, and appealed to Victoria for help and advice. Lord Palmerston, on hearing of this appeal, treated the trouble as a mere Coburg family affair, and, laughing his mirthless laugh and rubbing his hands together, declared that the whole peril was due to Dietz, a native of Coburg, who occupied the same position as adviser to the Queen of Portugal as that filled by

[1] Strachey, *op. cit.*, p. 133.

Stockmar at the British Court. The throne, he declared, could only be saved by Dietz being dismissed immediately, and he dictated a letter full of exhortations, solemn warning, and unwelcome advice, which must be copied in the Queen's own handwriting, and sent to her unhappy cousin. This roused great wrath in the Coburg family, who denounced Lord Palmerston as "ill-tempered, coarse and threatening".[1]

Nor did matters stop there. Late in 1847, the King of Prussia sent a private letter to Queen Victoria, in which he asked that she should declare her approval of his shifting efforts to dominate the whole of the German federation. This letter was sent through the medium of his ambassador, Baron von Bunsen, to be delivered into the Queen's own hands. But Lord Palmerston had as many ears as Argus had eyes, and somehow or other he came to hear of the letter, and, having told the Baron frankly that it was improper for an English sovereign to have a private correspondence with the monarch of another country, unless they were related, he obliged Prince Albert to draft with him what Sir Sidney Lee called "a colourless reply", with the result that the Queen, to her great indignation, found herself under the appearance of going back on what had always been Prince Albert's avowed opinion, asserted over and over again in private correspondence with the King of Prussia.

It was no use to remonstrate, for when, on one occasion, Lord Palmerston was called to order by the Prime Minister with regard to something that had annoyed the Queen, that reprehensible old person merely replied in his jaunty manner: "Unfortunately the Queen gives ear too easily to persons who are hostile to her government, and who wish to poison her mind with distrust of her ministers, and in this way she is constantly suffering under groundless uneasiness."

The Queen protested against her private correspondence

[1] *Memoirs of Ernest II, Duke of Saxe-Coburg-Gotha*, Volume I, p. 288. Lee, *op. cit.*, p. 212.

being opened at the Foreign Office—it was very impertinent of the offending official, she considered. Naturally, naturally! Lord Palmerston would see to the matter at once. It should not happen again. But it happened continually.

With Lord Palmerston at the Foreign Office, the Queen of England looked forward to migratory flights of ambassadors, nor was she to be disappointed. In 1850, Lord Palmerston, by despatching the British fleet to Grecian waters, obliged Greece to comply with the British demands that she should compensate Don Pacifico, a Portuguese Jew and, as a native of Gibraltar, a British subject, because his house in Athens had been stormed and pillaged by a mob, and, as well, Mr Finlay the historian, who had laid a claim for certain moneys against the Greek government. In the course of this fracas, the Queen was forced to inquire if Lord Palmerston felt he was justified in calling the Greek Minister of the Interior "a notorious defaulter to the amount of 200,000 drachms", and, if so, whether it was the proper thing for the Queen's Foreign Secretary to make this statement in a public despatch. In the end Lord Palmerston succeeded in offending France, as well as Greece, over this affair, and as a result the former power, who was at the moment occupied as mediator, promptly withdrew her ambassador from London, and once again we found ourselves on the verge of war.

In the same year, Lord Palmerston aroused the Queen's displeasure by his refusal to take seriously the attack made on the Austrian General Haynau by the draymen of Messrs Barclay and Perkins, the brewers. This odious old gentleman had caused women to be flogged during the Hungarian war, and had committed numberless other cruelties, and he was so hated in consequence that, when he came to England and in the course of his stay visited this brewery, the draymen mobbed and assaulted him, and he was forced to fly from them in a very undignified manner. He received no sympathy however from Lord Palmerston, who, when he was obliged to send an official letter of apology to the Austrian government, hastened to do so before the Queen could see it, in order that he could insert a paragraph offensive to Austria. In answer to the Queen's reproof, he told her that he had felt obliged to state his sense of the want of propriety shown by General Haynau in coming to England, since the state of public feeling in England about General Haynau's cruelties in Italy and Hungary was perfectly well known. Indeed Baron Koller (the ambassador) had told Lord Palmerston that he had begged the General "to cut off those long moustachios", in order that he might not be identified. Lord Palmerston naturally regretted a breach of the law, but the draymen were merely actuated by their anger at the General's cruelty, and in any case he had escaped with a torn coat, a lost cane, and a few severe bruises, and an attempt to rob him of his moustaches. The English were remarkable for their hospitality towards foreigners, and their forgetfulness of past animosities—witness their behaviour towards Napoleon, and Marshal Soult.... "But General Haynau", he added, "was looked upon as a great moral criminal; and the feeling in regard to him was of the same nature as that which was manifested towards Tawell" (the South Hill murderer) "and the Mannings"; only with this difference, that the General's crimes were committed upon a much larger scale. Indeed, Lord Palmerston could assure Her Majesty that "those feelings of just and honourable indignation have not been confined to England, for he had good reason to know that General Haynau's previous and unmanly treatment of the unfortunate inhabitants of Brescia and of other towns and places in Italy, his savage proclamation to the people of Pest, and his barbarous acts in Hungary, excited almost as much disgust in Austria as in England, and that the nickname of 'General Hyaena' was given to him at Vienna long before it was applied to him in London".[1]

[1] *Letters*, Volume II, pp. 267-9.

In reply to this, he received a withering letter from the Queen, who informed him that she was unable to imagine that Baron Koller had addressed his note to Lord Palmerston in order to receive an expression of his *own personal opinion*; and that she could no more approve of Lynch Laws in England than she could of the *violent* vituperation which Lord Palmerston used in condemning public men in other countries.[1]

But that jaunty old gentleman was unsnubbable; and, though he was by now thoroughly unpopular with the Queen and the Prince, he was equally beloved by the people, who trusted him implicitly.

A year after this time, Kossuth, the Hungarian revolutionist, arrived in England, and we find the Queen imploring Lord John Russell to try and prevent Lord Palmerston from seeing him, or at all events to have it understood that it was a private act of Lord Palmerston's which had not been sanctioned by the government—for otherwise immense harm would be done abroad. Lord John told the Queen he was sorry to say he could not interfere any further in the matter. As a last resort he could only humbly advise the Queen to *command* Lord Palmerston not to receive Kossuth, for in answer to Lord John's "positive request" that he should not do so Lord Palmerston had replied: "There are limits to all things. I do not choose to be dictated to as to whom I may or may not receive in my own house....I shall use my own discretion....You will, of course, use yours as to the composition of your Government."[2]

In the end Lord Palmerston gave way gracefully, but a little late, for the Queen felt assured that he had already received Kossuth, since meetings of Radical admirers in Islington and Finsbury sent notes of thanks to him for his reception of the Hungarian patriot, and, at the Foreign Office, he, as Minister for Foreign Affairs, received a deputa-

[1] See *Letters*, Volume II, p. 270. [2] *Letters*, Volume II, p. 393.

tion which presented an address in which the Emperors of Austria and Russia were called "merciless tyrants and despots" and "odious and detestable assassins".

Lord Palmerston either from the Queen's point of view ignored her orders altogether—defying them entirely and going to the opposite extreme in order to avoid following them—or he obeyed them in such an excessive manner that it would have been better, almost, had he disobeyed them. When Louis Napoleon brought off in 1851 his *coup d'état* in France, and the official policy of England was one of complete neutrality, Lord Palmerston's broad-mindedness was such that he told the French Ambassador that he thoroughly approved of the President's act, and, this having been repeated by the Ambassador to his government, England found herself in the strange position of being at once completely neutral and highly approving.[1] He teased Lord Normanby, the British Ambassador, about his fears at the time of the *coup d'état*, laughing openly because, when the Club House was fired upon, Lord Normanby was "pathetic over a broken looking-glass", "forgetting", as Lady Normanby told Colonel Phipps,[2] "that the same bullet grazed the head of an Englishman...who was between the window and the glass". In short, Lord Palmerston's conduct was a perpetual source of astonishment, and nobody could foresee what he would do next. As a result of this last adventure, the long-suffering Lord John Russell called his Foreign Minister to account, and, as he either could not or would not explain the affair, he was dismissed from office. The Queen and the Prince were in the seventh heaven of delight, and the former foresaw that Lord Palmerston would be obliged to "rest upon his laurels".

Not at all! In two months' time, this ancient will o' the wisp had encompassed the fall of the government! "I have

[1] See Benson, *op. cit.*, p. 164.
[2] *Letters*, Volume II, p. 40.

had my tit-for-tat with John Russell," he wrote, "and I turned him out on Friday last."[1]

In less than a year after the time when the Queen was rejoicing at his overthrow, he was back again in office, this time as Home Secretary, a position in which he was able to exercise his full energy. We find him, in 1853, for instance, during one of the appalling epidemics of cholera which swept over the country, devastating the Presbytery of Edinburgh with the following letter:

"Sir,

"I am directed by Viscount Palmerston to acknowledge the receipt of your letter of the 15th instant, requesting on behalf of the Presbytery of Edinburgh, to be informed whether it is proposed to appoint a day of national fast on account of the visitation of the cholera, and to state that there can be no doubt that manifestations of humble resignation to the Divine Will, and sincere acknowledgements of human unworthiness, are never more appropriate than when it has pleased Providence to afflict mankind with some severe visitation; but it does not appear to Lord P. that a national fast would be suitable to the circumstances of the present moment.

"The Maker of the Universe has established certain laws of nature for the planet on which we live, and the weal or woe of mankind depends upon the observance or the neglect of these laws. One of these laws connects health with the absence of those gruesome exhalations which proceed from over-crowded human beings, or from discomposing substances, whether animal or vegetable; and these same laws render sickness the almost inevitable consequence of exposure to those noxious influences. But it has at the same time pleased Providence to place it within the power of man to

[1] See A. E. M. Ashley: *The Life and Correspondence of H. J. Temple, Viscount Palmerston*, Volume I, p. 334. Lee, *op. cit.*, p. 228.

make such arrangements as will prevent or disperse such exhalations so as to render them harmless, and it is the duty of man to attend to these laws of nature and to exert the faculties which Providence has thus given to man for his own welfare.

"The recent visitation of cholera which has for the moment been mercifully checked, is an awful warning given to the people of this realm that they have too much neglected their duty in this respect, and that those persons with whom it rested to purify towns and cities, and to prevent or remove the causes of disease, have not been sufficiently active in regard to such matters. Lord P. would, therefore, suggest that the best course which the people of this country can pursue to deserve that the further progress of the cholera should be stayed, will be to employ the interval that will elapse between the present time and the beginning of next spring in planning and executing measures by which those portions of their towns and cities which are inhabited by the poorest classes, and which from the nature of things, must most need purification and improvement, may be freed from those causes and sources of contagion which if allowed to remain, will infallibly breed pestilence to be fruitful in death, in spite of all the prayers and fastings of a united but inactive nation. When man has done his utmost for his own safety, then is the time to invoke a blessing of Heaven to give effect to his exertions.

"I am, Sir, your obedient servant,
"Henry Fitzroy."

Altogether a difficult man; and it is not surprising that it was said of him that he treated Heaven as "a foreign power".[1]
But soon there was to be a still greater outlet for Lord Palmerston's energies.
In 1853, a storm swept over Eastern Europe. Russia, in

[1] Ashley, *op. cit.*

order to annex some more property of Turkey's, had decided
to protect the Christians in Turkey. This led to Turkey's
declaring war on Russia—which was exactly what Russia
wanted; and the other powers knew that they would be
obliged to intervene, since otherwise Turkey would be completely annihilated. Some short time before, the British
Mediterranean fleet was sent to the Bosphorus; but the orders
were that the fleet must not enter the Black Sea unless
Russia invaded Turkey. Louis Napoleon wished France to
ally herself with England and for the two countries to
declare war against Russia. But Lord Aberdeen, who was
then Prime Minister, was determined to preserve peace if it
were possible.

Lord Palmerston, however, believed that war was inevitable, and, since his colleagues did not agree with him, he
resigned from the Cabinet.

Meanwhile, the populace, longing for war, furious at the
delay, seized on Prince Albert as a scapegoat. He was a
German, he had been plotting with Russia behind the back
of the government. He had done so with Victoria's knowledge, he had done so without her knowledge. He was a
traitor. "There is no kind of treason to the country of which
I have not been guilty," he told Stockmar.[1] Mr Bolitho
relates that "the malicious scandal grew until it was said that
Prince Albert was a traitor to his Queen, that he had been
impeached for high treason, arrested and committed to the
Tower. The astonishing rumours drew the crowds of
London towards the river; they waited in thousands,
pressing against the Tower walls, to see the Queen and the
Prince brought in as prisoners."

The general insane clamour for war continued, and soon
the people were to have this wish fulfilled. The Cabinet at
last came to the same conclusion as that of Lord Palmerston,
with whom they became reunited, and who resumed his

[1] *Albert the Good*, p. 213.

office; and in February 1854 England and France declared war on Russia. The King of the Belgians exclaimed in a letter to his niece, shortly before: "How the Emperor could get himself and everybody else into this infernal scrape is quite incomprehensible; the more so as I remain convinced that he did not aim at conquest." And he reminded her that "the dear old Duke used to say: 'You cannot have a little war'".[1]

That was true; and the people, who had longed for it so ardently, were to find out the true nature of its glories. The story is so well known that it is scarcely necessary to repeat the details: the beginning, with the flying flags, the shouting and exultant multitudes, the Queen seeing off the troops at dawn[2] and leading out her fleet for the Baltic from Spithead —then the desperation of the Battle of Balaclava, and the soul-shaking horrors witnessed in the hospitals at Scutari, and in the ships which conveyed the wounded thither. In these ships—and the voyage, which should have taken only four days and a half, now took a fortnight or three weeks[3]—the wounded and the dying lay together in heaps, men whose limbs had just been roughly amputated, men with frostbite, men dying of cholera or of dysentery. In the Barrack Hospital the reign was that of Hell. Disease-laden vermin in huge crowds invaded walls and bedding, enormous sewers lay under the floor; there were insufficient beds for the multitudinous wounded and those who were dying of disease. Chaos and filth—nothing else seemed to exist.

And then came a young woman of thirty-four, named Florence Nightingale, with a small band of fellow workers, and by some miracle of devotion, by superhuman efforts put some order, some mercy into that abode of death.

The man whom the populace had declared to be a traitor because of his German birth—he too was working at high

---

[1] *Letters*, Volume III, p. 8.   [2] See Benson, *op. cit.*, p. 170.
[3] See Lytton Strachey: *Eminent Victorians* (Chatto and Windus), p. 128.

pressure and with his usual ardour. Many years afterwards (in 1882), Lord Wolseley, writing to the Queen,[1] said: "I hope your Majesty will forgive my reference to the memory of a great man who is no longer with us.... Who was it that we have to thank for being armed with rifles instead of old muskets when we landed in the Crimea? Who was it that advocated the reduction of the punishment of flogging?... in urging on the establishment of our great hospitals?... Those who have read through the pages of Sir Theodore Martin's work are now aware that the Army owes more to the late Prince Consort than to any other General Officer since the death of the Duke of Wellington."

Two months after the outbreak of war, the Queen wrote a letter that was particularly characteristic of her. She was "rather startled", so she told Lord Aberdeen, at the proposition that there should be a day of national humiliation,[2] as she felt very strongly on the subject. "To say...that *the great sinfulness of the nation* has brought about this War when it is the selfishness and ambition of *one* man and his servants who have brought this about, while our conduct has been throughout actuated by unselfishness and honesty"—this would be hypocritical and repulsive. Let there be a day of prayer, but let it be one thanking God for the great benefits the country had enjoyed, and for its immense prosperity, and asking the protection and the help of God.

[1] *Letters*, Second Series, Volume III, p. 389.
[2] See *Letters*, Volume III, p. 24. Benson, *op. cit.*, p. 171.

Chapter XVIII

THE GREAT EXHIBITION

The year 1850 brought many sorrows to the Queen and her husband, and these followed upon a great shock. On May 27th, as the Queen was leaving Cambridge House, Piccadilly, where the Duke of Cambridge was lying upon his death-bed, a man with a strange, skull-like, mad face and eyes with dilated pupils,[1] only a few months after a previous attempt had been made upon her life, made a sudden rush, and hit the Queen violently upon the head with the brass end of his stick. This was a particularly brutal attack, since her third son, Arthur, had only been born on the 1st of that month. An attempt was made to prove that the committer of this outrage, Robert Pate, an ex-officer, was mad; but it failed, and he was sentenced to seven years' transportation.

But far worse was to come. On June the 29th, the day after the Don Pacifico debate in the House of Commons, Sir Robert Peel, the beloved friend and adviser of the royal couple, whilst returning from a ride, was thrown from his horse on Constitution Hill, and after three days of agonizing pain died on the 2nd of July. It is characteristic of this strange, good, and uncharming man that his life might have

[1] Private information.

been saved by a warning from an acquaintance who realized that his horse was about to bolt, but the expression of his face was so forbidding that the acquaintance dared not speak. Yet, for him, alone of all statesmen, the poor wept, and there was not a begging-letter writer in all England who had not realized that he could safely be asked for five pounds. He remains to us now, in his monument—those Acts of Parliament which alleviated the lives of the workers—and in the portrait by Lawrence in which we see him still in his dancing-master attitude, one hip well stuck out, and with a finicking hand placed on the hip; his face is rather bleak and immobile, but the eyes are full of a gentle humanity, and a sort of childlike truthfulness.

The whole nation mourned for this good and honourable man, and the Queen's sorrow for the death of her once so dreaded minister was overwhelming, and she told the King of the Belgians that her husband felt he had lost a second father.

The loss was a bitter one, also, to Baron Stockmar, whose friendship he had possessed since 1819, and the Queen, writing to him three weeks after his friend's death, begged him to listen to her entreaties to come, and she added: "It will do you good to be with our beloved Prince. He longs for you. Since the night of your poor friend's death he wakes so early....Clark admits it is the mind."[1] For it was less than two years since his other great friend, Anson, had died,[2] and he felt friendless and alone.

Alas, still another cruel blow was in store, for on the 11th of October the good, gentle Queen of the Belgians died, aged only thirty-eight. The King, writing only four days before her death, said: "Her dear and angelic soul seems ever to shine more brightly at this moment of such great and

[1] Quoted, by permission, from *The Life of His Royal Highness the Prince Consort*, by Sir Theodore Martin. Volume II, p. 296.
[2] 24th November 1848.

imminent danger." But the soul left its wearied body and once more the King of the Belgians was alone.

In the midst of these sorrows, which almost overwhelmed his wife, the Prince found some consolation in the vast amount of work entailed in organizing the Great Exhibition—a plan which he had formulated long ago, and which had, for aim, not only the increase of prosperity in England, but the furthering of the cause of peace, inasmuch as the nations might come to understand how far the prosperity of each nation depended upon that of others. "The Exhibition of 1851", he declared,[1] "is to give a true test and a living picture of the point of development at which the whole of mankind has arrived in this great task of applied science and a new starting-point from which all nations will be able to direct their further exertions."

The difficulties of carrying out the scheme seemed, however, at one moment almost insuperable, since a large part of the press and public opinion were decidedly against it. It was enough that the Prince had planned it. He, the foreigner, was evidently determined that the country should be made to look ridiculous. "Peel cut down my income," he told his brother,[2] "Wellington refused me my rank, the Royal Family cried against the foreign interloper, the Whigs in office were only inclined to concede to me just as much space as I could stand upon." But the Prince won in the end, and all his astonishing powers of organization, his energy and will-power, were used to achieve the end he had in view.

In 1844 he had been much struck, when staying at Chatsworth, by the beauty of the enormous conservatory, which had been constructed by that strange man, Mr (afterwards Sir Joseph) Paxton, the Duke of Devonshire's gardener; and the thought had come to him that the Great

[1] *Speeches and Addresses of the Prince Consort*, p. 112. Benson, *op. cit.*, p. 150.

[2] Bolitho, *op. cit.*, p. 214.

Exhibition might flower under a conservatory still vaster
than this. The conservatory at Chatsworth was only three
hundred feet long and sixty-four feet high, but the design
that Mr Paxton now submitted to the Prince was for a
structure one thousand feet in length, and to be made
entirely of glass.

Mr G. M. Young, in a recent, most interesting essay on
Miss Violet Markham's *Paxton and the Bachelor Duke* (a book
which I have not yet, unfortunately, had the opportunity of
reading), said: "That the Crystal Palace is a great glass
house we all know. Had we realized that the structure, the
engineering side of it, was based on a careful botanical study
of the leaves, the lifting-power, of the Victoria Regia? A
brave new world, where such feats were within reach of a
man who had got his science by talking to George Stephen-
son."[1]

Five days before the great event of the opening, which
took place on May 1st, the Queen visited the exhibition and
came back, as she noted in her diary, "quite beaten, and my
head bewildered, from the myriads of beautiful and wonderful things, which now quite dazzle one's eyes!" The noise,
she added, was overpowering, for from twelve to twenty
thousand people were still working like bees, at a myriad
tasks.

The vastness of the house of glass can best be understood
if we realize that two of the tallest and leafiest elm-trees in
Hyde Park were no more hampered by the glittering dome
that covered them, than if they had been house plants.

On the day of the opening, the Queen and her husband,
the Prince and Princess of Prussia and their son Frederick,
the little girl of ten who, seven years after this time, was to

[1] The Victoria Regia was the great water-lily which was brought from
Guiana to this country in 1838, and bloomed for the first time in England
in 1849, when the flower was presented to the Queen. See Lee, *op. cit.*,
p. 52.

become his wife, and little Prince Edward drove in state carriages, at half past eleven, through the crowded streets, through the Green Park and Hyde Park to the gigantic house of glass, the

> *. . .miracle of rare device*
> *A sunny pleasure dome with caves of ice*

where waving palms, a myriad bright-coloured flowers, statues, and crowds of people filled the galleries. It seemed to the Queen as if all the beauty of the world was gathered there, as, led by her husband, and holding little Prince Edward with her other hand, she advanced to the middle of the Palace, where the great Crystal Fountain shed its spray. . . . The tremendous cheers, the joy of the people, the sound of the vast organ and the two hundred instruments and six hundred voices—all seemed part of the blessings showered by God upon her dearest Albert, and the work he was doing for her beloved country.

And indeed the blessings were many, for in planning the exhibition the Prince's wisdom, his strangely acute business sense, had been shown once more: the money taken was £186,000, 93 per cent. above the sum guaranteed.[1]

The triumph of Albert was complete, and the Queen's joy knew no bounds. At last the nation would realize the true worth of her beloved and wonderful husband.

And, soon after this success, the Prince was at work again, but this time on a much smaller scale; he was occupied with designing a new home.

Remembering her two enchanting visits to Scotland, the Queen was determined to have a home in that country, and in 1848 Balmoral, a small house in the Highlands, was taken on a lease. Then in 1852 it was bought, and the house was replaced by a castle of granite. This building was finished in 1854, and once more Prince Albert's gifts for interior decora-

---

[1] See Benson, *op. cit.*, p. 154.

tion were brought into play. The house became a thing of beauty. Lady Augusta Stanley, who was then lady-in-waiting to the Duchess of Kent, writing[1] to her sister the day after the royal family entered into residence, told her: "Yesterday was a very busy day—at 11.30 we went to Balmoral and watched the preparations till near luncheon time. Every trade connected with house-building and furnishing was carrying on its own particular business within those four walls, and how was it all to be completed before 6.30?...The general wood-work", she continued, "is light-coloured, maple and birch chiefly, with locks and hinges, etc., silvered. ...Besides there are beautiful things—chandeliers of Parian; Highlanders, beautifully designed figures holding the light, and which are placed in appropriate trophies—table ornaments in the same style, and loads of curiously devised and tasteful, as well as elaborately executed articles; the only want is a certain absence of harmony of the whole—in some matters such as the papering of the rooms."...And Lady Augusta added that the carpets were of Royal Stuart Tartan and Green hunting Stuart—the former lined with red; "the curtains of the same dress Stuart and a few chintz with a thistle pattern, the chairs and sofas in the drawing-room dress Stuart poplin. All highly characteristic, but not all equally *flatteuse* to the eye."

Then, just as Lady Augusta was looking over the last room, came "a joyous cry of welcome, and they" (the royal party) "drove up smothered in blue veils".

It was in this paradise, a year later,[2] that the young Crown Prince of Prussia, having asked the permission of the Queen and Prince Albert, gave the little fourteen-year-old Princess Royal of England a sprig of white heather, and "told her of his wishes". But, the Queen told the King of the

[1] *Letters of Lady Augusta Stanley* 1849–1863, edited by the Dean of Windsor and Hector Bolitho (Gerald Howe, Ltd.), p. 72.

[2] On 29th September 1855.

Belgians, this highly satisfactory and exciting event must be kept a secret for a time, as her child was not yet old enough to think of marriage. The news, however, leaked out, and caused considerable wrath in England. Less than a year later, in May 1856, the Princess made her début and the engagement was confirmed. In honour of both events, life then became a round of gaieties, and a ball was given in the new ball-room at Buckingham Palace, designed by Prince Albert and used for the first time on this occasion. In the same month, too, the Queen went to a ball at the Turkish Embassy, and, to the Ambassador's horror, chose him as her partner for the first country dance. Exquisite in movement as she had been and would be throughout her life, she danced minuets and country dances;[1] and a fortnight later, at a ball held in the Waterloo Gallery at Windsor, after having danced every dance, performed a Scottish reel to the bagpipes.

Meanwhile the Queen, to her intense astonishment, found herself on friendly terms with that alarming man Louis Napoleon—the man whom, after Palmerston, she had really distrusted the most.... And this happy state of affairs was brought about largely by her astute uncle Leopold, who thought that, if France and England were on friendly terms, Belgium would be in less danger of an attack on the part of France. So he set to work gradually, by sending his nephew Duke Ernest to stay with Napoleon, and both that gentleman and his beautiful wife spoke so enthusiastically about the domestic virtues and inspiring home life of Duke Ernest's brother and sister-in-law, professed such a keen desire to know them well—*really* well—that the Duke could not refrain from repeating these sentiments to those who had inspired them. And how could the Queen, who had, in the Emperor's unregenerate days, expressed a horror of his regrettable moral standpoint, fail to be touched by his ready

[1] See Lee, *op. cit.*, p. 267.

appreciation of the fact that her example and that of her husband had reformed every Court in Europe? It was obvious that it would be only kindly from a personal point of view, as well as wise politically, to cultivate their acquaintance. So the Prince paid the Emperor a visit at his military camp at St Omer, and the Emperor was so overwhelmed by his charm and by his great knowledge that the last barrier was broken down, and the Queen invited the Emperor and the Empress to stay with her at Windsor in the following April.[1]

The visit was an unparalleled success. The Queen found the Emperor very quiet, frank, and possessed of much fascination, whilst the Empress, who was afterwards to become one of her most intimate friends, was "very pretty and very uncommon looking". Mr Disraeli, however, who had been invited to some of the festivities, did not at first fall under the spell of this amazing beauty. "I was greatly disappointed with the Empress," he told Mrs Brydges-Williams. "For me she has not a charm. She has Chinese eyes, and a perpetual simper which I detest." Two years later, however, he was to revise this opinion. There was a review of the Household Troops in Windsor Park on the 17th, and the Emperor's flashing smile and immense moustaches and the Empress's nostalgic beauty were the admiration of all. The same evening a ball was given at the Castle, and the ghosts dreaming beneath the trees in the moonlit Park were disturbed till dawn by the sound of the gavottes, the mazurkas, the country dances, the valses, the Scottish reels. During the afternoon of the 18th the Queen presented the Emperor with the Order of the Garter. Then on the 19th the Emperor, resplendent in uniform, lunched at the Guildhall, and in the evening a state visit was paid to the opera, where *Fidelio* was being performed. On the 20th the whole party drove through the thronged streets to Sydenham, where the Crystal Palace

[1] 1855.

was by now on view; then the visit came to an end, as if, said the Queen, it had been a dream.

Mr Disraeli told Mrs Brydges-Williams that "there was immense embracing at the departure and many tears. When the carriage door was at length shut, the Emperor re-opened it himself, jumped out, pressed Victoria to his heart and kissed her on each cheek with streaming eyes," a fact which much astonished the observer.

The foundation of a lasting friendship had been laid; and, in August of the same year, the Queen and Prince, with the Prince of Wales and the Princess Royal, paid a return visit to the Emperor and Empress of the French—for the Emperor was particularly anxious that they should see the Great Exhibition that he, in his turn, had organized in Paris. They arrived in the midst of great heat, but, as the Queen said, the air was more bright and sparkling than in England, and so it did not tire her too much—and she was "*delighted*, *enchanted*, *amused* and *interested*" by everything. Maréchal Magnan told her that not even Napoleon the First on his return from his victories received a more wildly enthusiastic reception than was hers every time she appeared. Owing to her tiny stature and strange and incomparable grace, one critic wrote that "la Reine Mab nous a visité". But the Queen's costume caused astonishment in the French, and particularly in Maréchal Canrobert, who noted in his diary: "She wore a massive hat of white silk, in spite of the great heat. Her dress was white, and she had a mantilla and a parasol of downright green, which seemed to me to be out of harmony with the rest of the costume." On the other hand, the assiduity and devotion to duty of the French caused an equal astonishment and more consternation in the Queen's retinue, and Lady Bulteel suffered much from the excess of these valuable qualities in a footman who had been placed at her disposition: "Je suis aux ordres de Madame la Marquise, toujours prêt. Madame la M., je ne quitte pas ce fauteuil à la porte de Madame la M. Absolument à la disposition de Madame la M." And he was, apparently, as good as his word; for, having spent his time in fidgeting with the handle of the door whilst she was having a bath (the door having no lock), he "at all moments made good his entrance, despite her shrieks and remonstrances—'n'entrez pas,' (crescendo) 'n'entrez pas!' 'Oh, oui, oui, oui, oui, Madame la M.; il le faut, Madame la M. C'est pour expliquer à Madame la M.'" And, severe as were the sufferings of Lady Bulteel from the assiduity of one footman, those of Lady Churchill were worse, since she had three, whose devotion to duty was beyond all praise, and who never left her under any circumstances.[1]

These private troubles, however, were as nothing when compared to the public triumph—the entry into Paris, for instance. The Queen told the King of the Belgians that it was "quite overpowering—splendidly decorated—illuminated—immensely crowded—and 60,000 troops out, from the Gare de Strassburg to St. Cloud".[2] Then, too, how beautifully everything was managed at Court; the Queen and the Prince (unheeding of the footmen) were unable to resist comparing this quiet perfection with the confusion, noise, and bustle of poor King Louis Philippe's time. The Emperor's Court, explained the Queen, was far more regal. The visit was one of unending delights. The royal party had been to the opera, where they were greeted with "God Save the Queen"; they had visited the tomb of Napoleon the First by torchlight with the Prince of Wales, who was dressed in a tartan kilt, and who was told by her to kneel beside the tomb. At the very moment he did so a thunder-storm broke, and so impressive was the scene that the French generals burst into tears.[3]

[1] See *Letters of Lady Augusta Stanley*, p. 68.
[2] *Letters*, Volume III, p. 172.
[3] See Lee, *op. cit.*, p. 257.

THE GREAT EXHIBITION

The splendour of the fête at Versailles was, according to the Queen, beyond all imagination, and all these pleasures and excitements were heightened by the heat, the nostalgic sun, the Douanier-Rousseau-like, tropical-seeming trees with their great purring leaves, and the dark foreign faces. Then, too, how anxious the dear Emperor and Empress—the whole French nation—had been to please. The royal visitors' suite at St Cloud had been decorated in imitation of some rooms at Windsor; and one member of the royal suite, deeply impressed by the boudoir at the exhibition, "a *chef d'œuvre* of French upholstery", was assured that it was "an exact reproduction of the waiting-room at the Great Western Station, arranged for the Imperial visit".[1]

Nothing could have been more gratifying, and the Queen and Prince thoroughly enjoyed the visit. The former had fallen completely under the spell of the persons whom she had previously distrusted, she was enchanted with the Empress, and was in tears when the time came to leave them.

With what pleasure, then, did she receive the news, in August 1857, two years after her visit to Paris, that the Emperor and Empress were once more to be her guests, and this time at Osborne, and in a private capacity.

[1] *Letters of Lady Augusta Stanley*, p. 73.

Chapter XIX

FASHIONABLE INTELLIGENCE

B y the air-pale waves of the sea, where the gold spangles, the gold motes of the light seem sharp as the twanging of a mandoline, by the thick gold sand and the siren caves and the fountain caverns that are like honey-cells, the *calèches* and victorias are driving slowly, so that we may see the passing nymphs and their toilettes—these women like smiling statues or "the women of the ancient world—Stella, Palma, Obole, Œilleuse, Lily, Tsemad, Beryl, Dianella, Epave, Venusia, Digitalis, Lutécite, Hybrida, Virida, Pandora, Cosmopolita, Liane, Pistillarine—child-women who are half flowers, women who are half stars, waves of the sea, great waves born of love or of a dream, the flesh of poets, solar statues, nocturnal masks, white rose-trees flowering in the snow, chimeras, *vierges illuminées*".[1]

The carriages, the victorias and *calèches*, are driving slowly, for now it is late afternoon, and their occupants hope to see a victoria pass bearing the Queen and the Empress of the French. Here it comes, driving a little faster than the rest. The homely stubborn little figure of the Queen looks strange beside the Empress's exquisite air-bright beauty; yet still more strange is the fact that, having cast one look at the

[1] A rough translation of a prose poem by Paul Eluard.

[225]

beauty of the Empress, with her hair of rosy gold, her languid grace, all eyes return to the homelier figure, and this is not only because she is Queen of England, but because of her dignity and consummate grace.

The Queen is talking to her companion, showing her gums and laughing, and her enchanting voice sounds like that of a small bird as the carriage vanishes down an avenue of tall and great-leaved trees shining with the light of afternoon, arbutus trees, magnolia trees, pines, and ilexes. She is talking of the engagement of the Princess Royal, and of Prince Albert's visit to Brussels in July to attend the marriage of the ill-starred Archduke Maximilian, afterwards Emperor of Mexico, and Princess Charlotte of Belgium.

The air-pale petals of the foam seem like flowers from the Queen's hothouses at Osborne—the lyonia with its waxlike bells and its honey smell, the velvety sinningia with dark leaves, the long-petalled bouvardia from Izabal, the jessa-mine-flowered heinsia and the pale-flowered gloxinia with a blue shade on its snow.

The waves fade slowly, melt, and are gone, and with each wave another fashion dies and is born, in this most change-able of all centuries. Philhellenism, that rose with the Greek War of Independence, has faded like the beautiful Lord Byron, the romantic General von Norman, who also died in that "holy war", and like those strange and unworldly bankers, Eynard of Geneva and Hoffmann of Darmstadt, who poured out their money like waterfalls in the cause of Greece. Gone, too, is the Romantic Movement with that Prussian lord who, believing in the sacred duty of Knighthood, founded the Order of the Swan, whose Knights were dedi-cated to the battle against poverty. Gone are the ladies who renounced all for love—Charlotte Frederica of Mecklenburg, the wife of Christian the Eighth of Denmark, whose life as Queen was ended because of her love for her music-master, and who, after a long banishment in Jutland, died as a sister of mercy in Rome. Gone is poor foolish Lady Caroline Lamb, with her despair and her humiliation. Gone, too, are Constance Mayer, who in May 1821 cut her throat because of her despairing love for Prud'hon, and Charlotte Steiglitz, who in 1834 strangled herself in the hope of inspiring her beloved but very inadequately gifted husband, the poet Heinrich Steiglitz, with a great work. The Romantic Age is passing, and here drive a queen and an empress whose love is given to their husbands alone. Soon these fashions too will be over and forgotten, as the great summer roses when the year is over—for the summer a grey and white silk dress coloured like the rain, with great airy sleeves and a cape-collar with edges pointed like huge dark leaves—for cold-hearted December a pelisse like a dark swan's plumage, with a great cape, a bonnet and a muff embroidered with a thin foam of lace, and a dark serpentine boa that looks as if it were made of grebe's feathers. Those dresses are forgotten, and here, blown by the bright airs, come little light ladies with the pagoda sleeves of 1850, their leaf-dark hair smoothed into the Chinese style; here are ladies dark as the shadows beneath the trees, and with as light a foot, in mantillas, in camails, crispins, cardinals, redowas, and in the Aragonnaise or Andalusian half-cloak, for the names of all the lands of haunting winds and nostalgic suns and strange silent snows are mirrored in these fashions—in the Swedish cape (1846), the Moldavian mantle (1848), and later in the Algerian burnous and the Arab bedouin, the Russian bashlik and the Scottish tartan cloak—and with these are worn plumaged turbans whose feathers are stroked by the long golden fingers of the wind, and mittens fringed with gold.

Here are belles in the Phoebus and the Sultan pelerines, in all kinds of watered silks splashed by the great sprays of the foam, in foulard pekinet and *gros de Sidon*, and that *Chine de Syr* that is loved by the wind, and in Cashmere Alvandar, *barège Isabelle*, and *nacré Pékin* that is glittering and thin as the water—ladies in plaided Victoria and thin Clementine like the crinolined waterfalls.

In the dark airs beneath the trees walks a lady in watered muslin, with one in checked *barège* that looks as if lines of summer rain were crossing the cool and darkened air. But by the edge of the water the airs are bright and light and glittering as the stuffs of which these fashions are formed, as light as the gauze, the muslin, the jaconet, organdie, tulle, and tarlatan. But no airs whisper of the tragedies which as a result of these wind-thin stuffs will soon light the different countries with a terrible flame. Already, in 1851, the Duchesse de Maillé had been burned to death as she sat by the fireside in the Castle of La Roche Guyon, and a horrified audience had witnessed the burning to death of the actress Emma Livey. Backwards and forwards on the stage rushed that terrible pillar of fire, with its wild windlike hair, and there were none to help; only their screams mingled with her own. Soon, too, the Archduchess Mathilda, the daughter of the Archduke Albrecht, will die by fire. But the most terrible tragedy of all is yet to come, for in the burning of the church of La Compania at Santiago, in 1883, the flames will spread among those waterfall-bright dresses, and two thousand women, white rose-trees in the snow, solar statues, women half flowers, women half stars, will be changed to torches and be consumed to dust.

The *calèches* and victorias are driving slowly under the great gold rays of the nostalgic sun, spreading like palm-leaves across the sky.

In the satyr forests, ladies in gowns of green mohair trimmed with straw, and round straw hats bearing pheasant feathers, are walking; their high kid boots trample the leaves of the strawberries and buttercups among the thick gold dew. Through the green baize forests they walk, with other ladies in yellow petticoats looped over leather gaiters; their hair is thick and cream-coloured as ponies' manes as they walk

FASHIONS OF 1852

through the leaves that are green as country temples. Far away in Paris, the ladies sitting upon their balconies are reading the memoirs of Rigolboche and of Célestin Mogador, for the reign of the *demi-monde* has begun. Cora Pearl will soon be in fashion, and this is the age when Lola Montez obtains her ascendancy over Liszt and the King of Bavaria, Blanche de Marconnay marries a Bourbon prince, and Count Gustav Chavinsky, a member of a great Moravian family, falls under the dark spell of Julie von Ebergenyi who, we are told, "concealed her calling under the title of Canoness"— until at last, plunged by her into an eternal night, he poisoned her, and became the miserable, hallucinated ventriloquist-dummy hero of one of the most notorious murder trials of the century. Besides the Canoness, that terrible sphinx without a riddle, are other chimeras of the night, prostitutes masquerading as saints and prophetesses: the stigmatic peasant girl of Upper Bavaria who with an appalling and sinister blasphemy "begat the Host upon her tongue", and who at night could be seen sidling down the dark and deserted streets in search of a chance companion, without a face, without a name, to share her secret debauches; and the dark nun Patrocinia who by the light of her false prophecies led the Queen Isabella of Spain to the loss of her Crown and her kingdom.

But, in Paris, these dark chimeras of the night are ignored. To be "canaille", "avoir du chien"—to resemble as far as possible the *demi-monde*—this is the ambition of all fashionable ladies. Soon the Tuileries will echo to the sound of "rien n'est sacré pour un sapeur", "Vénus aux carottes", and "La Femme à barbe", for a princess will introduce Hortense Schneider and Madame Teresa, the music-hall artist, to the court presided over by the Empress of the French, and not only the manners but the toilettes of the *demi-monde* will be copied. In the languid summer evenings, walking past the bandstands set among the brilliant luxurious

leaves in the public gardens, to the begonia-bright sounds of
music by Messieurs Meyerbeer and Auber, we shall see the
most feminine of women wearing strange, amorphous
masculine attire—with men's paletots, men's collars, men's
cravats, and carrying walking-sticks. Later in the evening
some will flaunt military coats of yellow velvet covered with
Chinese embroideries, while others will wear red velvet
cloaks trimmed with black lace, or *caracos* of fiery satin
covered with "a whole planetary system of steel buttons, or
with icicles of cut glass"; whilst the hair of each lady is
dyed red, the colour of a cow's tail, and is "curled and frizzed
like a lap-dog's".

Now the sun is sinking into the wave, and the carriage
with the Queen and the Empress turns and drives homewards.
Late that night, like a white rose-tree in her muslin *peignoir*,
the Empress will spend two hours before her dressing-
table, that waterfall of muslin; outside the window are the
darkened sea and the sound of the sleepy waves, and the
little dark airs will blow away the scents of Guerlain that are
spread upon that dressing-table, amongst the pastes and the
washes and powders, the Essence Ethérée Balsamique, the
Bouquet de Fürstenberg, the Baume de Judée, Ruban de
Bruges, Papier de Vienne, Bois d'Aloès, Gomme d'Olivier,
Amidine de Guimauve, Ethiops Martial, Crépon, Spanish
Woll, Lait des Perles, Crème de la Mecque, Poudre de
Cygne, Poudre de Cypris, Lait d'Amandes, Extrait de Ben-
join, Amygdalin, Lait Virginal, Milk of Roses, Crème
froide de Concombres, Crème de Perse, Mellite Amygdalin
aux Pistaches, Pâte à la Reine et aux Quatre Semences, Pâte
Grenadine, Pâte d'Amande Royale, Serhis des Sultans, Opiats
Porphyrisés, Magyar Nemeiti, Bajuse Kenogs, Crème de
Cydonia, Eau Athénienne, Ambre, Arome synthétique de
Peau d'Espagne, Bellanova, Belle France, Bouquet d'Arabie,
Bouquet de la Néva, Cananga blanc, Chircé bouquet,
Cyparos, Damoiselle, Dypterix Outera, Elastic, El Djézir,

FASHIONABLE INTELLIGENCE

Erochloa, Erixcis, Fleurs de Serre, Florifera, Floxinia, Fol
Arome, Foin Coupé, Fumi Fulci, Gazaki, Grande Maréchale,
Impératrice, Jadis, Maréchale Duchesse, Marie Christine,
Marquise d'Auberive, Millaleuca, Moskowskaia Slava,
Nuée Blonde, Ourida, las Rosa, Parisiana, Plagia, Pré
d'Automne, Prés des Haies, Primauté, Primavera de España,
Rêve du Jour, Rita, Rococo à la Parisienne, Señorita, Senteur
du Soir, Stalizia Grandiflora, Stephanotis, Suaveolens,
Syringa de Japon, Tacona Gracilis, Zillia, Amiris Polyolens,
Anthaemta Nobilis, Ayapana, Azalea Millaleuca, Bananier,
Bergamote et Rose, Calaba des Antilles, Cédrat, Clématite,
Cyclamen, Cyotor Argyria, Cyparis Eraidon, Cytise Silvaria,
Dix Pétales de Roses, Dypterix Olitera, Essence Alpine de
Strawberry, Euxis, Flor d'Aliza, Fleur d'Ophélie, Al Fiori
di Como, Gloxinia, Honeysuckle, Iris Musqué, Jacapouda,
Jasmin de Siam, Lakynis Odorant, Laurus Camphora,
Lolium Agriphillum, Lys de la Vallée, Miel, Mimosa
Esterhazy, Mimosa Frangans, Portugal Water, Moss Roses,
Myrte Fleuri, Ocymum Dulce, Orange de Chine, Pao Rosa,
Palomis Aspienia, Polyante Suaveolens, Sweet Briar,
Thymelia Volcameria.

The little dark airs will blow all these away, among the
smooth leaves of the gardens; and soon those little pale
yellow rose-buds, the candle-flames on the Empress's
dressing-table, will fade too, and the Palace will be in darkness.

Chapter XX

TWO DEATHS

In a quiet sun-drowsy room in her house at Frogmore, an old woman sat, reading letters that had been written forty years ago. Outside, the shadows running over the grass seemed like children dressed in mourning for someone they had never known, playing some game they had learned in far-off gardens. In a little while those shadows would grow graver, deeper, and colder, and would speak to her in their unknown tongue of the secrets that would soon be hers; but the Duchess of Kent heeded them not; her thoughts were all of the past, and of the happy fleeting present. No longer was she bustling, self-assertive, moving in the midst of a hurricane of silks and feathers, but gentle and contented, dreaming away the remaining years of her life; though in perpetual pain from the disease from which she must die, she was happy now, "living on the love she gave".[1] Her daughter was restored to her, indeed loved her far better than she had done in the days of her childhood, the nephew who was that daughter's husband seemed like her own son, she was consulted about everything, and when the Court was at Windsor her grandchildren ran in and out of her house like the small happy shadows.

[1] *Letters of Lady Augusta Stanley*, p. 194.

Then, too, there were the summers spent at Abergeldie, near Balmoral, and the excitement of the Duchess's birthdays, so different from those of the past, when she was only a poor and neglected widow, and not the beloved mother of the Queen of England.... Early in the morning of those birthdays, the ladies-in-waiting would be roused by the sound of the national anthem being sung beneath Her Royal Highness's bedroom windows, followed by a pleasant sound like that of waterfalls, the chatter of the whole household as they clustered together, with the maids, in their white gowns bunched like cherry-trees, all wearing bouquets.[1] Then came the bagpipes and the gillies with their faces like harsh bucolic suns, and there were reels and sword-dances.

At night there would be a dance, with Maslin, the Duchess's page, "leading off a country dance of his own invention with the eldest Princess", and Lady Augusta Stanley fearing that the Duchess's hospitality and sentiments might "multiply the whisky toasts rather dangerously".

There was so much for the Duchess to think about; there were so many joys, little and fleeting, or great and eternal. The Queen's youngest child, Princess Beatrice, was born on the 14th of April 1857, so there was a new baby to be dandled; and the Duchess's eldest grandchild, the Princess Royal, was being prepared by her father for her duty as Princess of Prussia, so that there were all the arrangements for the wedding to be talked about and thought over. The Queen, meanwhile, had been much annoyed by the belief on the part of the Prussian people that the ceremony would take place in Berlin, and she told Lord Clarendon:[2] "the assumption of its being *too much* for a Prince Royal of Prussia to *come* over to marry *the Princess Royal of Great Britain* IN England is too *absurd*, to say the least... whatever may be the usual practice of Prussian Princes, it is not *every* day that

[1] See *Letters of Lady Augusta Stanley*, p. 53.
[2] *Letters*, Volume III, p. 321.

one marries the eldest daughter of the Queen of England. The question, therefore, must be regarded as settled and closed...."

At last the cold January day dawned when the little Princess Royal must leave England and the father to whom she had given all her childish love. He had wished her to make this marriage, it would be for her good, and she must obey him and go far, far away. But she told her mother: "I think it will kill me to take leave of dear Papa."[1]

After the wedding, Prince Albert went with his daughter and her husband to Gravesend. It was bitterly cold, and as they came on to the wharf snow was falling. The little Princess's face was very pale and she was shivering, and the flabby body of the ageing man of thirty-eight who walked beside her, flaccid as the result of his ever increasing burden of work, seemed bowed by the cold.

The Princess passed up the gangway of the ship and went below to the royal cabin, and, though her father stood on the wharf till the ship was out of sight, he did not see his daughter again. She did not come on deck to wave to him.[2]

The Prince felt, as he returned to London, strangely tired. There would be more work to be done tomorrow, he reflected; and, at the moment, the thought of that work seemed overwhelming. Fresh order must be put into the State, reforms must be instituted, the condition of the poor ameliorated—and the question of unemployment dealt with. Mr Bolitho, in his biography of the Prince, points out that his "philanthropy never remained in the realms of mere theory. When he was appointed Master of Trinity House, he became interested in the case of the ballast-heavers. The story of their emancipation is best told in their own memorial, written for the Queen after the Prince's death. 'Before he came to our rescue, we could only get work through a body of riverside publicans and middlemen, who made us drink

[1] Bolitho, *op. cit.*, p. 235. [2] See Bolitho, *op. cit.*, p. 238.

before they would give us a job....The consequence was that we were in a pitiable state; this truck-drinking system was ruining us, body and soul, and our families too....We got no help till we sent an appeal to your late Royal Consort....He at once listened to us...he could put himself down from the throne he shared to the wretched home of us poor men....He enquired himself into the evils that oppressed us...at once our wrongs were redressed, and the system that had ruined us swept away.'"[1]

So the years passed, each with its own burden of cares and overwork. The Crimean War was over, it is true; but a short time afterwards the Prince realized that England was slipping back into her old and habitual state of laziness; her armies were scattered, there was an unwise retrenchment in both the services, and the Prince foresaw that trouble might arise at any moment and England be unable to cope with it. So the Queen wrote to Palmerston, complaining of the retrenchments,[2] and urging him to follow a more active course.

The Prince's fears were soon to be proved only too well grounded, for in 1857 the Indian Mutiny broke out in all its fury. The Prince had foreseen this, and so had Mr Disraeli, who had already gained the confidence of the Queen. Mr Disraeli had issued warnings against the coming revolt, whilst Mr Gladstone had been too busy opposing the Divorce Bill to pay any attention to the reports of growing disturbances, and Lord Palmerston, usually so far-seeing, had no apprehension of coming danger, and told the Queen that, though the extension of the mutiny amongst the troops was regrettable, he had no fear of the results. But the revolt spread like fire, and every day there were new reports of unspeakable cruelties. The Queen told the King of the Belgians that "the horrors committed on the poor ladies—

[1] Bolitho, *op. cit.*, p. 242.
[2] See Bolitho, *op. cit.*, p. 243.

women and children—are unhuman in these ages, and make one's blood run cold".…

In the midst of the fury, the horror, and the confusion resulting from the Mutiny, Her Majesty, unlike most of her subjects, kept a level head, and remained entirely just-minded. We find her writing an extremely sensible and just-minded letter to Lord Clarendon, who had complained that the Maharaja Duleep Singh had not expressed his indignation at the atrocities. In the course of this letter, she reminded Lord Clarendon that the Maharaja could hardly "be expected to like to hear his country people called *fiends* and *monsters* and to see them brought in hundreds, if not thousands, to be executed".

Indeed, all Victoria's nobility of heart, all her feeling for justice, her consummate common sense, her gifts as a Queen, were shown in her attitude of mind towards India, and her Proclamation to the Indian People when the Mutiny had been quelled. "The Indian people should know", she wrote to Lord Canning, the Governor General, in December 1857, "that there is no hatred to a brown skin, none; but the greatest wish on the part of the Queen is to see them happy, contented, and flourishing."

The Mutiny and the Crimean War were over, each leaving a trail of wreckage and horror, and the years, as they passed, brought many changes. Lord Palmerston, for instance, who had once been the idol of the people, was treated now as if he were the villain of a melodrama. Should he rise to speak in the House, he was booed, and the members united as one man against any measure which he supported. "Without rhyme or reason," wrote the Prince, "he had been stamped the only *English* statesman, the champion of liberty, the man of the people, etc., etc., etc.; now, without having changed in any one respect, having still the same virtues and the same faults as he always had, young and vigorous in his seventy-fifth year, and having succeeded in his policy, he is now considered the head of a clique, the man of intrigue, past his work, etc., etc., etc.—in fact, hated."[1]

Young and vigorous at seventy-five! Was the Prince thinking of another man, weary and old at thirty-nine—nearly as old as those worn-out workers for whose welfare he had toiled so unremittingly—a man who also was distrusted, unpopular, and underrated?[2] But Lord Palmerston, unlike that other man, did not care if he was popular or unpopular. He laughed his jaylike laugh, and sported his green trousers and his blue coat, and dyed his whiskers just as jauntily as ever!

In the outer world these upheavals occurred, whilst in the family of the Queen there were changes of a gentler kind, reunions and births.

In August 1858, the Queen and the Prince paid a visit to their eldest child in Berlin; and early in the next year their first grandchild was born. Then, in 1859, the Prince of Wales, on attaining his eighteenth birthday, came of age. He was grown to manhood, but his father, who by now had the title of Prince Consort, realized with grief that in spite of this maturity he was quite unaltered. He still loved gaiety and light frivolous books, he would have liked to have companions of his own age, had he been allowed them—in short, from his father's point of view, he was a grievous disappointment. Still, it was the Prince Consort's place as a tender parent to shield him from all possible harm; and so, when he was sent for three terms to Oxford, he lived with his governor and tutor, in order that they might watch his every movement, and prevent him from making frivolous acquaintances. Smoking was forbidden, and not only was the Prince Consort informed, by memoranda, of his son's every action, but he made, as Mr Benson has said, frequent "surprise raids on the University to see that there was no slackness".

[1] Benson, *op. cit.*, pp. 188–9.   [2] See Benson, *op. cit.*, pp. 188–9.

TWO DEATHS

In 1860, however, the Prince of Wales was allowed to make a tour of Canada, and to visit Washington and New York, accompanied by the Duke of Newcastle, in his capacity as Colonial Secretary; and that charm which was such a source of grief and worry to his father made itself felt to such an extent that the Prince Consort, aware of this, hastened to assure his son, as soon as he reached England, that his popularity was only the result of his being the representative of his mother. And once again the Prince found himself imprisoned at Oxford and forbidden to smoke.

Meanwhile, the Prince Consort began to make inquiries about young ladies amongst whom he could choose a suitable bride for the future King of England. In this, he was helped by the indefatigable King of the Belgians, who, when his great-nephew was sixteen, had made a list of seven marriageable princesses.[1] The seventh name on the list was that of Princess Alexandra, daughter of Prince Christian of Schleswig-Holstein-Sonderburg-Glücksburg, and of the heiress to the Danish throne. The Princess Royal had already seen her, and so enthusiastic were her descriptions of the young Princess's goodness, charm, and delicate flawless beauty, that the Prince Consort, after further inquiries, changed her position from the bottom of the list to the top. He decided, too, that the sooner the Prince met his bride, the better; and the vacation at Cambridge—for the Prince was by now immured in that seat of learning—would, he thought, be a suitable opportunity.

These plans were already in the air, when the dark and mournful spring of the year 1861 dawned.

In February, the Duchess of Kent, ill and suffering, moved with her Court to Frogmore. On the evening of her arrival, Lady Augusta Stanley, one of her ladies-in-waiting, found the dying woman sitting, upright and proud, at her writing-table, taking out and handling her "writing treasures",[2] for

[1] See Benson, *op. cit.*, p. 197.   [2] *Letters of Lady Augusta Stanley*, p. 191.

a few days still remained in which she might chronicle the happy flying shadows and the moments fading like sun-motes, stretch out her withered hands to the warmth of the sun.

Next day, as usual, she played the piano; but the notes seemed faint like a little drift of dust. Her hand and arm hurt her increasingly, she said; once, indeed, the pain was so acute that her teeth chattered as if she felt the prescience of the eternal cold. She asked that she might be left alone for a while. So her ladies withdrew, but in a short time she called them to her, in her sad and flickering voice. Sir James Clark appeared, and, as he entered the room and saw the face of the Duchess, he knew that the end was near. Her voice was silent now, and her eyes "looked very pale and had a sad appealing look". Sir James Clark rushed to London to bring back the Queen and the Prince, but when they arrived, at 7 o'clock, the Duchess did not recognize them.

As the night advanced, the Queen, worn out with grief, promised to rest; but, time and time again, she stole down the stairs in her white dressing-gown, a lamp in her hand, and, entering her mother's room, knelt at her feet and, kissing her hand, spoke her name and tried to recall her.

Lady Augusta lay on the floor, others of the ladies lay on the couch or sat in the deep arm-chairs; but all were sleepless, waiting for that long farewell. At 4 o'clock, tea was brought, but it only made the ladies feel worse; then, at six, the Queen returned, and with her the Prince. "The cold grey dawn", wrote Lady Augusta,[1] "aroused the birds—soon we began to see the gardeners appear...it was very chilly."

The silence was now filled with a faint sad sound, like a little flickering light, as the dying woman drew her breath. Then, a little after nine, the flickering sound faded, until at last it ceased altogether, and once more the room seemed sunk in the deepest shade.

[1] *Letters of Lady Augusta Stanley*, p. 197.

TWO DEATHS

The Prince, bursting into tears, lifted the Queen from her place beside her mother's body, and moving together, slowly as if they were in a dream, their heads bowed, their faces filled with shadow, they left the room.

The succeeding days and weeks were one long round of self-torture and self-reproach for the Queen. "The constant crying", wrote the Queen, in her journal, "was a comfort and a relief"; and every memory of her childhood and her youth, every hour in which the Duchess's treasures were sorted and turned over—these were the excuse for a fresh outburst of tears. Could it be possible, the Queen wondered, that there had ever been a time, before the blessed coming of Albert, when she had not realized how dearly and passionately she had loved her mother? Oh, the bitter pain when, having realized the truth of this reproach, she found small faded books containing accounts of her babyhood, with little tender comments. Oh, to think that for a time *two people most* wickedly estranged the Queen from her mother....."I *dare* not think of it—it drives me *wild* now!"[1] Then, too, how touching it was to find diaries recording how deeply her dearest mama had loved her beloved papa (whose early loss, although she had never seen him, the Queen would never cease to mourn)—how she lived only to be reunited to him.

The Queen's grief became so alarming, her tears were so ceaseless, that at last the Prince Consort was forced to tell her that she must control herself and return to ordinary life. So the Queen, obedient to him in everything, dried her tears and after a while felt strong enough to receive royal visitors, and even, when the Court had moved to Balmoral, to enjoy the expeditions made incognito, and the picnics. The expeditions were the greatest fun, with herself and the Prince Consort travelling under the names of members of the Court; the fear of discovery, and the laughter when they

[1] *Letters*, Volume III, pp. 435–9. Benson, *op. cit.*, p. 199.

were discovered, the constant subterfuges—even the intense discomfort of the inns at which they stayed, the badness and insufficiency of food—were a constant joy. On one occasion[1] when they had put up at a certain inn, this was besieged by a crowd of commercial travellers in search of refreshment and rooms for the night; whereupon a member of the expedition was struck with the brilliant idea of announcing that the whole inn was occupied by a wedding-party from Aberdeen, and the commercial travellers retreated.

On these expeditions, a certain Highland gillie, one John Brown, was invariably the Queen's personal attendant, leading her pony, and waiting on her at table; indeed, as she told the King of the Belgians, "he combined the offices of groom, footman, page and maid, I might say, as he is so handy about cloaks and shawls."[2] Soon, his presence became so indispensable to the Queen's comfort that, when she left Balmoral for Windsor, he went with the royal household.

Life was so happy, so full of small joys and of laughter, that it seemed as if the darkness would never come, as if even the dust contained the germs of a new spring. Yet sometimes, as the Queen looked at her husband's face, she saw that it was filled with a faint and haunting shade. One morning in November, amidst increasing and torrential rain, the Prince drove to Sandhurst from Windsor, to inspect the Royal Military Academy and the Staff College, which were then being built. He did not return to Windsor till 2 o'clock, and then told the Queen that he was tired, and had felt the penetrating cold and the rain. For a fortnight he had known practically no sleep. On the 24th, two days after his visit to Sandhurst, he wrote in his diary: "Am full of rheumatic pains, and feel thoroughly unwell, have scarcely closed my eyes at night for the last fortnight."

[1] See Benson, *op. cit.*, p. 200.
[2] Benson, *op. cit.*, p. 200.

TWO DEATHS

Yet the next day, early in the morning, he went by train to Cambridge to visit the Prince of Wales, and to investigate some story, the truth of which has never been known. Again it was a piercingly cold and stormy day, and the Prince recorded that he was "still greatly out of sorts". On his return at half past one on the following day, he said that he was "very wretched"; nor could he walk with the Queen, as was his custom every afternoon, because of the pain in his back and legs. Next day, the pains and the feeling of discomfort had increased, but there was to be no rest for the worn-out, harassed man, for the news arrived of an American outrage on the British flag, and the Prince was obliged to deal with the matter. A Federal man-of-war, the *San Jacinto*, had, it seemed, fired upon an English mail and passenger steamer, the *Trent*; the captain of the man-of-war boarded her and stated that they had orders to arrest four Southern emissaries who were among the passengers; and this act would, if redress were not made at once, constitute a cause for war. Therefore the Foreign Secretary, Lord John Russell, drafted a despatch to the British Ambassador at Washington, with instructions to demand an immediate apology and, if this were not forthcoming, to ask for his passports. This draft was sent to Windsor on the evening of November the 30th for the Queen's approval.

Next morning at 7 o'clock, the Prince Consort—so ill that he could scarcely hold his pen, and wrote in a shaky and indistinct hand—was at work correcting the draft, softening its too peremptory quality,[1] making new suggestions. The business had to be gone through, in spite of his illness, his hopeless feeling of fatigue and despair. For the nation's welfare was at stake, and that was all that mattered. And so the man who was about to die dragged himself from his bed to his table, and sat there, correcting and reshaping the draft that was to save his country from a new war.

[1] See Benson, *op. cit.*, pp. 202–3.

And, that finished, he must accompany the Queen as she reviewed the Eton Volunteers.

It was a warm, close day; but, although the Prince was wrapped in a coat lined with fur, he felt as if cold water were being poured down his back. He walked slowly and with halting footsteps, as if the shade had become a tangible thing and was trying to drag him down into its company. That night, he could neither eat nor sleep, but lay shivering and trembling in that companionship; yet still the doctors saw no cause for alarm, and Sir James Clark assured the Queen that the illness was not low fever, that there was no reason to call in another physician as Lord Palmerston had suggested: it was only a question of waiting. Yet the shadow that filled his face grew deeper and greyer, he did not smile at the Queen, or take much notice of her, and she noticed that he had a strange, wild look.

On the 6th of December, the Queen wrote: "By eight he was up, and I found him seated in his sitting-room, looking weak and exhausted, and not better, and complaining of there being no improvement, and that he did not know what his illness could come from. I told him it was overwork, and worry. He said 'It is too much. You must speak to the Ministers.' Then he said that, when he lay awake there, he heard the little birds, and thought of those he had heard at the Rosenau in his childhood. I felt quite upset. When the doctors came in, I saw that they thought him less well and more feverish, and I went to my room and felt as if my heart must break."[1]

The doctors knew now beyond a doubt that they had been mistaken, and they broke to the Queen as gently as possible what was the nature of her husband's illness. He was suffering, they said, from gastric or low fever. Yet still they denied that there was any cause for alarm. The fever must take its course; it would last for a month, and all that was

[1] Martin, *op. cit.*, Volume V, p. 431. Bolitho, *op. cit.*, p. 281.

needed was care. But the Queen, moving through this dreadful dream, through these unreal days and nights, was haunted by a dread that had as yet no name.

Yet there were precious fleeting moments in which she thought that he must return to her, that it could not be true he was leaving her for ever. "He was so pleased to see me", wrote the Queen, "—stroked my face and smiled and called me 'liebes Frauchen'." One morning, as he took his beef tea, "I supported him, and he laid his dear head—his beautiful face, more beautiful than ever, has grown so thin—on my shoulder, and remained a little while saying: 'It is very comfortable so, dear child,' which made me so happy."[1]

On the 14th of December, at about six in the morning, one of the doctors came to the Queen and told her that "he had no hesitation in saying that the Prince was much better, and that there was ground to hope the crisis was over". "I went over at seven," wrote the Queen. "It was a bright morning, the sun just rising and shining brightly. The room had the sad look of night-watching, the candles burnt down to their sockets, the doctors looking anxious. I went in, and never can I forget how beautiful my darling looked, lying there with his face lit up by the rising sun, his eyes unusually bright, gazing as it were on unseen objects, and not taking notice of me."[2]

On this, the day when he must leave her, the hours seemed only a pattern of anguished despair and of wild hope. At 12 o'clock the Queen went on the terrace for air. Far away, the military band was playing a gay tune, as if it were not winter, and there were no shadow over the world. Hearing the little heartless gay tune, the Queen burst into tears and returned home. . . . Then came a new anguish as she waited for the doctors' report. "We are very much

[1] Martin, *op. cit.*, Volume v, p. 436. Bolitho, *op. cit.*, p. 283.
[2] Martin, *op. cit.*, Volume v, p. 438.

frightened", they said, "but don't and won't give up hope. The pulse keeps up. It is not worse."

Then came à change. There was, said the Queen, "a dusky hue about his face and hands.... Albert folded his arms, and began arranging his hair, just as he used to do when well and he was dressing. These were said to be bad signs. Strange! as though he were preparing for another and greater journey!"[1]

The Queen's agony of mind was terrible. The doctors tried to comfort her, to give her hope, but she knew, with the instinct of love, that this greater journey was about to begin. "About half-past five", wrote Her Majesty, "I went in and sat beside his bed. 'Gutes Frauchen', he said, and then gave a sort of piteous moan, or rather sigh, not of pain, but as if he felt that he was leaving me, and laid his head upon my shoulder."

Later in the evening, the Queen left him for a moment, in order that she might give way to her grief. But, when she had been gone for only a little while, Sir James Clark sent a message asking her to return. Entering the room, she knelt by her husband's side. At the foot of the bed knelt the Prince of Wales and Princess Helena and on the other side Princess Alice, while in the shadows of the background stood Prince Ernst of Leiningen, the doctors, the Prince's valet Lohlein, General Grey, and the Dean of Windsor.... A deep silence filled the room. Then, as the clock of the castle chimed the third quarter after ten, the worn and troubled face of the man upon the bed grew serene and shadowless—beautiful as it had been when, twenty-five years since, a boy of seventeen played in the leafy gardens of the Palace in Kensington....

[1] Martin, *op. cit.*, Volume v, p. 440. Bolitho, *op. cit.*, p. 285.

Chapter XXI

THE SHADOWED HOUSE

Osborne: 8th January 1862.... "Last year music woke us; little gifts, New Year's wishes, the children waiting with their gifts in the next room." This year there was silence, and the whole world seemed wrapped in a black veil.

In these featureless days of anguish that followed the Prince's death there were mechanical actions to be performed and decisions to be made, and amongst the former was the Queen's removal to Osborne on the day after the Prince's death, on the advice of King Leopold. Then, too, there was the site of a mausoleum to be chosen in the gardens of Frogmore, where one day she would lie once again by her husband's side, and there were meaningless state papers to be signed by an unconscious hand. Princess Alice and Princess Hohenlohe wept at her side; Prince Hohenlohe arrived at midnight on the 20th December, and the Queen, in a desolation of tears, met him on the staircase. Three days later, she looked upon her husband's face for the last time, and she knew that her life was over.

She wrote to Lord Derby (17th February 1862) that "to express the Queen's desolation and utter misery is almost impossible; every feeling seems swallowed up in that of unbounded grief. She sees the trees budding, the days lengthen, the primroses coming out, but she thinks herself still in the month of December. The Queen toils away from morning till night, goes out twice a day, does all she is desired to do by her physicians, but she wastes and pines, and there is that within her inmost soul which seems to be undermining her existence."

The rest of time would henceforth be to her only a memorial to the husband she had lost, a building up of duty on duty, in his honour and for his sake. He must, he should be known to her people for the man he was. Books must be written extolling his memory, statues and memorials must be raised with his image and bearing his name. Her cry, as she saw that beloved face for the last time, was "Will they do him justice now?" Every act, however great, however trivial, every thought, was dedicated to his memory. Till the end of her life, said her biographer, Sir Sidney Lee, his room remained unchanged; and, whilst she lived, the anniversary of his death was passed by the Court in rest and prayer; his birthday and the days when he was betrothed and married—these, too, were held as Saints' days. In these religious duties she found some outlet for her agony.

In her utter misery, in the "two dreadful first years of anguish", she would have liked to have obliterated every feature of the face that had once been so happy, lest she should see in the mirror some memory of what once had been. The presence of strangers, the duty of facing a crowd, these brought an additional pang, for they gave her the knowledge of her utter desolation, the realization that she, who until she was seventeen years of age had never walked downstairs without having her hand held, had now no one to direct or guide her. She was alone; and, had she but known it, would be alone for forty more long years.

We get glimpses of this anguish in *More Leaves from the Journal of a Life in the Highlands*, as, for instance, in the entry about the unveiling of the Prince's statue at Aberdeen (Tuesday the 13th October 1863). "I got out trembling, and when I had arrived, there was no one to direct me, and to say as formerly, what was to be done." Under the glossy, leathery brown leaves with their homely animal smell, in the hot familiar sunlight, the crowds of people were moving like waves of the sea, but yet the men with their apeish brown whiskers, their checked suits, the women with clouds of handkerchiefs waving in the air, and stiff gowns that looked as if they were made of bricks, might indeed have been some of Mr Scott's designs for the Midland Terminus; in spite of all their movement they had no more real life than these.

To face crowds, to make public appearances, caused the Queen anguish, since this emphasized her loneliness. She must drive from her Palace, and, haunted by the memory of the loved being who had once sat beside her, drive through unreal crowds, and then, once more, return to her Palace, alone. And the duty of opening Parliament seemed to her the hardest of all. She told Lord Russell (22nd January 1866): "To enable the Queen to go through what SHE can only compare to an execution, it is of importance to keep the thought of it as much from her mind as possible, and therefore the going to Windsor to *wait* two whole days for this dreadful ordeal would do her positive harm.... The Queen *must say* that she does feel *very bitterly* the want of feeling of those who *ask* the Queen to go to open Parliament. That the public should wish to see her she fully understands, and has *no* wish to prevent—quite the contrary; but why this wish should be of so *unreasonable* and unfeeling a nature, as to *long* to *witness* the spectacle of a poor, broken-hearted widow, nervous and shrinking, dragged in *deep mourning* ALONE IN STATE as a *Show*, where she used to go supported by her husband, to be gazed at, without delicacy, is a thing *she cannot* understand, and she never could wish her bitterest foe to be exposed to."[1]

[1] *Letters*, Second Series, Volume I, pp. 288, 295–6. Benson, *op. cit.*, pp. 225–6.

Then there was the Queen's visit to Lord Dalhousie;
though everybody was very kind, the Queen felt tired, sad,
and bewildered, and knew for the first time in her life that
she was "alone in a strange house without mother or
husband. How many visits", wrote the lonely woman,
"we paid together, my darling and I, and how we ever
enjoyed them. Even when they were trying and formal, the
happiness of being together and a world in ourselves, was so
great." Now he was gone, and the Queen felt "like a poor
hunted hare, like a child that had lost its mother, and *so* lost,
so frightened and helpless".[1]

There were days when she felt the door would open, and
he would enter, young and beautiful as when she first saw
him, his youthful face unstained by death. When Prince
Alfred was recovering from typhoid fever at Malta, she
wrote to the King of the Belgians: "I can't imagine *how*
anyone *can* recover from this dire fever if *he*" (her husband)
"*didn't*, and if dear Alfie (as unberufen) we may confidently
trust he will, *should* recover, I think my *own* darling must
return too."[2]

She lived, indeed, in an ever increasing desolation. In
July 1863, her "dearest, wisest, best, and oldest friend",
Baron Stockmar, died, and she told the King of the Belgians[3]
that the loss was "totally irreparable. To him my Angel looked
for advice and support, and *his* troubles and anxieties certainly
increased after Stockmar left. Again and again, he longed for
Stockmar. . . . Oh, beloved uncle! now that my darling is no
longer with us, I clung more and more ever to him, and
looked to him for advice and assistance in so many, many
ways, and I can't *at all* REALISE *what* this loss will be, or *at
all believe it*. It is *too* dreadful.

"One thought alone sustains me—it is the blessed one of

[1] *Letters*, Second Series, Volume I, p. 91.
[2] *Ibid.*, p. 68.
[3] *Ibid.*, p. 99.

the reunion of those two *blessed* spirits who loved each other so dearly, and understood each other so well, for dear old Stockmar said to me last year, looking at my darling's picture: 'I shall be so glad to see him again, my dear good Prince.'"

The whole of existence had changed to a mirage. There was, for instance, the lovely October day (October 3rd 1863), when the Queen, sitting on the shore of Loch Tay with her ladies and gentlemen, picking up glittering white quartz and eating her luncheon on the sand, saw the reflection in the mauve lake so clear, so strong, that it might almost be a real landscape. But nothing would ever be quite real again, now that her husband was not by her side, changing for her the pomp and splendour in which she must live to happy, intimate homeliness, the terrible years of history to happy and peaceful hours. How unreal was the history of nations beside the happy life of individuals—as unreal, perhaps, as the reflections in the lake. This she knew, the great Queen, who was the mirror of a million lives, of a million beings who live humble lives in happiness, placing all their treasures in love, regarding their homes as a refuge, not only against the winds of heaven, but against fate—a warm refuge, a shelter. Creation to her meant the bearing of children, her love for her husband was an earthly mirror of her love for the God whom she served so faithfully—a God made, perhaps, in her own image, but a God of goodness and gentle light. She was a mirror, as Mr Strachey has said; but she was not cold or hard as a mirror, being made of flesh that was at once warm and human, petulant and full of staying-power. Her strength was in her will, which resembled the roots of a tree, natural but uncomprehending, yet pushing upwards towards the light. There was nothing in her which could be touched by evil; when she heard of wickedness she hoped only that the perpetrators did not know what they were doing.

The moments were flying past, and they were as un-eventful, as humdrum—except for the huge wind of history outside—as when dearest Albert was alive. But oh, how different! Now the days were just holes full of light, the nights holes full of darkness.

At this period good, comfortable, indefatigable, resolute John Brown, her faithful personal attendant, seemed to be the only tangible reality, with his rugged strong appearance, so like that of Highland cattle, and his harsh eyebrows like the shaggy boughs of a fir-tree. The son of a Scottish farmer, he had been the Prince Consort's gillie for many years, and now his fidelity, his resolution, and his plain speaking made him prized by the Queen, who saw in him, perhaps, at once a kind of quintessence of the loyalty of her people, and a poor humble substitute for the character on which she had been accustomed to rely for help. He never failed her in any emergency, being ready at all times to seize a would-be assassin, or a pair of runaway horses, to drive away im-pertinent reporters, or to give commonsense advice. The knowledge of his presence in the background, so trust-worthy, so honest, so loyal, so manly, and so ordinary, gave the Queen an indefinable feeling of comfort, and every day when she drove abroad from Balmoral, by the dark green drake-plumaged waters of the small Highland streams and into the calm mauve distance, the cortège of black-veiled women and black-clothed men would be accompanied by this stalwart hirsute figure in a kilt.

When he was present, she felt safe, in spite of the dangers which surrounded her, and which increased month by month, owing to the general discontent, and the Fenian disorders. It had been brought to General Grey's notice, for instance—by Mr Hardy, the Duke of Buckingham, and the Duke of Cambridge, who had received an anonymous letter on the subject—that plans had been formed to kidnap the Queen whilst she was at Osborne. And General Grey told

Her Majesty that "whilst it is difficult to believe, where all seems so still and peaceful, that danger can lurk about the quiet woods and valleys of this island" he must repeat the expression of his honest conviction, that it was precisely in these solitary and peaceful places that real danger exists.... Would it not, therefore, be better for Her Majesty to remain at Windsor? Her Majesty replied that she intended to make no difference in her plans, and "must ask *not* to have this *again* mentioned".

But this was not the only peril. The Duke of Marlborough was rendered highly nervous by a telegram received from Lord Monck in Canada, warning him that eighty persons had set out in two shiploads from New York, with the intention of murdering the Queen and various members of the government. They intended, according to Lord Monck, to land somewhere in the Bristol Channel, and the Duke of Marlborough thought there might be considerable danger for the next three or four weeks, though orders had been sent to try and intercept these ships. "He said", explained Her Majesty in her journal, "that ships must watch the shore and troops be sent here." The Queen added that she walked in the afternoon with Princess Louise to the Swiss Cottage, and then drove in the woods; but that it was most unpleasant to feel one's liberty now so much interfered with, and that she could not help feeling nervous and upset. On the same day (20th December 1867) she wrote a letter to Lord Derby telling him that his fears about her late and distant drives after dark at Osborne were groundless, since they were very rare, and she always had an equerry riding in attendance. But that she did *not* consider Windsor safe, and that nothing would induce her to go to London, until the state of affairs was altered. The precautions taken at Osborne, she added, were such that she felt little better than a *State* prisoner. "She might consent to this for a *short time,* but she *could not* for long."

THE SHADOWED HOUSE

The thought of eighty persons with little boat-shaped hats, plugs of tobacco and chewing-gum, odd snarling accents, and nefarious intentions, landing from two ships and prowling about the gardens at Osborne, must have been an alarming one. It transpired, eventually, that these nefarious persons had never existed, excepting in the imagination. But in any case the presence and vigilance of faithful Brown, representing, as he did, all the loyalty of her people concentrated in one person, was undoubtedly a source of comfort.

Good Brown had also *in excelsis* the pleasing gift of being in a state of overwhelming distress on all melancholy occasions, and the same tendency to tearfulness which the Queen had admired in Lord Melbourne; so that it was not only a kindly condescension, it was a positive pleasure, to break bad news to him. Indeed, he peers at us from the gentle pages of Her Majesty's diary through a perfect cascade of tears, which were ever in readiness, and which spouted from his eyes on all suitable occasions, to the admiration of all beholders. We find the phrase "Good Brown quite overwhelmed" over and over again, and this state of affairs could be brought about as well by the present of a biscuit-box as by the news of a death. For instance, on September the 28th 1878, poor Sir Thomas Biddulph was very ill, and whilst the Queen was writing letters in the garden-house, at a quarter to one, a fountain of tears broke at her feet, and in the centre of it good Brown could be plainly discerned, saying "It's all over." The Queen added: "Good Brown so vexed and so kind and feeling". Again, on the "blessed anniversary", August the 26th, 1878, the Queen, having given Princess Beatrice a mounted enamelled photograph of "Our dear Mausoleum" and a silver belt of Montenegrin workmanship, sent after breakfast for her faithful Brown, and presented him with "an oxidised silver biscuit-box and some onyx studs. He was greatly pleased with the former and the tears came into his eyes and he said 'It is too much.'" But the

Queen said, "God knows it is not, for one so devoted and faithful."

It is a melancholy truth, and one reflecting no credit on human nature, that cynical and heartless persons, bewildered by good Brown's ever-ready tears, ascribed these, together with the fact that under the stress of strong emotion he had been known to totter in his walk, to causes other than grief. It is indeed reported of him[1] that on one occasion, bowed down under the weight of some overwhelming sorrow, he fell to the ground, and for some moments remained there, in what seemed to the observers to be a merciful oblivion; but when this phenomenon was reported to Her Majesty she replied, gently, that she herself had distinctly been aware of a slight earthquake shock. For good Brown's faithfulness was the only comfort amidst her desolation, and his tears seemed but an accompaniment of her sorrow.

Nothing, except humble fidelity such as this, seemed tangible or real. There was a day in Dufftown when "the people had turned out, the bell was rung, and the band played, but they seemed hardly sure till we had passed who it was". And it always seemed to be raining. "The rain is hopeless; the ninth day," wrote the Queen. Or, when it was fine and the Queen sketched, there was no light, no shade. Then there was a night[2] when the Queen gave a house-warming in the Glassalt Shiel—that small, compact house, so sure of itself, so sturdy, standing in the shadow of the mauve mountains whose "wildness" was a source of comfort and complacency to the Queen. The household danced five reels while the Queen watched; and then Brown begged that she would drink to the fire-kindling in whisky toddy, and she did. But after the "merry pretty little ball", though the men still went on singing in the steward's room, the Queen heard nothing, for "the little passage near my bedroom shuts everything off". So it was with her always. And she lay

[1] Private information.   [2] 1st October 1868.

awake in the darkness and thought of her husband and fancied she must see him, and in the end, half comforted or half drowsy, she said "I am sure his blessing does rest on it" (the house), "and on those who live in it."

In the empire of the shadows where the Queen lived, moved, breathed, no joy might rest. Reunions, the weddings of her children, the birth of grandchildren, these were now only an opportunity for a fresh outburst of tears. When the Prince of Wales returned from a long visit to the Near East, the Queen "was much upset at seeing him, and feeling his beloved father was not there to welcome him back. He would have been so pleased to see him so improved, and looking so bright and healthy."[1]

Then again, the night before Princess Alice's marriage to Prince Louis of Hesse-Darmstadt,[2] the Queen got scarcely any sleep; and hearing the preparations being made for the wedding tried her terribly. However, when the Princess came to her mother's room early in the morning, and asked for her blessing, this was given, together with a prayer-book such as had been given to the Queen by *her* dear mama on *her* happy wedding morning; and before putting on her "sad cap", as little Princess Beatrice called it, the Queen went to look at all the pretty decorations. Still, it was all a great trial, although the Queen restrained her tears and, in spite of a great struggle all through the wedding, remained calm.

But far worse even than the marriage of Princess Alice, was the public ordeal of the Prince of Wales's wedding. It is true that the Queen was enchanted with her future daughter-in-law, loving her, indeed, with all the warmth of her heart; yet it was impossible for her to see this future member of her family without bursting into tears, remembering all that had gone before, and her own sad loss.

[1] *Letters*, Second Series, Volume I, p. 84.
[2] 1st July 1862. See *Letters*, Second Series, Volume I, p. 40.

THE SHADOWED HOUSE

On a white and misty day[1] pierced by the sharp songs of birds, the future Princess of Wales arrived in England, accompanied by her parents and her sister. Early in the morning, the Prince of Wales left Windsor Castle for Gravesend to meet his bride, but it was not until dark that the bells began to ring, and the carriages and escort could be seen approaching. There was a general rush to the doors of the Castle, but the Queen walked slowly down the staircase, mournful and alone. At last, her future daughter-in-law appeared, looking like a rose, as the Queen said in her journal, and wearing a violet jacket trimmed with fur, and a grey dress. The Queen embraced her warmly, but, after a few moments in the White Drawing-room, went upstairs to her room once more, feeling desolate and sad. "It seemed", she wrote, "so dreadful that all this must take place, strangers arrive, and *he*, my beloved one, not be there." Three days afterwards—when the day of the wedding was over, and the Queen, who "so needed love and tenderness, sat alone and desolate, while our two daughters have each their loving husbands, and Bertie has taken his lovely pure sweet Bride to Osborne, such a jewel as he is indeed lucky to have obtained"[2]—she went over in memory all the events of the day. These had made but little impression upon her, for she could think of nothing but the Prince Consort; but she remembered putting on her weeds, with a silk gown trimmed with crape, and she remembered the huge crowds, and feeling cold with nervousness as they watched her. Princess Lenchen had worn a very pretty dress of lilac and white, with a long train, and "Sweet Baby" wore the same colours. Sweet Baby made a low curtsey when she saw her mama; but "to see them go alone was dreadful", and the Queen sat down feeling sad and bewildered. All round her were memorials of her beloved, but she was alone.

[1] 7th March 1863.
[2] *Letters*, Second Series, Volume I, p. 73.

THE SHADOWED HOUSE

The Queen did not at first notice Princess Alice when she appeared, looking very handsome in a violet dress, covered with her wedding lace, and a violet velvet train trimmed with the miniver the Duchess of Kent had worn at the Princess Royal's wedding. Last of all came the Princess Royal, dressed in white satin, and leading her little son Prince William by the hand (such a dear, *good* little boy—although he managed to get the cairngorm out of his dirk and throw it across the aisle, in order to annoy his young uncles...). When the Princess saw her mother she made her a very low curtsey, "with an inexpressible look of love and respect". Then the trumpets sounded once more, and the Prince of Wales entered, looking pale and nervous; he was accompanied by the Prince of Coburg and the Crown Prince of Prussia, and all wore their garter robes. He bowed to the Queen, and, during the long wait for his bride, looked frequently up at his mother with an anxious clinging look that touched her very deeply. Then at last, whilst the orchestra played Handel's Processional March, the young Princess appeared, lovely and pale as the spring day.

The Queen put down her pen, and sank into a dream. What more could she record of that long, bewildering day? She had, she remembered, walked down the Great Staircase for the first time since her life ended, so that she might meet her two dear children, and embrace them....There was the signing of the register, and a family luncheon of thirty-eight in the Dining-room; but the Queen lunched alone with little Princess Beatrice. After that came the long affecting farewell to the bride and bridegroom, during which everybody wept unrestrainedly, and the last glimpse of the young couple as they drove away in an open carriage, with the Prince of Wales standing up and looking up at the Queen lovingly....She saw him drive away, through the cheering crowds...and oh, *how* like it was to that other wedding journey, twenty-three years ago! Could these crowds be, in truth, shouting with joy for another bride and bridegroom? Or would she turn and find once more that beloved and youthful form of many years ago, standing by her side?...It was strange: now that he was gone, she saw only the young and lovely face, the. bright eyes with their look of hopefulness—never the bent and sagging body, the tired and dispirited face of the man who had died from over-work....But when she turned her head there was no one beside her—not even a shadow in the empty sunlight.

She stood waiting for a moment, and then, entering her carriage with Princess Lenchen, drove to the mausoleum and prayed by the resting-place of her beloved.

The trying day, so full of tears and of sorrow, was over; but the Queen determined that, next time one of her children married, there was to be no question of a separate household; and she told the King of the Belgians: "a married daughter I MUST have living with me, and must *not* be left constantly to look about for help, and to have to make shift for the day, which is too dreadful. I intend (and she wishes it herself) to look out in a year or two (for till nineteen or twenty I don't intend *she* should marry), for a young, sensible Prince for Lenchen to marry, who during MY *lifetime*, can make my house his *principal* home. Lenchen is so useful, and her whole character so well adapted to live in the house, that (unless Alice lived constantly with me, which she won't) I could *not* give her up, without *sinking* under the *weight* of my desola-tion. A sufficient fortune to live independently if I died, and plenty of good sense and high moral worth are the only requisites."[1]

Meanwhile, the great work of impressing on the people's minds, by means of the written word, the true character of one whom they had lost, went on apace. Sir Arthur Helps, labouring mole-like under the Queen's commands, produced

[1] *Letters*, Second Series, Volume I, p. 85.

mounds of the Prince's addresses and speeches. General Grey, also under Her Majesty's directions, produced the history of the Prince's life from his birth to his marriage, and for this work the Queen allowed him access to confidential documents, and added notes with her own hand. This book appeared in 1867; but the great work was still to come, Mr (afterwards Sir Theodore) Martin's complete biography of the Prince, which took fourteen years in the writing, the final volume not appearing until 1880. But even this work was not completed without some troubles and indecisions, which had to be smoothed away. We find, for instance, the Queen writing this highly mysterious letter [1] to Mr Martin on the 19th of January 1874: "Regarding the passage which she" (the Queen) "wishes omitted...she feels and knows how much such an allusion *might* hurt the feelings of faithful servants which she thinks should *always* be *as much* considered as *our own*. It may be that some footman who was with her did not understand her, and the dogs did not (most certainly) obey her as she well remembers, but this sweeping observation would be quoted and do *great harm*."

At length, however, in spite of all mishaps, Mr Martin's task came to an end, and from this enormous work a figure certainly emerges, but it is not the touching, suffering, loving human being, the man whose warmth of family love, whose passion of pity for the destitute, were almost unsurpassable, whom we find in Mr Bolitho's pages. It is true that all the virtues he possessed are chronicled, and none of the failings, but he appears as a rather flat and lifelessly perfect being, without light or shade—a character too perfect for our belief. [2] This was the case, indeed, with all his earlier biographers. Mr Tennyson added, as we shall see, the splendour of verse to the quieter prose eulogies, and as a result a figure emerged which was not the figure of the

---

[1] *Letters*, Second Series, Volume II, p. 301.
[2] See Strachey, *op. cit.*, p. 203.

Prince at all; it was a fairy-tale knight, it was the flat and shadeless saint in a stained-glass window.

Side by side with these eulogies, the question of the raising of buildings, of statues, of memorials, in the Prince's honour occupied the Queen's mind. A committee was formed and a meeting was called at the Mansion House a month after the Prince's death, to discuss whether to raise a statue or to build an institution to his memory in London. A subscription was raised and the Queen's wishes were consulted.[1] Her Majesty's preference, it seemed, was for a granite obelisk with sculptures at the base, rather than an institution. There were, however, technical difficulties in the way of this: an obelisk, the committee felt, must, to be really impressive, be a monolith; and where was the granite block to be found which would furnish a monolith of sufficient size?

It is at this point that Mr Gilbert Scott, the architect of the Memorial, appears on the scene, and it will not be out of place in this connection to examine some of this eminent man's earlier activities. He had, as Mr Strachey rightly points out, won his commanding position in the world of architecture as much by his personal virtue and simple piety as by his distinguished talents. Architecture was to him, above all, *a symbol*. He would have nothing to do, for instance (at least until Lord Palmerston brought him low), with the Classical style, which savoured far too much of the Italian nation and their unfortunate addiction to Roman Catholicism. Only by way of the "upward striving" of the English Gothic could one, he considered, find the path of light. This is explained very clearly in a letter to the editor of the *Ecclesiologist*, in which he points out that Mr Pugin, the gifted devotee of the English Gothic style, had "shown the particular rightness of the Gothic style for every building of a Christian nation". "He" (Mr Pugin) "adverts to the prevailing upward tendency of every feature in a Gothic

[1] See Strachey, *op. cit.*, p. 204.

building. He speaks of the clustered pillars as 'emblems of brotherly love, each helping to bear the other's burden, each assisting each other in its upward striving, till all meet in the heaven's vault above'; as the aim of all is the vault of heaven, so the soul of all is the free spirit of love—nothing servile is to be seen, no architrave checks with its oppressive burden the upward striving, everything, it is true, bears and serves, but it is the service of free love!"

No wonder, therefore, that, when Mr Scott sent in designs for the Government Offices in Whitehall, which were to be rebuilt, his aspirations were towards buildings of a Gothic character. And all would have gone well, had there not been a change of government, with Lord Palmerston as Prime Minister; for he, who had made Prince Albert's life a burden to him, now proceeded to make a martyr of Mr Scott, behaving, indeed, with a "quantity of poor buffoonery which only his age permitted". He must insist, he told the outraged Mr Scott, on his making a design in the Italian style.[1] And in the end, in spite of his horror at this lascivious suggestion, there was nothing for Mr Scott to do except to resign himself to the inevitable and, amidst the sympathy of the nation (as he tells us), prepare a pure, or impure, Classical design. It is at least a comfort to know that "even Mr Ruskin told him that he had done quite right". And it is even more comforting to know that in 1865 he was called upon to build the Terminus of the Midland Railway and the St Pancras Hotel, and that in these buildings he was able to embody his ideals, the upward striving, the ideals of free love, and of service, the pillars bearing each other's burdens.

So much for Mr Scott's other activities. But now the experience he had gained was to be used for a work which, if smaller in scale, had still more import than those which preceded it—the Albert Memorial.

[1] See Strachey, *op. cit.*, pp. 205-6.

From the very beginning, Mr Scott had been much attracted by the idea of the Memorial, though he regretted the form which it seemed likely to take, and, "for his own personal satisfaction and pleasure, at the time when a monolithic obelisk was thought of, endeavoured to render that idea consistent with that of a Christian monument by adding to the apex a large and magnificent Cross". Eventually, Mr Scott showed this drawing of the proposed monument to the Queen, though not, he hastens to assure us, till after the idea of the obelisk had been finally abandoned; and, to his great pride, he was chosen as architect for this, which under his direction had by now taken on a far more serious form. "My idea in designing the Memorial", we are told, "was to erect a kind of ciborium to protect a statue of the Prince; and its special characteristic was that the ciborium was designed in some degree on the principles of the ancient shrines. These shrines were models of imaginary buildings, such as had never in reality been erected."[1] This Memorial was, at the Queen's wish, placed as near as possible to the site of the Great Exhibition in London, and "in May 1864 the first sod was turned".[2]

Buoyed up by the encouragement of a dinner-party the workmen at last completed their great task, and, in July 1872, it rejoiced the sight of the Queen's loyal subjects. "This Memorial", said the *Daily Telegraph*, "is assuredly the most consummate and elegant piece of elegiac art which modern genius has produced. If we had dug up such massive pieces of fine thought and faithful toil in an Italian vineyard or on a Greek hill, the critics would not mistake them, perhaps, for the relics of the Periclean period; but they would, if they had eyes, hail the grace, the spirit, the beauty and reality of them. The 'America' is a poem of national progress in

[1] Strachey, *op. cit.*, p. 206. Sir George Gilbert Scott: *Personal and Professional Recollections*, p. 225.
[2] Strachey, *op. cit.*, p. 206.

eloquent marble; and the 'Africa', if Mr T. Theed had cut it for Dido or Sophonisba, would have been gladly paid for at its weight in Mauritanian silver.

"It is indeed a possession which ennobles the capital and which we may show to visitors from abroad. And they will not fail to admire and applaud it, above all, while they reflect that an age called money-seeking and ideal-less set up this exquisite and costly tabernacle of the Arts to the memory of one whose two chiefest glories were his perfect dutifulness in life, and in death the tears and the unchanging fidelity of his Widow. As long as it stands, the angels pointing downwards and pointing upwards will say aloud to all with 'ears to hear' that the best road to Heaven goes by way of duty quietly done on earth; while history will not forget to tell that it immortalises the unblemished troth of a true and virtuous husband and the love stronger than death of a perfect Wife."[1] But, deep as was the pleasure felt by the Queen in this noble achievement, her pride in that still greater monument to the Prince, the *Idylls of the King* and their dedication, was yet more profound. This dedication led to a friendship between the Queen and the poet; and, to trace the course of this, we must go back some years.

[1] *Victoriana:* A Symposium of Victorian Wisdom, edited by Osbert Sitwell and Margaret Barton (Gerald Duckworth and Co., Ltd.).

Chapter XXII

THE QUEEN AND THE LAUREATE

O n November the 19th, 1850, in the study of a house at Boxley near Maidenhead, a man whose appearance combined in almost equal proportions the grandeur of Homer and the rectitude of Mr Arnold of Rugby, the ruggedness of the Alps and the calm of an English sabbath (cow-bells intermingling, as one might say, with church-bells), sat reading a letter.

Outside the window, the gold-mosaic'd trees of autumn had the cold splendour of a mausoleum, the grass, thick as a beaver's fur, the Mendelssohnian waterfall, these were at once ordered yet wild, like the appearance of the poet. And Mr Tennyson gazed from the letter to the view with a distinct sense of satisfaction. Not long before this time, his friend Mr Carlyle had described him as a "life-guardsman spoilt by making poetry"; but the letter which had just arrived proved at least that the spoiling had not been complete from a worldly point of view, since it was a notification that Her Majesty had appointed Mr Tennyson as Poet Laureate.

This honour was conferred as the result of the Prince Consort's deep admiration for *In Memoriam*, and was, as well, a kind of prize won by the moral loftiness of the poet. He had, for instance, a truthfulness which could not be diverted under any circumstances, and his son places it on record that he was in the habit of saying: "I would pluck my hand from a man even if he were my greatest hero or my dearest friend, if he wronged a woman, or told her a lie." Indeed, it is reported of him that, when hearing, at a garden-party, a faint complaining sound, he turned to the lady next to him and said: "Young woman, your stays creak!" But such was his love of truth, that five minutes afterwards he made his way to the distant part of the garden to which she had fled, and added: "Young woman, I was wrong. It was not your stays, it was my braces." [1]

The same conscientiousness imbued every action, great or small, and was combined, strangely enough, with a sense of fun which came and went, but which was acute to a singular degree.

Mr Tennyson had had no expectation of this rise to power, for his predecessor Wordsworth had been dead for some months; it seemed to him, therefore, a strange coincidence that, only the night before he received the offer of the post, he should have dreamt that the Prince Consort came and kissed him on the cheek, in answer to which proof of affection the poet said in his dream: "Very kind, but very German." For some days Mr Tennyson was in doubt as to whether he should accept the Laureateship or not, but in the end he did, ascribing the decision to the fact that during dinner his friend Mr Venables had told him that if he became Poet Laureate he would always, when dining out, be offered the liver-wing of a fowl.

The post, as it turned out, was no sinecure, for, as soon as the news of the honour became known, every versifier in the

[1] Told the author by the late Sir Edmund Gosse. The information contained in this chapter is taken from *Alfred, Lord Tennyson*: A Memoir, by his son, Hallam, Lord Tennyson (Macmillan and Co., Ltd.).

kingdom bombarded the Laureate with letters, appeals for advice, and, worst of all, poems. "The two million poets of Great Britain deluge me daily," he sighed. On one occasion, this state of affairs led to the poet being brought face to face with twelve cantos written by a survivor of Waterloo to commemorate the victory, and including the line:

> *The Angels encamped above the field of Waterloo.*

The Laureate, however, performed the duties of his office unflinchingly. When called upon to commemorate the Great Exhibition at the Crystal Palace, he wrote the following lines, and incorporated them in the address to the Queen which is prefixed to the seventh edition of his *Poems*:

> *She brought a vast design to pass*
> *When Europe and the scatter'd ends*
> *Of our fierce world did meet as friends*
> *And brethren in her halls of glass.*

But the stanza, as Sir Sidney Lee remarks, gloomily enough, in his life of the Queen, was not reprinted. Seven years later, Her Majesty wished a stanza to be added to "God Save the Queen", in order that this might be sung at a concert to be given at Buckingham Palace on the evening of the Princess Royal's wedding day. The Laureate complied with two stanzas; these were published in *The Times* on January the 26th, 1858, and caused great satisfaction:

> *God bless our Prince and Bride!*
> *God keep their lands allied,*
>   *God save the Queen!*
> *Clothe them with righteousness,*
> *Crown them with happiness,*
> *Them with all blessings bless,*
>   *God save the Queen.*

THE QUEEN AND THE LAUREATE

Fair fall this hallow'd hour,
Farewell our England's flower,
God save the Queen!
Farewell, fair rose of May!
Let both the peoples say,
God bless thy marriage-day,
God bless the Queen.

Nor was this the only triumph. "The Charge at Balaclava" fired both soldiers and civilians to such an extent that we find Mr Tennyson telling John Forster: "My friend Chapman wrote to me thus: 'An acquaintance of mine in the department of the S.P.G. as he calls it (Society for the Propagation of the Gospel) was saying how a Chaplain in the Crimea writes to the Society: "the greatest service you can do just now is to send out on printed slips Mr Tennyson's 'Charge at Balaclava'. It is the greatest favourite of the soldiers—half are singing it, and all want to have it in black and white, so as to read what has so taken them."'"

A thousand copies of the poem were despatched by the Laureate, with the result that a survivor of the charge, who had since been kicked by a horse, and was in such a state of despondency that nothing, not even the application of leeches, could rouse him, was thrown into such excitement by hearing the poem that within three days he was discharged from the hospital as cured and fit for duty. Nor was this the only case recorded where the Laureate's poems proved to have healing qualities. On October the 18th 1855, immediately after his friend Mr Edward Lear had visited the poet and sung to him his setting of "Mariana", "The Lotus-Eaters", "O let the solid ground", and "O that 'twere possible", Mr Tennyson received an interesting letter telling him of a man who had been roused from a state of suicidal depression by "The Two Voices"; whilst the mate of a ship

[267]

in the Malay Archipelago, after reciting the poems of Mr
Tennyson almost unceasingly for a week, told a friend of the
poet that these had kept him from suicide by drowning.

Alas, he was not always so popular. Indeed the poem
Maud raised such a storm that Dr Dunn was constrained to
publish a work in defence (*Maud Vindicated*). It seems that
one critic had labelled the poem "a spasm", another discovered that it was "a careless, visionary, and unreal allegory
of the Russian War", a third was unable to make up his
mind if the poem should have been called "Mad" or "Mud"
instead of by its original name, a fourth found that "Mad"
was the right word, and that the madness was an excuse for
pitching the poem in "a key of extravagant sensibility".
Others again announced that it was "an epidemic caught from
the prevalent carelessness of thought and rambling contem-
plativeness of the time", and that it was the result of "a
political fever", whilst the phrases "obscurity mistaken for
profundity", "absurdity such as an even partial friendship
must blush to tolerate", "the dead level of prose run mad",
"rabid blood-thirstiness of soul" were hurled at the poet,
who finally, to his delight, received the following letter,
unhappily not signed: "Sir, I used to worship you, but now
I hate you. I loathe and detest you. You beast! So you've
taken to imitating Longfellow. Yours in aversion."

But worse was to come; aspersions were actually cast on
the poet's moral outlook, and the *Athenaeum* was so horrified
by the tone of *Enoch Arden* that we find this stern rebuke
figuring in its pages: "What are we to gain by putting such
poems before the public mind? Are the poets and novelists
bent on preparing the way for the introduction of polyandry?
Are the young ladies of a coming age to be trained in a com-
plaisant belief that it is rather a poetical incident than a dark
and shameful misery to have two husbands living at one
time? If not, why all this prostitution of art?

"Enoch on his return home could not stand off from his

wife and children, leaving them in another man's house, without a positive fraud, a criminal collusion. For the sake of everyone's purity of soul, it would have been better for him to have stopped it at once by announcing his return. That he should be represented as acting a heroic part in skulking by, in dodging about the pothouse and the port, in living a daily lie in the face of men, is one of the mysteries of a morbid epoch."

It is comforting to know that the *Lady's Magazine* was able to prove that Mrs Arden was guiltless of bigamy from a legal standpoint, since she had not heard of her first husband for over seven years.

This battle took place in 1864, after the Prince Consort's death, so that he was spared the shock of seeing this blemish on the Poet Laureate's moral reputation; but, in the midst of other storms, his admiration and that of the Queen's remained undiminished.

Farringford House, which had just been bought by Tennyson, was within distance of Osborne, and the Prince paid a visit to the poet, driving into the distance that was royal blue as a coachman's coat, where the floating trees seemed old as Wellington's generals. Under the great gold sun, amongst the green and babyish leaves, the inns seemed bright as a seedman's packet, or as bunches of marigolds and zinnias, candytuft and red double daisies. The countrymen drinking the bright and foxy beer raised a cheer, the little girls, in their bunched cauliflower-like dresses, curtseyed; everything seemed peaceful and happy as if the machine age had not begun, as if there were no problems of unemployment, no terrible Lord Palmerston, the man "who embittered our whole life", as if policies and overwork were just winter shadows.

The Prince's visit to the Laureate was unexpected, and his arrival frightened the servant who opened the door to such an extent that she was unable to admit him, and had to be removed from the doorway before he could effect an entrance.

Then, in the still half-furnished library, these two epitomes of much that was best in the Victorian age, of what was most selfless and most high-minded, most far-seeing and most enlightened, talked for a couple of hours; the equerry picked a small bunch of wild flowers to take home to the Queen, and then the prematurely aged man, who was soon to die, worn out before his time by the claims of duty, driven to his death by overwork, climbed into his carriage again and returned to Osborne.

Not long after this, the *Idylls of the King* appeared, a work of spotless purity, in spite of one or two very dangerous passages. The *Quarterly Review* felt moved to say: "The chastity and moral elevation of this volume, its essential and profound though not didactic Christianity, are such as perhaps cannot be matched throughout the circle of English literature in conjunction with an equal power....He has had to tread upon ground which must have been slippery for any foot but his. We are far from knowing that either Lancelot or Guinevere would have been safe even for mature readers, were it not for the instinctive purity of his mind and the high skill of his management."

The Prince Consort was delighted with the book, and wrote to the poet apologizing for the intrusion on his leisure, and asking him to inscribe his name in the Prince's copy of the book. The Laureate replied that the Prince's liking for the poems arose from his seeing in them, "unconsciously", his own image.

Three years afterwards, when the Prince was dead, the poet visited the Queen in her widowhood at Osborne. He said that "she stood pale and statue-like before me, speaking in a quiet, unutterably sad voice. There was a kind of stately innocence about her." She told him that "next to the Bible, *In Memoriam* is my comfort". Then they talked of the Prince and of Hallam, whom she thought from his portrait in *In Memoriam* greatly resembled him, even to his blue eyes. The Laureate said that he thought the Prince would have made a great king, and she replied: "He always said that it did not signify if he did the right thing or not, as long as the right thing was done."

The dedication of the "Idylls" to the memory of the Prince Consort strengthened the liking which the Queen had always entertained for the Poet Laureate; esteem grew into friendship, friendship into a genuine affection. She enjoyed both their correspondence and their conversations, although his letters always contained a note that seemed inspired by a sense at once of his high calling and of his office. Later in life, indeed, he added an extra elegiac dignity to these already rather pontifical letters to his sovereign, by referring to himself as a stranger, a separate being: "the old Poet", "your old Poet", "the old Poet sends blessings"; "your old Poet" was grateful for being remembered on his birthday. By these means he became spectator as well as protagonist, and could enjoy to the full the touching impressiveness of the correspondence between the honoured and beloved Sovereign Lady, "so alone upon the heights—it is terrible", and that subject who was the pride of the nation—the great poet whose noble and aged head was bowed beneath the weight of his laurels.

The Queen's attitude towards the poet shows all the warmth and simplicity of her nature, her capacity for reverence; and the friendship that grew between them was an honour to both. It is sad to think that, nine years before his death, his increasing infirmity and the distance between them made his visits impossible. She, in her private journal, records that on Tuesday August the 7th, 1883, she saw the Great Poet Tennyson for the last time in dearest Albert's room for nearly an hour; she noticed that he was grown very old, and that he was almost blind. She asked him to sit down, and they talked of the many friends he had lost, and of immortality, he speaking "with horror of the unbelievers and philosophers who would make you believe there was no other world, no Immortality, and who tried to explain away all in a miserable manner". They spoke, too, of Ireland, and of "the wickedness of ill-using poor animals". "I am afraid", said Lord Tennyson (for by this time he had been raised to the Peerage), "I think the world is darkened. I dare say it will brighten again." The Queen told him once again what a comfort *In Memoriam* had been to her, to which he replied that "she could not believe the number of shameful letters of abuse he had received about it". "Incredible!" wrote the Queen in her private journal. On his leaving, she thanked him for his kindness, and said she needed it, for she had gone through much, and he said, "You are so alone on that terrible height....I've only a year or two to live, but I shall be happy to do anything for you that I can. Send for me whenever you like."

On his return, the Laureate sent the "Dear and Honoured Lady, My Queen" a letter of appreciative grief, in which, after commenting on the likeness of the Queen's state to those mentioned by Shakespeare:

> *O hard condition, twin-born with greatness*

and:

> *What infinite heart's-ease must kings neglect,*
> *That private men enjoy!*

and after touching lightly on "the loneliness of the throne, and your Majesty's many losses", he made a touching reference to "this latest" (loss) "of your faithful servant". For John Brown had recently died. Letters were still exchanged, the Queen sent her poet photographs of a *tableau vivant* of "Elaine", which were suitably admired; but she never saw him again. Illness and the difficulty of visiting in the bad weather deprived her of that solace, him of that comfort, though nine years lay between him and the immortality in which they both believed.

It is a comfort to know that when the end came, it was worthy, as Her Majesty tells us in her journal, of so remarkable a man, since he died with his hand on his Shakespeare, and the moonlight shining over him.

Chapter XXIII

THE QUEEN, MR DISRAELI,
AND MR GLADSTONE

In December 1868, to Her Majesty's politely disguised dismay, Mr Disraeli, who, after serving ten months as Prime Minister, had already insinuated himself into the Queen's favour, went out of office, and she found herself faced with the necessity of asking Mr Gladstone, who, when in private conversation with her, spoke to her as if he were addressing a public meeting, to form a new ministry.

During the ten months of Mr Disraeli's premiership the Queen had shown signs of an animation unknown since her widowhood; she held a Drawing-room at Buckingham Palace in March; on June the 20th she reviewed 27,000 volunteers in Windsor Park, and, two days later, she gave a public "breakfast" or afternoon party in the gardens of Buckingham Palace.

But now, with the coming of Mr Gladstone, a sober sabbatical calm, intermingled with hard work, reigned in the palace.

There was a wide gulf between the characters of these two men, each in his own way possessing the quality of greatness, but of a strangely opposed kind. The fire which was their native element burned in shapes which were utterly different.

THE QUEEN, DISRAELI, AND GLADSTONE

Mr Gladstone's rugged appearance yet seemed covered or glazed over with a sleek gloss; Mr Disraeli's face and form seemed on the point of complete ossification, and lacked glaze altogether. Sir John Skelton, in *Talk of Lothair*, describing a meeting with Disraeli, in 1862, wrote that "the potent wizard himself with his olive complexion and coal-black eyes, and the mighty dome of his forehead (no Christian temple, be sure), is unlike any other living creature one has met. I had never seen him in the daylight before, and the daylight accentuates his strangeness. The face is more like a mask than ever, and the division between him and mere mortals more marked. I would as soon have thought of sitting down at table with Hamlet, or Lear, or the Wandering Jew.... They say, and say truly enough, what an actor the man is! And yet the ultimate impression is of absolute sincerity and unreserve. Grant Duff will have it that he is an alien. What's England to him, or he to England? There is just where they are wrong. Whig or Radical or Tory don't matter much, perhaps—but this mightier Venice—this Imperial Republic on which the sun never sets—that vision fascinates him; or I am much mistaken. England is the Israel of his imagination, and he will be the Imperial Minister before he dies—if he gets the chance."

These then were the two men, equal in their patriotism, though from widely opposite points of view, who now controlled, in turns, the destiny of the nation. The habit of their lives, too, was diametrically opposed. Consider young Mr Gladstone proposing to the lady who afterwards became his wife (and to whom he had first been attracted by her piety) by moonlight at the Coliseum, and repeating the proposal in an English garden, where she—overcome by emotion at his revelation that he had longed to become a clergyman, but that, on his father opposing this wish, he had resigned himself to a political career because he realized that a politician could consecrate his life to enhancing the glory of the Church—accepted him. Consider Mr Gladstone, at 5 o'clock on the day of his marriage, reading the Bible with his wife; contemplate Mr and Mrs Gladstone engaging a cook only after they had had a long conversation with her on religious matters.[1] And then think of that aged but ever brilliant firefly Mr Disraeli—of whom his biographer, Mr Sichel, said that "he was a kind of Mediterranean Byron, for the stock of the Disraelis were Semites who had never quitted the Midland Coasts, and were powerful in Spain before the Goths"—dancing, when in old age, a Highland fling, clad in his nightshirt, with Mrs Disraeli, clad in her nightgown, because they had received the news that a stroke of good luck had befallen one of their friends. Consider these differences, and we shall realize why these political opponents could never have been personal friends, although Gladstone cherished an affection for Mrs Disraeli which she returned.

Again, Gladstone's sympathies lay, it may be said, with the middle class; his were middle-class virtues; whereas Disraeli's sympathies lay with the workers, for whose welfare he toiled unremittingly, and with the older aristocracy, whose society he preferred to that of the new. Pitt, he declared, "created a plebeian aristocracy and blended it with the patrician oligarchy. He made peers of second-rate squires, and fat graziers. He caught them in the alleys of Lombard Street, and clutched them from the counting-houses." For this worship and aggrandizement of Property he had no liking, and he disapproved of this more than ever when it led to the exploitation of the poor. Long ago, in his speech of 1848, he had shown that the radical Hume was "taking *property* as the basis of suffrage, fully as much as the Whigs had done in 1832", and that "the same bourgeois predominance would ensue".

"Now sir," he continued, "I for one think property is

[1] See André Maurois: *Disraeli*, translated by Hamish Miles (John Lane, The Bodley Head, Ltd.).

sufficiently represented in this House.... The House will not forget what that class has done in its legislative enterprises. I do not use the word 'middle class' with any disrespect; no one more than myself realises what the urban population has done for the liberty and civilisation of mankind; but I speak of the middle class as one which avowedly aims at pre-dominance, and therefore it is expedient to ascertain how far the fact justifies a confidence in their political capacity. It was only at the end of the last century that the middle class rose into any considerable influence—chiefly through Mr Pitt.... Their abolition of the slave trade was a noble and sublime act, but carried out with an entire ignorance of the subject, as the event has proved. How far it has aggravated the horrors of slavery, I stop not to enquire.... The middle class emanci-pated the negroes, but they never proposed a Ten Hour Bill. ...They turned their hands to Parliamentary Reform, and carried the Reform Bill. But observe, in that operation they destroyed, under the pretence of its corrupt exercise, the old industrial franchise, and they never constructed a new one. ...They next tried Commercial Reform, and introduced free imports under the specious name of Free Trade. How was the interest of the working classes considered in this third movement? More than they were in this Colonial or their Parliamentary reform? On the contrary, while the interests of capital were unblushingly advocated, the dis-placed labour of the country was offered neither consolation nor compensation, but was told that it must submit to be absorbed in the mass."[1]

There is no doubt that Mr Disraeli, who was not only a Mediterranean Byron, but also an oriental aristocrat, dis-liked the middle class, as far as so just a man could be said to dislike anything which possessed any virtue. He also de-tested utilitarianism, and, with that strange power of pene-trating into the future which was one of his greatest gifts, not

[1] Walter Sydney Sichel: *Disraeli* (Methuen and Co., Ltd.).

only showed us, in the character of Duncan Macmorragh, the utilitarian in *The Young Duke*, a flawless portrait of a certain mentality, but gave us, as well, a foreshadowing of our present robot civilization. "Duncan Macmorragh", he wrote, "cut up the Creation and got a name. His attack upon mountains was most violent, and proved, by its personality, that he had come from the lowlands. He demonstrated the inability of all elevation, and declared that the Andes were the aristocracy of the globe. Rivers he rather pulled to pieces, and proved them to be the most useless of existence....He informed us that we were quite wrong in supposing ourselves to be the miracle of the Creation. On the contrary, he avowed that already were various pieces of machinery of far more importance than man; and he had no doubt in time that a superior race would arrive got by a steam-engine on a spinning-jenny."

It is true that Mr Gladstone was also an idealist; but his idealism was of a very different temper to that of his political opponent, and Mr Buckle is right in saying, in the life of Disraeli[1]: "Each admired and respected the great Parliamentary qualities of his rival, but Gladstone's respect was combined with an alloy of deep moral disapprobation—a frame of mind which was fostered by what Disraeli had called the 'finical and fastidious crew of high anglicans' among whom Gladstone familiarly moved. To them and to him Disraeli's elevation was an offence."

Mr Gladstone and Mr Disraeli had met for the first time in 1835, at a dinner-party at the Lord Chancellor's. Mr Gladstone, who was then aged twenty-six, seems to have been overcome by his opponent's effulgence—the clouds of glory which Mr Disraeli trailed from the houses of great hostesses, the "fantastic glitter of dubious gems", as Lord Morley ex-

[1] *The Life of Benjamin Disraeli, Earl of Beaconsfield*, in 6 vols., by W. F. Monypenny and G. E. Buckle (quoted by permission of Messrs John Murray, the Publishers).

pressed it—for he made no mention of him. Mr Disraeli, on the other hand, told his sister that he had met "young Gladstone", but went on to say that the best company at the table was "a swan very white and tender and stuffed with truffles".

Even at that time, Mr Gladstone was distinguished by a very high sense of duty and of seriousness. He would not, for instance, dine out on a Sunday, even though Sir Robert Peel were to be his host. Yet he was, as Lord Morley [1] tells us, "closely attentive to the minor duties of social life, if duties they be; he was a strict observer of the etiquette of calls and on some afternoons he notes that he made a dozen or fourteen of them."

The close of the calls, must, I think, have been hailed with a certain degree of relief by some of the lighter-minded hostesses; for conversation with Mr Gladstone was invariably of a serious and even improving character, and this seriousness increased as he grew older. Indeed, in later life, we read of him visiting Mr Tennyson one Sunday, and discussing the Goschen parish-council plan, and other social reforms, Lacordaire, and liberal collectivism. With Queen Victoria, however, the conversation—as, by the rules of etiquette, this must be led by the Queen—necessarily took on a more frivolous courtier-like tone, and the subjects discussed were (I quote from a letter from Mr Gladstone to his wife) Prince Humbert, Garibaldi, Lady Lyttelton, the Hagley boys, Lucy, smoking, dress, fashion, Prince Alfred, his establishment and future plans, the Prince of Wales's visit to Denmark, the Revenue, Lancashire, foreign policy, the newspaper press. the habits of the present generation, young men, young married ladies, clubs, Lord Clarendon's journey, the Prince Consort on dress and fashion, the Prince of Wales on ditto, Sir Robert Peel, Mrs Stonor, the rest of that family,

[1] *The Life of William Ewart Gladstone* by Lord Morley (Macmillan and Co., Ltd.).

misreading foreign names and words, the reputation of English people abroad, and the happy absence of foreign-office disputes and quarrels.

"Nature", wrote Lord Morley, "had bestowed on him many towering gifts. Whether Humour was among them, his friends were wont to dispute. That he had a gaiety and sympathetic alacrity of mind that was kin to humour nobody who knew him would deny; of playfulness his speeches give a thousand proofs; of drollery and fun he had a ready sense though it was never quite certain beforehand what sort of jest would hit or miss."

Reading, too, was no light matter with Mr Gladstone. In the year 1885, this seventy-six-year-old scholar digested Bodley's *Remains*, Bauchamont's *Anecdotes*, Cuvier's *Theory of the Earth*, *Whewell on Astronomy*, *The Life of R. Gilpin*, Hennell's *Inquiry*, Schmidt's *Social Effects of Christianity*, Miss Martineau's *Autobiography*, Anderson's *Glory of the Bible*, and Borrow's *Towards the Truth*.

Three years later, he was to be attracted irresistibly to a far more important work than these: "Mama and I", he wrote to his daughter Mrs Drew, "are each of us engaged in reading *Robert Elsmere*. I complained of some of the novels you gave me to read, as too stiff, but they are nothing to this. It is wholly out of the common order. At present I regard with doubt and dread the idea of doing anything on it, but cannot yet be sure whether your observations will be justified or not. In any case it is a tremendous book." Later, he told Lord Acton: "I find without surprise that it makes its way slowly into public notice. It is not far from twice the length of an ordinary novel, and the labour and effort of reading it at all, I should say, sixfold, while one could no more stop in reading it than in reading Thucydides......has brought this book before me, and being as strong as it is strange, it cannot perish still-born. I am tossed about with doubt as to writing upon it."

Such was the phenomenon who now took up his position as Her Majesty's adviser in place of Mr Disraeli, who, although he had only been Prime Minister for ten months, had already established himself in the Queen's favour by his extreme willingness to save her work, by his lightness, his flashing personality, his wit, his habit of lightening official letters with pieces of gossip which he knew would amuse Her Majesty, and by his delicious flattery which, although the Queen knew it was only meant in fun, still did, even at this early date, undoubtedly throw a glamour on the relationship.

Both Mr Disraeli's and Mr Gladstone's attitudes towards her dear dead husband had been filled with respect, and "the Prince", Mr Disraeli told Her Majesty, "is the only person whom Mr Disraeli has ever known who realised the Ideal. None with whom he is acquainted have ever approached it. There was in him an union of the manly grace and sublime simplicity, of chivalry with the intellectual splendour of the Attic Academe. The only character in English history that would, in some respects, draw near to him is Sir Philip Sidney: the same high tone, the same... vigour, the same rare combination of romantic energy and classic repose." Nor was this all: to know the Prince had been, said Mr Disraeli, "one of the most satisfactory incidents of his life: full of refined and beautiful memories, and exercising, as he hopes, over his remaining existence, a soothing and exalting influence".[1]

The Queen saw nothing exaggerated in this praise, and quite forgetting that not many years ago the writer of the eulogy had been "that dreadful Mr Disraeli" she sent it to Sir Arthur Helps, in order that he might see what a beautiful letter she had received, and Lord Derby told Mr Disraeli that she had found it "certainly as eloquent, in the language employed, as any of those beautiful and glorious orations". And indeed perhaps it had been entirely sincere. For Mr Dis-

[1] Buckle, *op. cit.*, Volume IV, p. 382. Strachey, *op. cit.*, p. 210.

raeli, in a pamphlet written many years ago, had proclaimed that "a great mind that thinks and feels is never inconsistent and never insincere....Insincerity is the vice of a fool, and inconsistency is the blunder of a knave."

Mr Gladstone's manner when he spoke about the Prince, whilst being equally respectful, was less warm; his eulogy, at the time of the Prince's death, gave the Queen great satisfaction; but in a private memorandum (though naturally, being private, it never came to the Queen's knowledge) he had written: "My praise will be impartial: for he did not fascinate, or command, or attract me through any medium but that of judgement and conscience. There was, I think, a want of freedom, nature, and movement in his demeanour, due partly to a faculty and habit of reflection that never intermitted, partly to an inexorable watchfulness over all he did and said, which produced something that was related to stillness and chilliness in a manner which was notwithstanding invariably modest, frank, and kind, even to one who had no claims upon him for the particular exhibition of such qualities."[1]

It is true that in 1845 Mr Gladstone had "rather a nice conversation" with the Prince about an Anglo-Prussian copyright convention,[2] but his principal memory—a painful one—was of a very interesting but disappointing conversation at Windsor respecting the papal decree imposing the belief in the Immaculate Conception. The Prince had said he was glad of it, as it would tend to expose and explode the whole system; Mr Gladstone contended that "we all had an interest in the well being and well doing, absolute or relative, of that great Christian communion, and that whatever indicated or increased the predominance of the worse

[1] Morley, *op. cit.*, Volume II, p. 90.
[2] See Philip Guedalla: *The Queen and Mr Gladstone* (Hodder and Stoughton, Ltd.), Volume I, p. 30. Frank Hardie: *The Political Influence of Queen Victoria* (Oxford University Press), p. 42.

influences within her pale over the better was a thing we ought much to deplore". "No assent, even qualified," continued Mr Gladstone sadly, "was to be got."[1]

Apart from such disappointments as this, Mr Gladstone had never *really* cared for staying at Balmoral, although he enjoyed the "black-green fir and grey rock, and the boundless ranges of heather". (Mr Disraeli, on the other hand, enjoyed the parrot-green stretches of smooth shaven grass outside Her Majesty's windows.) It is true that many years before (in 1845) he had done his best to fit into the rather unseemly lightness of the after-dinner pastimes, and had played commerce, at which luckily (for he had locked his purse up in his bedroom before dinner) he was never the worse hand, and so was not called upon to pay; on the contrary, he found that he had won 2s. 3d. at the end, of which eightpence was paid him by the Prince. But now all attempts at brightness had vanished, and Sundays were a disappointment. Mr Gladstone had inquired in vain and with the greatest care about episcopal services; but there did not seem to be one within fifteen miles; it was true that there was something like family prayers and a service after tea in the dining-room, but that only lasted for forty minutes. However, on the following Sunday, Mr Gladstone felt more cheerful, for there was a service in the Free Kirk Schoolroom for Girls; but, as against this advantage, must be set the fact that there was *no* chaplain at Balmoral that day, and so no dining-room service. Mr Disraeli, on the other hand, enjoyed every moment of the day; his dinner with the Queen in the library—"with good books, very cosy"—enchanted him; it struck him that it was like dining with a bachelor in very good rooms at the Albany, and he added with no touch of gloom: "The Duke of Edinburgh talked much of foreign fruits, and talked well."

Then too, there was the great bond of authorship between

[1] Morley, *op. cit.*, Volume II, p. 91.

the Queen and her former Prime Minister. Sir Arthur
Helps had sent Mr Disraeli an early copy of the *Journal in the
Highlands*, and Mr Disraeli told Sir Arthur that he had read it
"with unaffected interest. Its vein is innocent and vivid;
happy in picture and touched with what I ever think is the
characteristic of our royal mistress—grace.

"There is a freshness and fragrance about the book like the
heather amid which it was written."[1]

This praise was naturally gratifying, and when Mr Disraeli followed it up by presenting the Queen with all his
novels, and inserting in his conversations with her the phrase
"we authors", the conquest was complete. Still, it seemed at
first as if Mr Gladstone, though heavier in his manner, was
equally conscious of the need to please his sovereign. For
some time he had been receiving advice from the Dean of
Windsor as to the exact way in which to deal with the
Queen's nervous hypochondria, her extreme reluctance to
appear in public, and this *preux chevalier* replied: "Every
motive of duty, feeling and interest that can touch a man
should bind me to study to the best of my small power the
manner of my relation with Her Majesty. She is a woman,
a widow, a lover of truth, a Sovereign, a benefactress to her
country. What titles!"[2]

It must, however, be admitted that it was not such fun to
be a woman, a widow, a lover of truth, a benefactress to her
country, as it was to be the Faery, Titania, a tiny creature ruling
by enchantment; and this feeling was enhanced when the
benefactress of her country was sent two papers "on the
general policy and effect of the measure" (the Bill for the Disestablishment of the Irish Church) and "a dry recital of the
purport of what would be the leading clauses of the Bill".
Once she had mastered these, Mr Gladstone would come to
Osborne, and the matter could be discussed further. But the

[1] Buckle, *op. cit.*, Volume V, p. 94.
[2] Benson, *op. cit.*, p. 243.

Queen could not master them, nor could Mr Theodore Martin, to whom she appealed in her dilemma; and when the Queen asked Mr Gladstone to unravel the mystery he "replied under six carefully reasoned heads".[1]

It was evident that Her Majesty was not only to be bored, but also overworked; for, in addition to Mr Gladstone's heaviness, he had no consideration whatever for her enfeebled health. In vain did the Queen send him reports of her symptoms, in vain did Sir William Jenner, her physician, interview him, and send him bulletins; his insistence that she should appear in public never wavered. And, had she but known it, her own private secretary, General Grey, was actually not only agreeing with him, but urging him to make further efforts. Mr Gladstone even went so far as to try to interfere with her periods of rest at Balmoral. During one of these intervals, the Khedive Ismail, to whom the Prince of Wales, when in Egypt, had paid a two months' visit, was on his way to England. Would not Her Majesty entertain him? Yes, Her Majesty would invite him to stay for one night at Windsor, if he was not bringing a large suite with him. But she must "strongly *protest against* the pretension raised that she should at her *own* expense, in the *Only Palace* of her own ...entertain all Foreign Potentates who chose to come here for their own amusement".

Lord Russell and Lord Palmerston both strongly felt that, as a lady, *without a husband,* with all the weight of government thrown upon her, with weakened health, *quite incapable* of bearing the *fatigues* of representation, she could not be expected to entertain Princes as formerly...."It makes her quite ill to be *unable* to do the *right* thing, and yet she cannot do so."[2] Really, if Mr Gladstone was going to worry her to entertain foreign royalties as well as to open Parliament, the fatigue entailed would be endless. Nor was this all.

[1] Benson, *op. cit.*, p. 244.
[2] *Letters*, Second Series, Volume I, pp. 600–1. Benson, *op. cit.*, p. 245.

THE QUEEN, MR DISRAELI,

Would Her Majesty open a bridge at Blackfriars...in the July heat, and with her health in such a precarious condition. Mr Disraeli would never have suggested such a thing. Her Majesty replied, with some firmness, and with so many words underlined and spelt in capitals, that her letter appeared like a stormy sea on which the frail barge of her thought was being driven to an unknown and incalculable bourne—that she would NOT.

The question of the Irish Church was being discussed in Parliament. Should this lead to a crisis, would not Her Majesty delay her return to Balmoral in the middle of August? Her Majesty replied that, if it was absolutely necessary, she would postpone her visit for two or three days.

Tireless and pursuing, Mr Gladstone pressed her further. Balmoral, he pointed out, was many hundred miles away, and it was inadvisable for the sovereign to be at that distance, when Parliament was still sitting. As for Blackfriars Bridge, would she not reconsider her decision? The people liked to feel they were in personal touch with their Queen, and it was not only wise, it was a duty for her to make public appearances from time to time. She yielded so far as to consent to open the bridge—not in July, for the heat would really be too tiring, but in November—and, in spite of her reluctance, found herself almost, if not quite, enjoying the ceremony. "This most successful and gratifying progress and ceremony", "the great crowds of people bowing and cheering", "enthusiasm which was very great", and all "the friendly faces". She had never, she said, seen more enthusiastic, loyal, or friendly crowds, and this, in the very heart of London, when people were said to be intending to do something, and were full of all sorts of ideas, was very remarkable.

The Queen noted that "she felt so pleased and relieved that all had gone off so well. Nothing could have been more gratifying." But there comes a darker note: "it was a hard trial for me *all alone* with my children in an open carriage, amongst such thousands!"[1]

Mr Gladstone, with his tremendous energy, and his determination, had scored a semi-victory, but the Queen was not pleased; and for the next five years (1869-74) she was to live in an ever increasing state of displeasure. Mr Gladstone and his ministry were never weary of introducing reforms—reforms in the Irish Church and the Irish land system, in parliamentary elections, and in the administration of justice. It is true that over and over again Mr Gladstone had come loyally to her defence—when, for instance, it was supposed that her income was so large that she could provide for her children on their marriage, without an extra grant from Parliament. He sympathized with her, too, in her anxiety about the Prince of Wales's increasing tendency to travel—a tendency which she ascribed to restlessness, and which led sometimes to strange dangers. (When in America, he narrowly escaped being wheeled in a wheelbarrow by Monsieur Blondin over a tight-rope stretched across the Niagara Falls.) Nor could it be said that Her Majesty was averse to reforms; at the time of the Bill for the Disestablishment of the Irish Church, for instance, she was deeply immersed in the question as to whether the Navy should be allowed to wear beards or not....

No question concerning the management of her kingdom was beneath the Queen's interest; in later years Lord Rosebery, at her request, inquired into the rumour that Lord Aberdeen, who was the Governor General of Canada, with his wife, family and staff, dined in the servants' hall once a week—a rumour which, though Lord Rosebery was able to reassure Her Majesty on the subject, was repeated many years afterwards when Lord Aberdeen became Lord Lieutenant of Ireland. Whereupon it was found that nothing of the kind occurred—that Lord and Lady Aberdeen merely

[1] *Letters*, Second Series, Volume I, pp. 630-1.

joined their servants in social evenings at the Haddo Dance Club, where, from time to time, Lord Aberdeen would lecture on such subjects as Railways and Railway Work, his valet would sing "Will o' the Wisp", and an odd man attached to the estate would recite "Caught In His Own Trap".

Her Majesty, as I have said, was by no means averse to reforms, but she felt that those instituted by Mr Gladstone were tiring.[1]

She could not help feeling that Mr Gladstone held subversive views—*was not safe*; though it was not, according to Lord Gladstone's account, until the year 1876, when Beaconsfield's personal ascendancy over the Queen was firmly established, that the first signs of her displeasure with Mr Gladstone were shown.[2] In 1852 the Queen, with the Prince Consort, was partly responsible for Gladstone becoming Chancellor of the Exchequer. But, as the influence of Beaconsfield grew, so did he flatter what Lady Ponsonby, in a letter to her husband, described as "the superstition in the Queen's mind about her prerogative"—and to that superstition Gladstone was firmly opposed.[3] This fact, and his unceasing efforts to induce her to exert herself, his obvious despair at his failure, were at the bottom of much of her personal distaste for him…."Upon the whole," he told Ponsonby, "I think it" (the Queen's neurasthenia) "has been the most sickening piece of experience which I have had during nearly forty years of public life. *Worse* things may easily be imagined; but smaller and meaner causes for the decay of Thrones cannot be conceived. It is like the worm which bores the bark of a noble oak tree and so breaks the channel of its life."[4]

[1] See Strachey, *op. cit.*, pp. 212–14.

[2] See Viscount Gladstone: *After Thirty Years* (Macmillan and Co., Ltd.), p. 320.

[3] Mary Ponsonby: *A Memoir, Some Letters and a Journal*, edited by Magdalen Ponsonby (John Murray), p. 144. Hardie, *op. cit.*, p. 55.

[4] Guedalla, *op. cit.*, Volume I, p. 304, Gladstone to Ponsonby.

Nor were matters helped by a speech made by Mr Disraeli defending the Queen's withdrawal from public ceremonies. The contrast between the two men was only too marked, and when, in the month following this speech, Mr Gladstone paid a visit to Balmoral, the Queen found that the state of her health did not allow her to see him for some days. When she did, at last, grant him an audience, he felt, for the first time, "the repellant power which she so well knows how to use". And, in spite of the fact that her ill health prevented her from appearing at public ceremonials, it did not prevent her from "running across to Baden"[1] for a holiday.

Mr Gladstone, grieved at his reception, and impeccably loyal to the Queen, felt that the matter of her continued seclusion grew even graver. And he told Granville[2] that an instinct told him that much would have to be said about it, and that the question of putting forward the Prince of Wales would have to be broached, since this was preferable to forcing upon the Queen a duty against which she set herself with so much vehemence. Mr Gladstone was right in his apprehension; yet when the question of sending the Prince of Wales as representative of the Queen to Dublin was brought forward, in 1871, it widened the gulf between the Queen and her minister to an unbridgeable degree.[3]

With what relief, then, did she hail the return to power, in 1874, of Mr Disraeli. Gone were the lectures to which she had been subjected, the long and dull reports, the perpetual pestering to appear in public. Now, all was romance, she was the Faery once more, and Mr Disraeli lived only to serve her. It was undoubtedly delightful, instead of being begged to overwork herself, to be implored on no account to do anything which might tire

[1] Guedalla, *op. cit.*, Volume I, p. 70. *Ibid.*, p. 327. Hardie, *op. cit.*, p. 61.

[2] See Guedalla, *op. cit.*, Volume I, p. 71.

[3] See Hardie, *op. cit.*, p. 62.

her.... "He hopes[1] Your Majesty remembers your gracious promise not to write at night or at least not so much. He lives only for Her, and works only for Her, and without Her all is lost."[2] It was pleasant, when her Prime Minister was ill, to be told that he thought, if he did not see Her Majesty, he would never get quite well, and, on another occasion, that "during a somewhat romantic and imaginative life, nothing has ever occurred to him so interesting as this confidential correspondence with one so exalted and so inspiring".[3] Then too, he had such a charming and romantic way of thanking her for the flowers she sent him: "Truly he can say they are more precious than rubies, coming, as they do, at such a moment from a Sovereign whom he adores";[4] and it was quite evident that he regarded her, not only as his sovereign, but as a supernatural being, brought about by enchantment. Osborne was not so much a small place marked on the map, as Your Majesty's Faery Isle, and the primroses which had arrived from the Isle in question had been plucked, by the command of the Faery Queen, by the fauns and dryads of her woods. "Yesterday eve," he declared, "there appeared, in Whitehall Gardens, a delicate-looking case, with a royal superscription, which, when he opened, he thought, at first, that Your Majesty had graciously bestowed upon him the stars of Your Majesty's principal orders. And, indeed, he was so impressed with this graceful illusion, that, having a banquet, where there were many stars and ribbons, he could not resist the temptation, by placing some snowdrops on his heart, of showing that he, too, was decorated by a gracious Sovereign.

"Then, in the middle of the night, it occurred to him, that it might all be an enchantment, and that, perhaps, it was a

---

[1] March 1878.
[2] Buckle, *op. cit.*, Volume VI, pp. 254-5.
[3] Buckle, *op. cit.*, Volume VI, p. 238.
[4] Buckle, *op. cit.*, Volume VI, pp. 246-7.

Faery gift and came from another monarch: Queen Titania, gathering flowers, with her Court, in a soft and sea-girt isle, and sending magic blossoms, which, they say, turn the heads of those who receive them!"[1] Then too, how amusing he was, blending absurdity with romance in the most delightful manner, as in the letter written to the Queen, on St Valentine's Day, 1880, in which "he wished he could repose on a sunny bank like young Valentine in the pretty picture that fell from a rosy cloud this morn—but the reverie of the happy youth would be rather different from his". It was amusing to be told of a certain minister that he had the wisdom, as well as the form, of an elephant. No wonder that the Queen declared she had never received such letters before, and that for the first time in her life she was told *everything*. Her trust in him was complete, and she told Mr Theodore Martin, after the government had bought the Viceroy of Egypt's shares in the Suez Canal for four millions—thus giving England complete security for India—that it was entirely Mr Disraeli's doing. And she added that Mr Disraeli had *very large, clear*, and *very lofty* views of the position this country should hold because his mind was so much greater, larger, and his apprehension of things great and small so much quicker than that of Mr Gladstone. Then too, how charmingly, he had announced the news to the Queen: "You have it, Madam!...It is yours!" so that it became not only an official, but a private triumph.

Every enchantment, which was born of that oriental mind, was placed in the path of the Queen of England; Mr Gladstone had seen her as a woman, a widow, what titles!...but Mr Disraeli saw more deeply still. In an incautious moment he had suggested that the Faery's title should be, not only the Queen of England, but Empress of India. The glamour of the idea struck Her Majesty, and in a short time Mr Disraeli found himself faced with the necessity of espousing an excessively unpopular bill altering the royal title

[1] Buckle, *op. cit.*, Volume VI, pp. 464–7. Strachey, *op. cit.*, p. 226.

from that of Queen of Great Britain to that of Queen of Great Britain and Empress of India. After a terrific struggle the bill was passed, and the triumph was celebrated by a dinner-party at Windsor. At this, the newly created Earl of Beaconsfield was welcomed by the Faery who had for the moment discarded her usual plain attire, and was, as became the Empress of India, covered with jewels presented by her subject Princes.

When the dinner-party was ended, Lord Beaconsfield, that epitome of Her Majesty's eastern empire, with his strange age-old wisdom, his delicate hands with their velvet touch, their grip of steel, congratulated the Empress of India on her new title in a long and flowery speech. Smiling and responsive, she answered him with a half curtsey.[1]

Years afterwards, when he had long been in his grave, his Queen wrote of him as "that kind wise old man". And she understood human character to an extraordinary degree. She might, perhaps, because of the very nature of her duty towards her people, underrate or underestimate the work of such men as Gladstone, but it was impossible, in her later life, for a charlatan or a man with a mean or small mind to impose upon her. She had the great and unfailing interest of royal nature, the sight of an eagle, the heart of a lion. This kind wise old man had given her his devotion; he loved her because of her great nature, because of her wise heart, her eagle's view, the glamour that surrounded her, the incredible majesty and splendour of her walk, her natural love for her people. In return, she gave him a noble friendship.

And, indeed, could she be the same woman who, such a short time ago, had felt that she could not undergo the strain of being seen in public? Now, at her minister's request, she opened Parliament, visited hospitals, distributed medals. But there were moments when this added vigour was a source of danger. Beaconsfield's foreign policy, his desire for the

[1] See *Quarterly Review*, cxxxix, 334. Strachey, *op. cit.*, p. 229.

aggrandizement of England, his imperialism, had not been looked upon with favour by Russia, and, when war broke out between that country and Turkey, the danger that England might be involved was great. It was clear to Beaconsfield that boldness and caution were both necessary, coupled with an absolute certainty of movement and an extraordinary nerve.[1] But now came the difficulty. The Queen, remembering her old hatred of Russia, engendered at the time of the Crimean War, was resolved to help Turkey. Night and day, the already harassed Prime Minister was bombarded with letters and telegrams, urging him to vigorous action. "The Queen", she wrote, "is feeling terribly anxious lest delay should cause us to be too late and lose our prestige for ever! It worries her night and day."[2] "Oh, if the Queen were a man," said a later letter, "she would like to go and give those Russians, whose word one cannot believe, such a beating! We shall never be friends again till we have it out. This the Queen feels sure of."[3] Indeed "The Faery", as her Prime Minister told Lady Bradford, "writes every day and telegraphs every hour; this is almost literally the case."[4] He was urged to action by his Queen, and to moderation by his Foreign Secretary, who would not hear of a violent course being taken. And matters grew worse. The Queen threatened, not once, but several times, to abdicate, for "If England", she told her minister, "is to kiss Russia's feet, she will not be a party to the humiliation of England, and would lay down her crown," and Lord Beaconsfield was at liberty to warn the Cabinet of Her Majesty's determination.[5] "This delay," she exclaimed, "this uncertainty by which, abroad, we are losing our prestige and our position, while Russia is

---

[1] See Strachey, *op. cit.*, p. 230.
[2] Buckle, *op. cit.*, Volume VI, p. 144. Strachey, *op. cit.*, p. 231.
[3] Buckle, *op. cit.*, Volume VI, p. 217. Strachey, *op. cit.*, p. 231.
[4] Buckle, *op. cit.*, Volume VI, p. 150. Strachey, *op. cit.*, p. 231.
[5] Buckle, *op. cit.*, Volume VI, p. 132. Strachey, *op. cit.*, p. 232.

advancing and will be before Constantinople in no time! Then the Government will be fearfully blamed and the Queen so humiliated that she thinks she would abdicate at once. Be bold!"[1] And she exclaimed: "She feels she cannot, as she said before, remain the Sovereign of a country that is letting itself down to kiss the feet of the great barbarians, the retarders of all liberty and civilisation that exists."[2] Three letters demanding war were written in one day, when the Russians had reached the outskirts of Constantinople, and the harassed Prime Minister told Lady Bradford that only one thing prevented him from resigning his post—and that was the thought of the scene at headquarters. Mr Strachey adds,[3] sadly: "This was no longer the Faery; it was a genie whom he" (Lord Beaconsfield) "had rashly called out of her bottle, and who was now intent upon showing her supernal power." But, in the end, he triumphed; the Queen's martial ardour subsided, Lord Salisbury took the place of Lord Derby, and Lord Beaconsfield, at the Congress at Berlin, gained another victory for England. When he returned to England, he told the Queen that she would very soon be "the Dictatress of Europe".

But alas, the days of his triumph were numbered. In 1880, the Liberals were returned to power. And in one year's time, a still more cruel blow befell. Lord Beaconsfield, the kind wise old man who had been the Queen's friend, who had served his country so nobly and well, lay on his death-bed. "I have suffered much," he told his doctors. "Had I been a Nihilist, I think I should have confessed all."

[1] Buckle, *op. cit.*, Volume VI, p. 148. Strachey, *op. cit.*, p. 232.
[2] Buckle, *op. cit.*, Volume VI, p. 217. Strachey, *op. cit.*, p. 232.
[3] *Op. cit.*, p. 232.

Chapter XXIV

EIGHTEEN-SEVENTY

O n the 15th of July 1870, far away in Berlin, Prince
Bismarck leaned back in his chair and sighed; but
the sigh was one of contentment, not weariness.
The war between Germany and France, for which he had
long waited and plotted, for which he had set the train, had
begun, that war which should unite all the kingdoms of
Germany under the supreme domination of Prussia.

Soon, the air of Europe would be an echoing hell of
shrieks, and the earth would be wet and red, but Count
Bismarck saw only the end of his ambition, the triumph of
his life's work. And how skilfully the plot had been laid,
which should make France appear in the wrong; he had
sought a quarrel, but the quarrel must seem to be the fault of
France, and now at last the opportunity had come. For
Spain, in her search for a king, had been half inclined to
accept a Catholic Hohenzollern, Prince Leopold of Hohen-
zollern-Sigmaringen, as a candidate, and Count Bismarck,
knowing well that France would not tolerate the idea of a
member of this house as King of Spain, urged Marshal Prin,
who had supported the plan, to persevere; with the result that,
after many months' delay, Prince Leopold accepted the
Crown, with the King of Prussia's permission.

The dismay felt in France at this news was unbounded; the Emperor at first seemed undecided what course to pursue, but Gramont and the whole of the Paris press raised a cry of protest, and in this they were supported by the Chamber. The Queen of England and her government, and the King of the Belgians, alarmed at the turn of events, at length persuaded Prince Leopold to withdraw from his position, but the French government, the French people, who had by now lost their heads, insisted that the King of Prussia should not only associate himself with the withdrawal, but should promise that the candidature would not be renewed. The King, in answer to this demand, declared that he approved of the withdrawal, but that he could make no promises for the future. And now came the opportunity of his minister. When the telegram containing this news arrived from Ems, where the King was taking the waters, Bismarck reissued it in such terms that both France and Germany became infuriated, and war was certain.

It is difficult to know where lies the blame, for in this war, as in all wars, both sides, if we except those in power at the chancelleries, believed themselves to be innocent. In all probability, leaving aside Bismarck's plotting, the blame might be equally apportioned; as Lord Granville wrote to Queen Victoria: "Everyone seems to have been in the wrong"—everyone except the wretched men who were thus doomed to a horrible death.

Two days before war broke out, the Crown Prince of Prussia assured Queen Victoria that Prince Leopold of Prussia's renunciation of the Spanish Crown removed all pretext for war on the part of France; adding that all fair observers must admit that the King of Prussia had acted in such a way as to show his sincere love of peace.

Both the Germans and the French had, indeed, the feeling that they were perfectly right, and both felt assured that their very existence was threatened. The Crown Princess of

Prussia, writing to her mother three days after war was declared, said: "The enthusiasm which seems to be the same with young and old, poor and rich, high and low, men and women, is so affecting and beautiful that one must forget oneself.

"The odds are fearfully against us in the awful struggle which is about to commence, and which we are forced into against our will, *knowing* that our existence is at stake." And the Princess added that she wished no evil to France or to anyone; her only wish was that Europe could unite once and for all to prevent France from ever again having it in her power to force a war upon another nation....[1] "Oh, why", she said, in another letter, had not England prevented war "by declaring in concert with Russia, Austria, and Italy that she would take up arms against the aggressor?"[2]

But the war continued. Many thousands of men, each side believing their country to be in the right, and that they were making a war to end war, died, or were maimed; then, after a few weeks, came the Battle of Sedan, and the capitulation of MacMahon's Army, and the news that the furious mobs of Paris had rushed into the Senate and had declared the overthrow of the Dynasty....Gone was the brilliant bubble, Napoleon, and in place of the Empire they proclaimed a Republic.

On a cold raw day in November—oh, how unlike the lovely summer afternoon, not so many years ago, when the Queen and her friend the Empress Eugénie drove on the seashore at Osborne—Victoria drove to Chislehurst in Kent, where the Empress had taken refuge.

It was a sad moment. The once air-bright beauty, on whose loveliness a shadow had fallen, stood waiting for her friend at the door. She was dressed in black, very plainly, and with no ornaments; her hair too was simply done, in a net at

[1] See *Letters*, Second Series, Volume II, pp. 42–3.
[2] *Letters*, Second Series, Volume II, p. 48.

the back. She spoke of the terrors of the revolution and of how, before she fled from Paris, the crowds had already invaded the gardens, and there had been no troops to resist them; the night before she left, she told the Queen, she had lain down on the bed fully dressed. Then the little Prince Imperial came in, "a nice little boy, but rather short and stumpy". "It was a sad visit", the Queen wrote in her diary, "and seemed like a strange dream."

Then, in March, the Queen received the Emperor, who by this time had joined his wife in England, and she noted, sadly, that he had grown very stout and grey, and his moustaches were no longer waxed or curled as formerly.

In Germany, the triumph seemed overwhelming. The Crown Princess of Prussia, writing to the Queen of England, exclaimed that such a downfall was a melancholy thing, but was meant to teach deep lessons. The war, it seemed, had been ordained by Providence more or less in order that the French people might learn whither frivolity, conceit, and immorality inevitably lead. What a contrast, she exclaimed, was this frivolity to the poverty, the dull towns, the plodding hard-working *serious* life of the Germans, which had made them strong and determined. The French, she explained, had despised and hated the Germans whom they thought it quite lawful to insult, and now they had been punished.

As for the war, the Crown Princess did not know whether it would continue or not, but, she added naïvely, "as there is no French army left, I do not know with whom we are to fight."[1]

Realizing this insuperable difficulty, Bismarck set about the task of dictating the terms of peace, and the Queen of England, who was constantly appealed to by both sides for some expression of opinion which would be useful to them, who was anguished by the horrors of war, and who had

[1] See *Letters*, Second Series, Volume II, p. 59.

written a most noble letter to the King of Prussia during the Austrian-Prussian quarrel imploring him to do all in his power to avert the danger of any conflict, noted in a memorandum, dated the 9th September 1870, that any interference on the part of England would only have the appearance of wishing to prevent Germany from making a lasting peace by obtaining such securities from France as would prevent such a war from occurring again. And Her Majesty added that "a powerful Germany can never be dangerous to England". And she spoke of the risk of allowing the German people, our natural allies, to "think that we despised them and did not wish for their development".

Meanwhile, her son-in-law, the German Crown Prince, prayed that the ground might gradually be prepared upon which might arise the natural alliance binding England and Germany, and embracing, as well, Austria. With these three mighty empires in alliance, he told his mother-in-law, it was undoubted that they would be able to ensure a lasting peace. For who was more anxious for peace than Germany (or France, or England?). The Crown Prince concluded by a fervent wish that England would come to understand the peaceful spirit of Germany instead of imputing to her Force and Militarism.

Nor was this the only noble spirit. Not to be outdone by her husband in this respect, the Crown Princess, invariably warm-hearted and conscientious in her conduct, had determined to show the fallen Empress of the French these qualities at their highest. She therefore sent[1] a large packet to the Queen, to be delivered by her into the Empress's own hands. This packet contained a screen which had stood in the Empress's boudoir at St Cloud.[2] It seemed that when, as the Crown Princess explained, the French shells set fire to the house, the Prussian soldiers had, with the best intentions, entered, and

[1] On 4th January 1871.
[2] See *Letters*, Second Series, Volume II, p. 104.

had risked their lives to save the valuables of various kinds that lay within; and amongst these was the screen, which, after it had been delivered to General Kirchbach, had, by the King of Prussia's permission, been sent to the Crown Princess. But the Crown Princess felt that although St Cloud was not the private property of the Emperor and Empress, but of the State, and consequently no longer belonged to them, still she could not regard this as a trophy of war, and did not feel she had a right to keep it. The poor Empress, too, had been *so* kind to the Crown Princess, who would beg her dearest mama to restore the screen to her. She could not offer it as a present, whilst the two nations were at war, and besides, she considered it merely returning a piece of property to its rightful owner. And she added that she did *not* approve of war trophies, at least of ladies possessing them; for soldiers they are lawful, of course, and every army in the world considers them so.

Lord Granville, on being consulted by the Queen as to the course of conduct to be pursued in the matter, was deeply touched at the good and elevated feeling shown. But "a night's reflection" caused him to write a second letter to Her Majesty, in which he declared that war trophies, in the opinion of England, were understood to be flags and guns; and that the articles of value taken from palaces and country houses, and which Lord Granville understood to have been sent in great quantities from France to Germany, would un-fortunately, as seen by a nation not at war, be regarded as acts of plunder, or looting. There might, he added, be a slight distinction in an article which had been removed from a palace belonging to the State and set on fire by the French themselves; but to certain people it might have looked better if the Crown Prince had refrained from appearing to sanction this habit on the part of the German Army. Lord Granville thought, too, that Her Majesty would be put in a difficult position by accepting a present, which was acknowledged to have been taken from the palace of a friendly state, or by handing it to the Empress in England when it belonged to the State of France. He really thought, therefore, that the best, and certainly the safest, plan, would be for Her Majesty to explain to the Crown Princess that, though her good feelings were much appreciated, the Queen would prefer the screen to remain unpacked until the war was over, when the Crown Princess could decide on its future.

Nearly three years after this time,[1] when the unity of Germany had been begun, we find the Queen writing to her daughter to the effect that she had never been able to feel the same towards King Victor Emmanuel of Italy since he had undermined his own uncle's kingdom, and taken that, as well as other people's; and how grieved she was that she could no longer say with pride that her daughter's father-in-law would never, like the King of Italy, become the tool of his minister. The Queen had wished for the unity of Germany, and so had her dearest husband—for one head, for one army, and for one diplomacy—but not for dethroning other princes and taking their property and palaces. The Queen could never, were she the Empress or the Crown Princess, bring herself to live in the palaces in question. In answer to this the Crown Princess sent her beloved mama many affectionate thanks for her dear letter, and remarked that, whilst everything she said about the King of Italy was quite true, what she felt about the Emperor and the taking of the palaces was not. "*Palaces*", she added, "my father-in-law never *took*, he PAID for them and they are legally *his*. . . . We never should have put our foot into a palace about which there was the *slightest doubt*. *Those* in which *we have* been, we had as much right to inhabit as you to wear the Kohinoor or place the Indian arms in the Armoury at Windsor.

"The right of conquest", she continued, "is a very hard one.

[1] On 1st October 1873.

"God knows I am *not* one who admires it, but *it has* often been, OFTEN, of the Greatest use. England's Empire over the East is the best example of it, and even *there* Englishmen have NOT always shown themselves as scrupulous, humane, civilised, and enlightened as they *should* have done. So really I do not think we deserve more reproach, although you will object that Orientals are *not* Europeans, and cannot be treated in the same manner!

"I am more attached to the cause of liberty and progress than to any other, and I *do* believe that the events of '66 and '70 are a step in that direction, in SPITE of those who brought them about...." [1]

I do not know what was Her Majesty's reply to this remarkable letter. The Crown Princess did, indeed, take an extreme interest in the expansion of both her native, and her adopted country, abroad. And, six years after the letter about the Koh-i-noor, she wrote to her beloved mama reminding her that, owing to the "Oriental War", *all* lovers of England were *so* anxious that she should not miss this unparalleled opportunity of annexing Egypt. She added: "I hear some people in England think that Prince Bismarck has an *arrière-pensée* when he expresses his conviction that England *ought* to take Egypt. He has no other *arrière-pensée* but that he considers a *strong* England of great use in Europe, and we can only rejoice that he thinks and feels so. As to a wish to annex Holland and let France take Belgium, I assure you it is nothing but a *myth*, and a very ridiculous one."

Her Majesty, however, did not see eye to eye with her daughter on this question—nor did Lord Beaconsfield, who was shown the letter, and said it might have been dictated by Prince Bismarck—and she told her darling child that such a suggestion, *coming from her*, had surprised her very much. She was unable to understand why England should make such a wanton aggression, since neither Turkey nor Egypt had

[1] See *Letters*, Second Series, Volume II, pp. 283-4.

done anything to offend her. Remembering, perhaps, the remark about the Koh-i-noor, and the Indian Emblem, she added that it was not *our* Custom to *annex countries* (as it is in *some others*) unless we are obliged, as in the case of the Transvaal Republic; and that to do so would be a most greedy action. How, the Queen inquired, would it be possible for England to protest against the aggression of Russia, if we ourselves were guilty of the same fault?

For Russia, the menace of Russia, the fear of Russia—these were the incessant notes that hammered at the back of the Queen's brain. And her persistent cry to her ministers was "Be prepared! Soon, it may be too late."

Chapter XXV

THE RETURN

O n a damp and chilly afternoon at the end of November 1871, a silent procession of carriages, driving slowly through the sandy wastes of Norfolk, past the plantations of thin fir-trees, the wind-stricken commons, stopped at a house which stood, amidst its dark gardens, quite close to the road. The door of the house opened, and a young and lovely woman, silent and with tears in her eyes, stretched out her arms to the small figure dressed in widow's weeds, shrouded in veils as thick as the mists drifting over the dreary country, who descended from the first carriage.[1] Hand in hand, the Queen and her daughter-in-law walked upstairs through passages that seemed like avenues leading between dark-leaved, cold-leaved trees, into a darkened room where only one small light was burning; hand in hand they stood and looked down upon the figure lying in the bed and dozing fitfully. Ten years ago, thought the Queen (*could* it be ten years, when the blackness of that dreadful night still clung about her heart?) she had stood looking down on another beloved one, drifting away over an unknown sea. And now her eldest son was lying stricken by the same illness that had taken her husband from her.

[1] See *Letters*, Second Series, Volume II, p. 171.

THE RETURN

Her journey to Sandringham, and her return to Windsor, the long days with their alternations of fears and hopes, seemed like an endless dream, and the nights brought back many memories with sleep, restored to her a beloved face and form that had long been dust—then, with an anguishing cruelty, withdrew it from her again.... Albert, standing beside her in a sun-flooded room at Windsor, holding his eldest son in his arms, dandling him for the Queen to see— Edward as a tiny child running towards a dark and waving sea that was rushing to engulf him.... Oh! what a fall! The waves will be over him.... But Albert will run and pick the little boy up, and hold him high, so that the dark sea cannot touch him. But no, Albert was not there, and somebody was crying.... Who could it be? All dark! Two o'clock in the morning, and it would be hours before the Queen could hear the latest news. One could not hope for improvement before the twenty-first day, and it was now only the sixteenth day since her son fell ill. It was the 8th of December.

With the morning came worse news, and the Queen travelled to Sandringham once more, and was met again by that sad and silent figure at the door. The voices of the doctors were low, and the one lamp in her son's bedroom seemed feebler than ever. Next morning, at 5.30, as she lay in a fitful sleep, she was awakened by the doctors. The Prince had had a very severe spasm...and no sooner was this said than Sir William Jenner returned, saying that there had been a second attack, and of so serious a nature that at any moment her son might die. Would the Queen come at once? Putting on her dressing-gown, she hurried to the room where her daughter-in-law, Princess Alice, the doctors, and the two devoted nurses were standing whispering together. It was very dark, thought the Queen; there were but few candles, and they seemed flickering low. The Prince lay breathing heavily, and he was covered with a cold sweat.

[305]

After a while, the doctors said her son's condition seemed easier, so she returned to her bedroom and breakfasted, and the long day passed, with gusts of whispering voices like a fitful wind, and more fearful stretches of silence.

Next day, the 13th of December, the Prince was worse;[1] still weaker and with constant delirium. In an interval when he was sleeping, his mother left the house and walked amongst the pleasure gardens for a short time; but the air was very damp, and the snow upon the ground was thawing. A few Christmas roses, their delicate beauty ruined by the heavy mist, showed green against the melting snow; but the Queen knew nothing save the coldness of the mist, and the cold desolation at her heart. Returning to the Prince's room, she found his wife and his sister Alice in the greatest alarm and despair, and then, at last, breaking into tears, the three women cried: "There can be no hope." The Queen went up to the bed, and taking her son's hand in hers kissed it again and again, stroking his arm. He turned and looked wildly at her. "Who are you?" he asked....Then, after a long while, said "It's Mama." "Dear child," she replied, in little more than a whisper. Later he said "It's so kind of you to come"—his voice drifting strangely on the silence. It is getting nearer and nearer to the 14th, she thought with anguish. That terrible black and engulfing time is approaching, and oh, today is becoming a nightmare ghost of that day, ten years ago, when my world was lost to me—yet it is different too.[2]

But the next day, instead of dawning upon another death-bed, which the Queen had believed was certain, brought the news that her son had slept quietly at intervals. The tide had turned, and no longer was that dark sea creeping onward to engulf him.

Two months after that time, on the 27th of February 1872,

[1] See *Letters*, Second Series, Volume II, p. 178.
[2] See *Letters*, Second Series, Volume II, pp. 80 *et seq.*

the Queen, looking from the window of a room in Buckingham Palace, early in the morning, saw the crowds assembling to welcome her and her son, his wife, and his children on their drive to St Paul's Cathedral for the service of thanksgiving for the Prince's recovery. In an open landau drawn by six horses, they drove through the roaring cheering crowds —the Queen in a black silk jacket over a dress trimmed with miniver, and the Princess of Wales in blue velvet trimmed with sable, sitting facing the Prince of Wales and Princess Beatrice, with little Prince Eddie. Millions of people thronged the streets; it was a world of flags dancing in the young sunlight.[1]

It seemed to Victoria, as she watched those crowds gathered together for love of her, that the world she had known was changing beneath her eyes. The voices prophesying revolution, crying out for a republic, these were dying down into a sullen muttering, and soon would fade into silence; for, with the illness of the Prince, the Queen had been restored to the love of her people, who saw in her once again a suffering human being, subject to the same laws, the same love, and the same hopes and fears as themselves. No longer was she a costly figurehead, an unreal being existing only in order to draw money from the land over which she reigned.

The discontent with the Royal House which had been felt in some quarters, the small but menacing Republican movement—these were due to various causes, but above all to the Queen's seclusion, and to the belief that she was amassing vast sums of money for her personal use. Separated from her people by the mist of tears which had arisen round her, she had, for the time, lost their love. In later life, when her indomitable will had come to her aid, when she had rebuilt herself and, greater than she had ever been, had come back to her people as guide, as prophet, as mother, she was

---

[1] See *Letters*, Second Series, Volume II, pp. 198–9.

to be loved by them as no sovereign of our race had yet been loved; but until the illness of her son had brought her back to them as a living being, she was a stranger, not speaking their language, but that of a grief they could not share.

She would rarely take part in any public function, and it was felt, indeed, that the only time at which she was willing to appear among her people, was when she was about to ask for a fresh grant of money to be made by Parliament to her children.[1] On these occasions, she would consent to open Parliament and to perform public duties, but the people were fully aware of the reasons for these departures from her usual habit. It was true that the engagement of Princess Louise to Lord Lorne had lulled the discontent for a short time, as this was the first time an English sovereign had sanctioned the marriage of a princess to a subject since the marriage of a daughter of Henry VII with the Duke of Suffolk. But this again led to a fresh demand for money, and when, a week after the Princess's wedding (which took place on March 21st 1871), Her Majesty drove in an open carriage from Paddington to Buckingham Palace with her daughter and son-in-law, although the crowds were great, and cheered politely, the wind struck the Queen as being very cold.

Gladstone, loyal and chivalrous as ever, had feared—and had warned the Queen—that Parliament might oppose her demand for a grant of £30,000 to Princess Louise; on this occasion he was wrong; but when it was suggested that Prince Arthur, on his majority, should receive an income of £15,000 a year, fifty-three members of the House of Parliament voted to reduce this sum to £5,000, whilst eleven voted against any allowance being made. Pamphlets were published comparing the very large income of the Queen with the modest £10,000 which was the yearly allowance made to the President of the United States. One publication of the kind—*Tracts for the Times, or What does she do with it?*

[1] See Lee, *op. cit.*, pp. 410 *et seq.*

by Solomon Temple, Builder—pointed out that, in addition to the annual allowance of £385,000 provided for the Queen by the nation, she had inherited £1,000,000 from the Prince Consort, as well as £500,000 from a millionaire of the name of Neild, who had left his entire fortune to the Queen.[1]

The writer complained, as well, that the Queen did not spend her official allowance on the purpose for which it was granted, that of maintaining for the Queen "a Court and a Royal Establishment on the same scale as that of William IV"— since a splendid court and lavish entertainment would have stimulated the trade of the nation. The Queen, it was stated, was setting aside a large part of her allowance in order to amass a gigantic fortune which amounted already, it was believed, to five million pounds.[2] She had no right to these savings; indeed, the pamphlet claimed that her conduct in this matter amounted to malversation of public moneys.

Against these misrepresentations, it was useless for Gladstone, her constant and loyal champion, to protest; the lies were there, and they spread, being seized upon eagerly by the Republicans in this country as a means of propaganda against the Queen. For the rise of a Republic in France had not been without its influence on this country and, perhaps for the first time, an English Republic was advocated openly in some quarters. This feeling was fostered by the change in the attitude of the English people towards France. When the Franco-Prussian war began, English sympathy had been with Germany, since Bismarck's plotting was unknown to the general public, and the provocation came, ostensibly, from the French. But after the war had ended these sympathies changed. The revengefulness of Prussia, the harshness of the terms imposed by her, contributed to this alteration in outlook, and with this change came a tendency to blame the

[1] See Frank Hardie: *The Political Influence of Queen Victoria* (Oxford University Press), pp. 208–9.
[2] See Hardie, *op. cit.*, p. 207.

Queen. Knowing nothing of her noble and clear-sighted letter to the King of Prussia, entreating him to impose upon his fallen enemy only terms which could be accepted; knowing nothing of the fact that her only reason for not making a still greater appeal was the fear that Germany, misunderstanding it as an attempt to wrest from the latter the spoils of victory, might become still more bitter and harsh,[1] the people believed that she might have interceded with Prussia and might so have lessened the horrors that were to fall upon the people of France. The Queen's husband had been a German; she was in communication with her two daughters who were married to German Princes; and this, it was supposed, was sufficient to prove that her sympathies lay with Germany.

And so the discontent grew, until, in 1871, it reached its height. In April of that year, a meeting was held in Hyde Park as a mark of sympathy with the Paris Commune. It could not be claimed that this was an entire success, for, whereas the organizers had claimed that one hundred thousand persons would be present, only six hundred attended. In November, however, a more sinister event took place. On that date, a Member of Parliament, Sir Charles Dilke, made a speech at Newcastle in favour of an English Republic. According to his own account, this was drawn forth by the question of dowries for the Queen's children, and "contained references to this subject which were accurate but possibly unwise".[2]

Subsequently the Queen, in a cold rage, told Mr Gladstone[3] that whilst she was aware that he had alluded to this speech, and had stated his preference for the present form of government to that which Sir Charles Dilke advocated, yet, if the

---

[1] See Benson, *op. cit.*, p. 253.
[2] Stephen Lucius Gwynn and G. M. Tuckwell: *The Life of the Rt. Hon. Sir Charles W. Dilke*, Volume I, p. 139. Hardie, *op. cit.*, p. 211.
[3] See *Letters*, Second Series, Volume II, p. 164.

Queen understood Mr Gladstone, the end of his speech had conveyed the impression that the matter was one open to discussion. Though Sir Charles was a person of little weight, yet the Queen felt that his attack on the system of monarchy, and his personal attack made upon herself, might have led Mr Gladstone to administer a stronger rebuke to the person guilty of this offence.

To this, Mr Gladstone replied[1] that the matter had given him grave anxiety, since it was a cause for alarm that even a person of such moderate weight as Sir Charles Dilke should have been able to propound these views in a public speech, and should have received a vote of thanks. Though the persons attending the meeting were not many, yet, a few years ago, even this small number of Republicans did not exist. Mr Gladstone felt that the best course would be to deal "very lightly with the signs, but seriously with the causes of the distemper"! It was for this reason that he had spoken slightingly of Sir Charles's foolish Republicanism, whilst praising the monarchy in the strongest terms.

Mr Gladstone was, in fact, alarmed, for Sir Charles Dilke's speech gained for the movement several enthusiastic supporters. Mr Joseph Chamberlain, for instance, of the flashing, dashing, fox-terrier-sharp appearance, proclaimed: "The Republic must come, and at the rate at which we are moving it will come in our generation. The greater is the necessity for discussing its conditions beforehand, and for a clear recognition of what we may lose as well as gain."[2]

The supporters of the idea of an English Republic were, however, few, and when, early in 1872, Dilke brought a motion in the House of Commons for inquiry into the Civil List it was defeated amidst great disorder.

In May 1873, a Republican conference was held at Birmingham; Mr Joseph Chamberlain was absent, and Mr Hardie

[1] See *Letters*, Second Series, Volume II, p. 166.
[2] Gwynn and Tuckwell, *op. cit.*, p. 140. Hardie, *op. cit.*, p. 211.

tells us that "Bright specifically dissociated himself from the movement. The leading figures were Bradlaugh and George Odger." It is true that in 1883 Mr Chamberlain gave vent to a new outburst of Republican feeling, in the presence of twenty thousand people celebrating the Jubilee of John Bright as Member for Birmingham, but in Mr Hardie's opinion "his more considered view" on Republicanism was contained in a speech which he made as Mayor of Birmingham in 1874, just before the city was to be visited by the Prince and Princess of Wales!

"If to be a Republican is to hold, as a matter of theory at all events, that that is the best government for a free and intelligent people in which merit is preferred to birth, then I hold it an honour to be associated with nearly all the greatest thinkers of the country and to be a Republican. But if a Republican is one who would violently uproot existing order, who would thrust aside the opinion and affront the sentiment of a huge majority of the nation, merely to carry to a logical conclusion an abstract theory, then I am as far from being a Republican as any man can be. . . . At the same time, gentlemen, there may be an exaggerated loyalty as well as an exaggerated Republicanism."[1]

The Republican movement in England was dead—killed by the sympathy which had been evoked by the Prince's illness, and the anger aroused by an incident which occurred two days after the thanksgiving service. At the time when the Prince's life was in danger, even the Home Rule Association, as the Viceroy of Ireland hastened to assure Her Majesty, "adjourned on account of the illness". And now, two days after the ceremony which celebrated the Prince's recovery, the fury of the whole nation was to be aroused. On the 29th of February 1872, the Queen returned to Buckingham Palace in an open landau accompanied by two of her sons and a lady-in-waiting. The equerries had dis-

[1] *Mr Chamberlain's Speeches*, Volume I, p. 46. Hardie, *op. cit.*, p. 217.

mounted, good Brown had got down and was about to let down the steps of the carriage, the lady-in-waiting was on the point of getting out—when a shadow appeared at the Queen's side. At first she thought it was that of a footman, about to lift the cover, until, turning her head, she saw an unknown face peering at her, an unknown voice speaking. A hand was lifted. Then, for the first time in her life, the intrepid Queen of England, worn out by sorrow and anxiety, showed fear. "Save me," she cried, and threw her body across that of her lady-in-waiting. As she did so, she heard a scuffle, and voices, and in a moment recovered herself sufficiently to stand up and look round. Good Brown was holding a young man tightly in his grasp, there was a violent struggle, then Brown and the equerries laid the man on the ground, Brown still holding him for fear he should escape before the arrival of the police.[1] By this time, the Queen had recovered all her self-command; but in a moment, all the onlookers were overcome with horror—white as sheets, as the Queen remembered afterwards, the lady-in-waiting half crying, Prince Leopold looking as if he were about to faint; for Cannon the postillion, pointing to the ground, cried out "There it is"; and looking down, the Queen and the onlookers saw a small shining pistol.

It was to good Brown and his unfailing presence of mind, said the Queen, that she owed her life, for he had seen the boy dash forward, and had followed him. And though the pistol was not loaded, it well might have been.

It appeared, on examination, that the seventeen-year-old boy O'Connor, who had threatened her, had intended, by terrifying her, to force her to sign a document, freeing the Fenian prisoners. He was sentenced to a year's imprisonment and a whipping.

It had seemed to the people, during the long years of the

[1] See *Letters*, Second Series, Volume II, p. 198.

Queen's seclusion, that the unseen figure shrouded in mourning was kept from them because it was but an unreal and unliving substitute, a doll dressed in the garb of the living woman.

Yet the life was there, and even in those years the strange greatness which, when the glory or the welfare of her country was concerned, changed her utterance from a little household sound, trivial yet touching, to the gigantic sound of the wind of history, blowing all before it—this was heard. It lived in every line of her reply to Earl Russell at the time of the Schleswig-Holstein question,[1] in which she observed that it was unnecessary to remind the Queen of the honour of England, since this concerned her more nearly than anyone else; but she added that she was equally aware of her responsibility as Queen, and that she refused to allow England to be involved in a war for purely imaginary interests, or for a point of honour which did not exist, or to sanction measures which might only too probably lead to a conflagration over the whole of Europe, perhaps ending in universal anarchy.

Time and time again, it was Victoria with the eagle vision, the strange foresight and wisdom, who saved Europe from a fresh bath of blood. Calm, unwavering in resolution, unafraid because of the power of her vision, she held the balance in strong hands. In May 1875,[2] hearing of the menacing behaviour of Germany towards France, and the rumours that Germany had said she must attack France before the French could begin a war of revenge, the Queen told Mr Disraeli that the conduct of Germany was intolerable, that the talk of a war of revenge was sheer nonsense, and that England must, at the head of the other powers, inform Germany that Europe could not and would not stand another war.

[1] See *Letters*, Second Series, Volume I, p. 158.
[2] See *Letters*, Second Series, Volume II, pp. 391–2.

THE RETURN

Before that unconquerable will Germany gave way, and the peace of Europe was saved. Endowed as she was with greatness and an unsurpassed courage, not all the miseries of the hypochondriacal condition which followed her husband's death could dim these, and the time had come when that greatness would be recognized.

Chapter XXVI

THE PASSING YEARS

═══════════

How quickly the years had flown, changing the young body of the Queen, the youthful happy face, casting them into the heavy sagging lines of middle age. But now the face which, in her girlhood, had been "so dear and homely", which in early middle age had been lined by grief, annoyance, self-pity, and petulance, had grown noble and wise—the shadow of the mountain peaks lay upon it. Her character had widened and her sympathies, always deep, were enlarged by experience. No detail which affected the welfare of her people was too small to escape her notice. An extra tax, for instance, must not be put upon matches, for matches were made by the very poorest people, including very little children, whose livelihood might thus be taken away. Her grief for the loss of her husband was ever present, but she no longer greeted every marriage of her children, any birth of a grandchild, any simple ceremony in her home, or public ceremonial amongst her people, with an outburst of tears.

The years had taken much that was lovely and beloved from the Queen of England—wise voices whose sound had upheld her, gentle voices that seemed part of her lost youth, or of her happy married life. In 1865, the King of the Belgians, whose fatherly love had comforted her childhood, died after a short illness; one by one, all that bound her to her youth had vanished. Her beloved half-sister Feodore, so much admired by King George IV for her beautiful manners —Feodore who on her little sister's tenth birthday had longed to fly through her window like a bird, just to tell her how much she loved her—Feodore, the young and laughing creature who, it had seemed, would never grow old—she too had gone. And good wise Dr Macleod, her friend at Balmoral, who had understood so well her feelings about the mausoleum, and had helped her to find consolation in religion, he was dust. Tears rained down the Queen's face as she sat at her dressing-table, mechanically smoothing her hair. It was the 14th of December 1878, the seventeenth anniversary of that black and polar day when her husband had been taken from her, and on this, of all days in the year, her daughter Alice had died, struck down by diphtheria caught while nursing her children. The night had been passed by the Queen in fitful sleep, and when morning came at last, she went to her husband's room, which was her custom on this day, and prayed. As she left the room, she met John Brown, with a stricken look on his face, holding a telegram in his hand...Alice standing beside her father's bedside on that night when the Queen's world had ended...Alice entering her mother's room on her wedding morning, stooping for her kiss....The Queen pressed her fingers over her eyes, as if to keep those memories for ever within them.[1]

The years had passed so quickly, for all their heavy burden of sorrows. They had brought her, too, bright flashing pleasures, and little joys. Above all, they had given her a clearer understanding. The Prince of Wales, shut out for many years from playing any real part in public affairs, had

[1] See *Letters*, Second Series, Volume II, p. 654.

now, owing to the constant demands of Gladstone and Beaconsfield, taken his place as heir apparent, and had gone to India as the Queen's representative in 1875. Indeed, it seemed to her now that the time could not have existed when she had lived without the support of her son.

Then, too, with the Queen's recovered health, her renewed interest in life, came a delight in those state visits which, not so long ago, she had dreaded. On the 20th of June 1873 [1] the Shah of Persia, accompanied by the Grand Vizier and a large suite, had paid her a visit at Windsor. It was highly desirable that England should be on good terms with Persia, because of the expansion of Russia in Asia; and, so that cordial relations should be established both with Russia and with Persia, the Czarevitch and his wife were invited to visit the sister of the latter, the Princess of Wales, at the time when the Shah was due to arrive at Windsor. [2]

Ten years ago, the Queen would not have believed it possible that she could have derived so much enjoyment and amusement from her party for the Shah; the whole day was filled with delights, and the Shah's jewels—the enormous rubies he wore as buttons, his sword-belt and epaulettes made entirely of diamonds, the diamond aigrette in his hat—flashed in the blue daylight of summer till he seemed a second sun. The monarchs exchanged Orders, and when the Shah put one round the Queen's shoulders he nearly knocked her cap off—but it was put straight again by the Grand Vizier and Princess Beatrice; and then the doors were flung open and the whole procession walked slowly into the Oak Room where luncheon was served. The Shah ate fruit all through luncheon, and drank a great deal of iced water, and talked to the Queen about the *Journal of our Life in the Highlands*, which he had caused to be translated into Persian in order that he might read it. Then, after lunch, the Queen left the

[1] See *Letters*, Second Series, Volume II, p. 258.
[2] See Benson, *op. cit.*, pp. 265-6.

Shah, who went to rest, attended by his servants, his Cup-bearer, and his Pipe-bearer; and at about half past three, looking from her window, she saw him, minus his aigrette and wearing a pair of spectacles, drive away with his whole suite to visit Virginia Water and the Fishing Temple, where, forty-seven years before, a little princess had driven in an open phaeton with a very different monarch, the First Gentleman in Europe.

Not only the Queen's activities as hostess, but the marriages of her children established her influence more and more deeply. Three weeks after this time, while the Queen was having tea with Princess Beatrice near the pines and ilexes at Osborne, a telegram arrived from the Duke of Edinburgh announcing his engagement to the only daughter of the Czar.[1] And on March 7th of the following year[2] the Queen, nervous and trembling at the ordeal of seeing her new daughter-in-law, welcomed the Duke and his wife at Windsor Station. All the bells were ringing, and all the bands were playing, the guns were firing and the flags were flying, as the bride, in a light blue dress with a long train, and a white tulle bonnet with white roses and white heather, stepped out of the car-riage; and she was so charming with her pleasant kindly face, her bright eyes, and her friendly manner, that the Queen quite forgot to tremble, and kissed her tenderly.

It seemed strange that her son should have married the daughter of the young Grand Duke, that dear, charming young man with whom, "speaking jokingly", she really thought she was a little in love. Could it really be thirty-five years since they had danced together, had talked together, had said good-bye with tears in their eyes at Windsor? In two months' time from the arrival of his daughter in her new home, he paid the Queen a state visit; but, although he was very kind, she knew that he was terribly altered, and his face,

[1] See *Letters*, Second Series, Volume II, p. 261.
[2] See *Letters*, Second Series, Volume II, p. 328.

she noted in her journal, was so sad, so careworn, and so old! [1] On the following day a great dinner was given in his honour, and, seated side by side, the Queen and the Czar talked of those youthful days in which they had danced together, ridden together, and in which, perhaps, both had fancied that they were a little in love. Once again—it reminded her of the day, thirty-five years ago, when they had said good-bye— the Queen saw tears in his eyes; but this time they were evoked, not by a parting, but by the goodness the Queen had shown to his daughter; and the young Duchess of Edinburgh, she too was so overcome that her mother-in-law must stretch her arm across the Czar and, seizing her hand, press it encouragingly. Little reference was made to the past trouble between England and Russia, although the Czar said meaningly "You were ill served!"—referring, as the Queen supposed, to Palmerston.

The visit passed pleasantly, but the Queen's dread of Russia's growing powers, and labyrinthine intrigues, remained, and eighteen months after the Czar's visit those fears were to be realized to some degree. A revolt of the Balkan subject races against the Porte was used by Russia, jealous of the power of Turkey, as an excuse for furthering her own ambitions. Russia announced her intention of coming to the rescue of her fellow Christians, as she had done in 1854, and Beaconsfield, realizing that British interests in India rested, to some degree, on the Sultan retaining his authority, accepted the fact that England must, at all costs, protect Turkey from Russia. As we have seen in the chapter on Beaconsfield, the Queen not only upheld him in his view, but urged him to the most extreme policy, praying him for God's sake to "hold" the firmest language when dealing with Russia, to remember that the honour and dignity of England were involved and that her great Empire must be upheld,[2] whilst Lord Derby, her

---

[1] See *Letters*, Second Series, Volume II, pp. 337–9.
[2] See *Letters*, Second Series, Volume II, p. 595.

Minister for Foreign Affairs, was told that the Queen would hear of neither difficulties, nor impossibilities, but that the rights of England must be secured.

The result of this line of policy was that the Viceroy of India was able to assure the Queen[1] that England appeared once more to the eyes of India in her old and noble character of lawgiver and judge, and that the land which, only twenty years since, had mutinied against the English rule, now wished to place all her resources in men and money at the disposal of England.

Lord Beaconsfield's triumph at the Congress of Berlin, which finally restored peace to Europe, had, the Queen felt, restored the prestige, the greatness, of England. His boast, that he would live to see his Queen the Dictatress of Europe, was no idle one. But Mr Gladstone had shown himself in a very different light, for, having announced his intention of retiring from public life, he had chosen the moment when Her Majesty's government would least wish to be harried, to return, and to rouse the British people to a state of fury against Turkey on account of her atrocities. The Queen remarked in her journal that Mr Gladstone's policy really made it appear as if England would never hold her old place again....For, by this time, these two great but wholly irreconcilable natures were hopelessly at variance. Mr Gladstone was able to understand, to some degree, the Queen's nature, but for all the generosity, all the breadth of comprehension which went to make their greatness, neither could be attuned to the key of the other.

Mr Gladstone's second administration was to increase the Queen's distrust; during its existence, she urged perpetually that the Afghan and South African wars, inherited by this government from that which preceded it, must be brought to a triumphant conclusion. She feared reduced armaments, a reduction of the army. Tireless in her duty, she reviewed

[1] See *Letters*, Second Series, Volume II, p. 618.

troops, inspected the battleship *Juno* which was to carry reinforcements to India, urged her Ministers to more energetic action. At length Sir Frederick, afterwards Lord Roberts, reduced the Afghans to submission; and the Queen's attention was turned to the Boer war, which had broken out in December 1880. When, at last, the government made what the Queen considered a weak and inconclusive peace, restoring to the Boers practical autonomy, she felt that even Mr Gladstone's unsatisfactoriness could scarcely go further. On no point could they agree, save on that of the wickedness and folly of women's rights, though the Queen still continued to take a kindly, if remote, interest in Mr Gladstone's health, and the various adventures in which he became involved. Many years after this time, for instance, the Queen's sympathies were aroused when, towards the end of August 1892, Mr Gladstone had a miraculous escape from the sinister attentions of a cow. It appears from a letter written to the Queen by Mrs Gladstone[1] that this highly reprehensible animal rushed at Mr Gladstone and threw him upon his back, after which she stood over him, glaring in a most threatening manner. Mr Gladstone glared back, and some moments had been spent in this mutual pursuit before the statesman, who, according to his wife, had never lost his presence of mind for a moment, was able to rise to his feet and dart behind a tree—whereupon the cow forgot him immediately and strolled away. The cow was shot. This affray seemed, indeed, almost in the nature of a symbol.

Both Mr Gladstone and the Queen had, for some time before this incident, been alarmed by the increasing tendency in the female sex to forget that gentleness which is their principal charm; both had been equally dismayed by the appearance in 1851 of Mrs Amelia Bloomer of Seneca County, Ohio, in voluminous trousers. This lady, it seems, was "a smart society woman" and the editress of the *Lily*, a New

[1] See *Letters*, Second Series, Volume II, p. 157.

York journal of a high moral tone. Her trousers—reaching to her ankles, and there secured by elastics—were intended as a rebuke to "the indelicacy of raising dresses a dozen times a day to avoid the mud, etc., of the streets". But this was not generally understood, and when she appeared in England they caused such a sensation that public meetings were held to discuss the matter, and the stir only died down after the owner of a large brewery had dressed all his barmaids in the replica of the lady's costume.

At the time of the incident of the cow, and for twenty years before, the Queen had been, as she assured Mr Martin, occupied in "checking this mad, wicked folly of 'Woman's Rights', with all its attendant horrors, on which her poor feeble sex is bent, forgetting every sense of womanly feeling and propriety. Lady—", added Her Majesty, "ought to get a *good whipping*. It is a subject which makes the Queen so furious that she cannot contain herself. God created men and women different—then let them remain each in their own position. Tennyson has some beautiful lines on the difference of men and women in 'The Princess'. Woman would become the most hateful, heartless, and disgusting of human beings were she allowed to unsex herself, and where would be the protection which man was intended to give the weaker sex?"[1]

Mr Gladstone's horror at this menace fully equalled that of Her Majesty. At the time when Mr Disraeli was warning the government that a mutiny was about to break out in India, Mr Gladstone was too busy in combating the bill, which would permit women to divorce their errant husbands, to pay any attention to the gathering storm. The bill, indeed, from Mr Gladstone's point of view, showed a lamentable tendency towards a looseness of principles, since, if passed, it would enable poor persons to obtain

[1] Strachey, *op. cit.*, p. 260. Sir Theodore Martin: *Queen Victoria as I knew her*, pp. 69–70.

a relief which until now had been only possible to the rich.

The dislike of feminism was, however, the only bond between Her Majesty and her minister. Mr Gladstone did not think imperially; and it seemed to the Queen, also, that his attitude towards Home Rule showed a tendency towards revolution. He went abroad, on a yacht, with his friend Tennyson, without first obtaining the Queen's permission; he had no foresight; he was not concerned for the honour of England.

The Queen's anger against him however reached its height in 1884. Three years before this time, a native of Dongola, in the Sudan, proclaimed that he had received inspiration from Heaven, ordering him to confound (and massacre) the wicked man, the hypocrite, and the unbeliever, to gather under his banner the god-fearing tribes of the southern Sudan in order to fulfil this mission. Unfortunately, this virtuous ideal did not meet with the approval of Her Majesty's government. After prolonged discussion, it was decided to evacuate the Sudan. A strange figure, as fanatical as the Mahdi of Dongola, as warlike, as heaven-inspired, and as brave, was sent to perform this task—Chinese Gordon, who lived according to the commands of the Bible, who loved solitude, and courted danger, who cared nothing for worldly goods, and who gave all he possessed to charity.[1] His appearance was as unusual as his character; short and spare in figure, with a brick-red complexion and fiery blue eyes that yet held a look of childlike innocence, he walked with a rather mincing, tripping movement which seemed to be absolutely at variance with his nature.

Such was the man who, on February the 18th 1884, made a triumphant entry into Khartoum as Governor General, ordered the ancient instruments of torture to be broken in

[1] In the following pages, I am deeply indebted to Mr Strachey's brilliant *Eminent Victorians*.

the public square, but yet, at the same time, made the public announcement that slavery had been sanctioned.[1]

From the moment he entered Khartoum, all thoughts of evacuating the Sudan left his head, and he, who had been sent from London in order to report upon the best means of doing so, now could think and talk of nothing but "smashing up the Mahdi with the help of British and Indian troops".[2] English public opinion, meanwhile, veered round to his side, and after a while Lord Wolseley strongly advocated the annexation of the Sudan. Sir Gerald Graham was sent, therefore, with a large force to Suakin. But then the policy of the government wavered again, for had not General Gordon wished Zobeir, the rebel chieftain of Darfur, the greatest slave-hunter who ever existed, a man against whom Gordon had warred for years, whose son he had executed, to be "given an English subsidy and the control of the Sudan"?[3] Would it be possible to reconcile this with the English public conscience? The Anti-Slavery Society set up a loud outcry, but General Gordon persisted in his demand; for the idea that Zobeir, should he join him at Khartoum, would be the means of smashing the Mahdi was as he explained "a mystic feeling", and as such could not be distrusted. Unfortunately the government was out of touch with mysticism, and their enthusiasm for Gordon began to wane; the imperialistic feeling in England was subsiding too, and then, suddenly, the Cabinet took a decisive and terrible step: Sir Gerald Graham and his British army were recalled from the Sudan,[4] the Mahdi was supreme, and his forces, with none to oppose them but Gordon and the Egyptian garrison, gradually advanced upon Khartoum.

Then, at last, the danger was understood in England; but, long before it was generally known, the Queen was remind-

---

[1] See Lytton Strachey: *Eminen Victorians*, p. 366.
[2] *Eminent Victorians*, p. 267.   [3] *Eminent Victorians*, p. 268.
[4] See *Eminent Victorians*, p. 269.

ing her ministers of their responsibility.... "It is alarming," ran her telegram to Lord Hartington on March 25th. "General Gordon is in danger, you are bound to save him.... You have incurred fearful responsibility...." Public meetings were held, urging that Gordon must be saved at all costs; Lord Wolseley was sent in command of an expedition to relieve Gordon; but it was too late. Already, beleaguered, the people were dying of starvation, already Gordon had had gunpowder put in the cellars of the palace so that, rather than surrender to the Mahdi, the place should be razed to the ground. But even this was in vain. One morning, from the roof, where Gordon was standing in his dressing-gown, he saw the first attack begin. There was just time for him to rush to his bedroom, put on his uniform, and seize his pistol and his sword, before the gates of the palace were burst open and the dervishes rushed in. At the top of the staircase stood the man they were seeking. There was a moment's silence. The foremost dervish, in a loud voice, cried "O cursed one, your hour is come!" and plunged his spear into Gordon's body. A moment later he was hacked to pieces, his head was cut off and, by order of the Mahdi, was nailed between the branches of a tree on the high road, where all who went by might stone it.

When the news reached England the wrath and grief of the Queen knew no bounds. Gladstone had neglected all her warnings, had deserted her faithful servant; his death, she declared, was on Gladstone's head. Such was her fury that she sent telegrams, *en clair*, so that they might be read, one to the Prime Minister, Mr Gladstone, one to Lord Hartington: "These news from Khartoum are frightful and to think that all this might have been prevented and many persons' lives saved by earlier action is too frightful."

These telegrams were read by the post-office clerks, and the Queen's anger then became known. Mr Gladstone, deeply wounded by this public expression of her distrust in him, replied by pointing out that the delay which led to the death of Gordon was due to the fact that the military authorities were unable to make up their minds which route should be taken; but the Queen was not appeased. She wrote: "Mr Gladstone and the Government have—the Queen *feels it dreadfully*—Gordon's innocent, noble heroic blood on their conscience. *No one* who reflects on *how* he was *sent* out, how he was *refused* can deny it! It is awful...may they feel it, and may they be *made to do so*."[1]

The Queen never forgave her Minister; he remained, in her eyes, a man at once vacillating and obstinate, violent and weak, possessing spells of furious energy alternating with periods of a spineless immobility, a statesman without foresight or judgment; and these faults of character were, in her opinion, as much responsible for the Phoenix Park murders as for the death of Gordon. Had Mr Gladstone shown firmness in dealing with the Irish rebels, Lord Frederick Cavendish and Mr Burke would not have died.

Mr Gladstone was unable to agree with Her Majesty in her estimate of his guilt; and, writing to a colleague long after Gordon's death,[2] he explained that he must continue to suffer in silence. "Gordon was a hero, and a hero of heroes, but we ought to have known that a hero of heroes is not the proper person to give effect at a distant point, and in most difficult circumstances, to the views of ordinary men. It was unfortunate that he should claim the hero's privilege by turning upside down and inside out every idea and intention with which he had left England, and for which he had obtained an official approval....My only opinion is that it is harder to justify our doing so much to rescue him, than our not doing more. Had the party reached Khartoum he would not have come away (as I suppose), and the dilemma would have arisen in another form."

[1] *Letters*, Second Series, Volume III, p. 597. Benson, *op. cit.*, p. 298.
[2] Letter dated 10th January 1890.

THE PASSING YEARS

Such were the men, each so typically English, yet so utterly opposed—Mr Gladstone with his calm and obstinate resolution and ordinariness, General Gordon with his fieriness, obstinacy and eccentricity—who came to make the increasing glory of England and of her Queen.

Chapter XXVII

THE DAY OF TRIUMPH

Since dawn broke, the troops massing, the bands playing, the cheering crowds, were heard in Buckingham Palace. And now the waiting and expectant multitudes saw two plump and beringed hands draw aside the curtains of the Chinese Room, and a short stout figure in black appear in the opening; only for a moment, and then it was withdrawn again.

The Queen of England looked at her people, gathered to cheer her on the anniversary of the day when, fifty years ago, she had come to reign over them; then, turning away from the window, she walked to the dressing-room to prepare for the ceremony of thanksgiving at the Abbey.

It was nearly fifty years since a little figure in cloth of gold had stood with the crown on her head in the Abbey, and had asked for the blessing of heaven on her work for her people. Now, a little old lady in a black dress trimmed with white *point d'Alençon* and covered with Orders, with a widow's bonnet, and pearls round her neck, she walked down the staircase of Buckingham Palace and out into the great courtyard, to join her people in their thanksgiving; and beside her moved in triumph her proud and never-forgotten Dead—those beloved ones who had helped to make her what she was—her husband, immortally young and ever faithful, her uncle Leopold, her two dead children, that kind wise old

[329]

man Lord Beaconsfield, dear Lehzen and faithful Stockmar, poor Lord M— purified of their human faults by death, beloved and loving.

The day was bright, warm, and glittering as she entered the gilt landau drawn by six cream ponies.[1] Opposite her sat her daughter the Crown Princess of Prussia and the Princess of Wales; immediately in front of the carriage rode twelve Indian officers, and, before them, the Queen's three sons, five sons-in-law, nine grandsons and grandsons-in-law, whilst following the Queen's carriage were others containing her three other daughters, three other daughters-in-law, her granddaughters, one granddaughter-in-law, and some of their suite. The other royalties, the King and Queen of Belgium, the King of Denmark, the King of Saxony, the King and Queen of Portugal, the Archduke Rudolph of Austria, and many other princes, drove in a separate procession. The Matriarch, the grandmother of the future Emperor of Germany and of the future Empress of Russia, felt the shadow of her greatness spreading over the earth. The crowds were vaster, or so it seemed to the Queen, than those that had greeted the little eighteen-year-old Queen fifty years ago—and now they were filled with love for her, all their discontent and their disbelief forgotten. How magnificent was the sight of the royal escort, the brilliant uniforms of the troops, the marching bands, the huge and overwhelming crowds, all cheering and calling her name and waving their handkerchiefs—and surely there could not be so many flags in the world as were flying to-day! In the happy sunlight, there was not a shadow that could rest on the face of her dear Fritz—she knew, for she had watched him anxiously. He looked so well and so handsome. The doctors were wrong, they had made a mistake; he *could* not be so ill as they said... yet it was only five weeks since that dreadful day of anxiety when those anguished letters and telegrams from the Crown Princess had reached her,

[1] See *Letters*, Third Series, Volume II, pp. 322 *et seq.*

begging her to send fresh specialists to examine the Crown Prince's throat. How kind Lord Salisbury, her minister, had been when the Queen confided her anxiety to him; he was always a support to her; his help, his sympathy, were invaluable. Nobody could ever replace dear Lord Beaconsfield—but, now that he was gone, she felt that she could at least find refuge with his pupil.... The Queen smiled as she saw Princess Beatrice's young husband, Prince Henry of Battenberg, whom she had married on July 23rd 1885, wearing his British uniform for the first time, and looking so handsome. The Queen loved him as if he had been her own son; he was so gay, so affectionate, he had brought such happiness into her home, in which he lived. Then, too, he loved music, arranged concerts in the Palace, caused Mr Sullivan's bright new operas to be performed at Court; life was quite different since he had come, and the Queen could scarcely believe that only a few years ago she had greeted every small or great event with an outburst of tears.

By now the procession had arrived at the Abbey, and there stood the Archbishop of Canterbury and the Dean, in those very same copes of velvet and gold that had been worn nearly fifty years ago at her Coronation. Entering the shadow of the Abbey, she walked slowly, with that incomparable majesty that was her genius, and, accompanied by the sound of music, up the nave and to the chair where she must sit alone, without the man who had been the solace of her queenship; and as she sat there on her throne she thought again of her beloved dead. When the ceremony was over, her sons and sons-in-law, her grandsons, stopped before her and bowing kissed her hand; she kissed her daughters, and then, rising from her throne, walked back through the shadows into the sunlight and the company of her people.

The heat of the sun, she noted on her return, had been very great. When she reached the Palace, she went to her room to remove her bonnet and put on her cap, and it was not till four o'clock that luncheon was served, and she walked into the dining-room on the arm of the King of Saxony. After luncheon, she stood on a small balcony of the Blue Room looking out on the gardens, and saw the bluejackets march past, and then went to the small ball-room, where she received her children's present, a piece of plate, and many other gifts, including a strange present from the Queen of Hawaii, consisting of very rare feathers arranged as a wreath round her monogram, which was also in feathers on a black ground.

The heat, the excitement, had been so great that the Queen was by now exhausted and felt that she might faint; so she was wheeled back in her rolling-chair to her room, and when there lay on the sofa, opening and reading the telegrams which came from every part of her Empire. And presently her dear little great-grandchildren came to say good-bye.

An exhausting day! And now it was time to dress for dinner and the great ceremony which must succeed it, in a gown embroidered with the rose, the shamrock, and the thistle in silver, and in all her diamonds. The King of Denmark led her in to dinner, and she sat between him and her cousin the King of the Belgians. After dinner she received the Indian Princes, the Corps Diplomatique, and the foreign envoys until she was half dead with fatigue. It was very late when, at last, she could slip away and be rolled back to the Chinese Room to see the illuminations. The lights in the room were extinguished, the door was shut, and the Queen was alone in the blue moonlight that flooded the room; all the sounds in the Palace seemed far away, but outside the noise of the crowd, which had begun the day before, still sounded in her ears, and continued until the small hours of the morning. How disappointing it was, thought the Queen, that although she could still hear the crowds cheering and talking, she could see but little of the fireworks.

Next morning, when she breakfasted in the Chinese Room,

there was no crowd to be heard, no sound of music, and yesterday seemed a dream. But later in the day she knew that the dream was not over, for there was a great luncheon party, and afterwards she received the members of her household and that of Princess Beatrice and accepted their presents. Then, worn out, she rested on her sofa and had a cup of tea, and it was not till five-thirty that she left Buckingham Palace for Windsor. The streets of London were crowded with flags, and there were schoolchildren singing "God Save the Queen" all out of tune, and a dear little girl gave her a bouquet with ribbons on which were printed *God bless our Queen*, not *Queen* alone, but *Mother, Queen and Friend*. The Queen left the train at Slough, where she was presented with an address, and at Windsor, which was dancing with flags, and where the Eton boys were dressed as Templars. There was a family dinner-party at the Castle, and then the Eton boys formed a torchlight procession, and the Queen called out "Thank you" as loudly as she could—and the Round Tower was illuminated, but the Queen was too tired to see anything.[1] Lord Rosebery, writing to the Queen shortly afterwards, assured her that all was worthy of Her Majesty and of the Empire over which she reigned; the whole ceremony, he continued, had strengthened and deepened the foundations of a monarchy which overshadowed the world, and which represented the union and the aspirations of three hundred million people. The Queen replied that she knew, now, that her fifty years of care and of hard work, her sympathy with the sorrowing, the suffering, and the humble, had been appreciated.[2]

The Queen was, indeed, nearer to the various races over which she reigned than ever before. The Jubilee ceremonies in Calcutta had brought to the astonished Indians, who were, as the Viceroy, Lord Dufferin, assured the Queen, passion-

[1] See *Letters*, Third Series, Volume I, pp. 326-7.
[2] See *Letters*, Third Series, Volume I, pp. 339-40.

ately fond of pyrotechnic displays, fireworks which exceeded their wildest expectations—the Queen's head traced in lines of fire, the Prince and Princess of Wales in the midst of a gigantic rose-bush of flame. Could it be wondered at that a burst of loyalty followed, in which images of the Queen were carried about the streets, and processions shouted her praises?

On the 30th of June, the Queen received a company of Indian princes at Windsor, and presented them with enamel portraits of herself and the Grand Cross of the Indian Empire. In return, Sir Partab Singh took a pearl ornament from his pungaree and presented it to her, after laying his sword at her feet and assuring her that all his possessions were at her service; the Maharanee of Kuch Behar gave her a carved ruby set with huge diamonds; and when she stepped out from the entrance the Thakur of Morir rode up on a young horse of the Chettawa breed, which was completely covered with a coat of mail, and which had an amulet on one leg, and, dismounting, begged her to accept it.

A year before this time, the Queen had received in audience at Windsor various representatives of distant races dwelling beneath her rule [1]—some Cingalese, who struck her as exceedingly black,[2] some splendid-looking Kaffirs, dressed in blankets only, which displayed their magnificent legs and arms, some wretched-looking little Bushmen, Malays established at the Cape, and some natives of British Guinea, who struck the Queen as hideous, and who wore for the most part no clothes, but only a little band round their loins. There were, as well, some interesting-looking Chinese from Hong Kong, and some Cypriots. Most of these persons burst into song or played instruments as a sign of loyalty, and it was some time before the Queen felt she could retire. She bore the ordeal, however, not only with slight amusement but

[1] 8th July 1886.
[2] See *Letters*, Third Series, Volume I, pp. 157-8.

with pleasure and gratitude, for were not all these persons signs of the growing power of her Empire, and was she not happy in the possession of their loyalty? Her lands were great, her power was increasing; and she told Lord Salisbury that Lord Beaconsfield had raised up the power of England in a marvellous manner, from '74 to '80, that Mr Gladstone and Lord Granville had pulled it down again during "those five years of their mischievous and fatal misrule", but that already, in only seven months, Lord Salisbury had raised it high, once again, in the eyes of all the world.[1]

The Queen had long wished for Mr Gladstone to retire into private life, for she considered that the violence of his attacks on his former colleagues, and the fact that, according to her, he could never believe for a moment that he was in the wrong, or that others were in the right, had done him so much harm that for his own sake, as well as for the sake of England, he ought to resign.[2] Then, again, there were his attacks on the wealthy and educated classes, which were deeply to be deplored, as the Queen pointed out to her offending minister. But that obstinate old gentleman retorted merely that for a long course of years he had noticed that on all the greater questions which were dependent on broad considerations of humanity and justice those persons possessed of wealth and rank had invariably been wrong, and the masses right.[3] What was to be done with such a man? He was incorrigible; it was obviously impossible to argue with him; and when, in January 1886, he had displaced Lord Salisbury and had become Prime Minister in his stead, though only for a short time, the Queen realized that he intended to institute an Irish Parliament; and she added bitterly: "imagining thereby to avoid Revolution".[4]

[1] See *Letters*, Third Series, Volume I, p. 196.
[2] See *Letters*, Third Series, Volume I, p. 160.
[3] See *Letters*, Third Series, Volume I, p. 156.
[4] *Letters*, Third Series, Volume I, p. 32.

Now, however, the Queen felt she could breathe again; for his place had been taken once more by that firm, wise, just, urbane, cultured and amusing character Lord Salisbury —Lord Salisbury who knew how to wait for an opportunity, and to take it when it came, Lord Salisbury who knew how to act with firmness, how to return a straight answer or an evasive one, Lord Salisbury who was so incurably interested in new inventions and scientific discoveries that Hatfield House was nearly blown up by an explosion, whilst the feet of his guests were always in danger of becoming entangled in telephone wires—but who knew how to prevent explosions and entanglements in Europe.

The Queen was satisfied when Lord Salisbury became her minister, but Lord Salisbury was less so, for he explained[1] that he would be perfectly capable of managing two departments, but that, owing to the cruelty of fate, he was obliged to manage four: the Prime Ministership, the Foreign Office, the Queen—and Lord Randolph Churchill. And unfortunately the last two departments were at war, for the Queen considered Lord Randolph odd, mad, impertinent, disloyal, and unreliable.[2] The harassed Lord Salisbury was, at one moment,[3] informed that "the Queen was *quite* furious at anyone" ("anyone" being Lord Randolph) "daring or presuming to say *she* wanted to make war on Russia to replace Prince Alexander", the brother of Prince Henry of Battenberg, who had been deposed from the throne of Bulgaria through the intrigues of Russia. Lord Randolph, it seemed, had repeated his language in the clubs of London, and he must be made to feel how deep was the Queen's indignation.

With such difficulties was Lord Salisbury faced. But the Queen was thoroughly satisfied with her new minister; for was not his foreign policy in direct descent from that of Lord

[1] See Lady Gwendolen Cecil: *Life of Robert, Marquis of Salisbury* (Hodder and Stoughton, Ltd.), Volume III, p. 180. Hardie, *op. cit.*, p. 123.
[2] See Hardie, *op. cit.*, p. 125.   [3] 20th January 1887.

THE DAY OF TRIUMPH

Beaconsfield? In January 1887, the Queen and he were in-
strumental in preventing a fresh outbreak of war between
France and Germany,[1] for, hearing from Lord Salisbury that
Bismarck had declared that Germany must go to war if
France did not cease her preparations, the Queen begged
Lord Salisbury to urge the two countries to swear to England
and the other great powers that they did not intend to
attack each other. In the course of this transaction, Lord
Salisbury had a curious interview with the German Ambassador, in which, after assuring the Prime Minister that
Germany had no wish for war, the Ambassador told him
that "no more salutary thing could happen to England than
to be involved in a good war".[2]

Lord Salisbury was, as the Queen remarked, so just and
generous, he felt so much for her being so alone and cut off,
he was so firm in his assurance that he would do everything
in his power to help her,[3] that the Queen felt comforted by his
presence. And she was, indeed, much in need of support, for
her private life had contained of late much anxiety. There
had been, for instance, the distressing case in which Sir
Charles Mordaunt, divorcing his wife who had become insane, had cited the Prince of Wales among the co-respondents. There was ample proof that the Prince had been completely guiltless, but the other co-respondents cited were
among the Prince's friends. The charming, affectionate, easy-
going child who had written to Baron Stockmar about his
interest in thugs was, now that he was a man, interested and
amused by persons whom his father, had he lived, might
have thought scarcely superior to these in moral worth.

But, in spite of the Queen's personal worries, nothing
could dim her pride in the growing glory of England. Every
year fresh lands came under British protection or were

[1] See *Letters*, Third Series, Volume I, pp. 261 *et seq.*
[2] See *Letters*, Third Series, Volume I, p. 262.
[3] See *Letters*, Third Series, Volume I, p. 46.

annexed to the Empire, and her influence in Europe increased with every marriage of her children, grandchildren, and great-grandchildren. And, with the passing of time, the inventions of science welded her lands more closely together, as the means of communication were made more possible. One night after dinner at Osborne, nine years before the Jubilee,[1] the Queen saw and heard that strange new invention the telephone; Professor Bell explained the whole process, which, it seemed, was most extraordinary. The contraption had been put into communication with Osborne Cottage, and the Queen was able to have a conversation with Sir Thomas Biddulph; she also heard some singing quite plainly; but it was rather faint, although the Queen held the tube quite close to her ear. This invention struck the Queen as very astonishing, although the telegraph wire had long been in use—indeed, one of the first telegrams sent had been one from the Emperor Napoleon III congratulating the Queen on the capture of Delhi.[2]

With her renewed interest in life, the Queen began to take delight in travel, and in April 1888 visited Florence.[3] On her arrival, the King and Queen of Italy paid her a visit at the Villa Palmieri where she was staying, and at 4 o'clock on the same day she drove to the Pitti Palace to return their visit. On the following morning she received the Emperor and Empress of Brazil and their young grandson Prince Pedro; but she noticed that the dark faces of their Imperial Majesties looked very aged and ill; it seemed that the shadows of all their forests were cast upon them. When they had gone, she drove through Florence to lunch with the King and Queen of Italy at the Pitti Palace, where she was much struck by the absolute lack of *savoir-faire* of their radical minister Signor Crispi, who remained in the room, staring at her incessantly

[1] See *Letters*, Second Series, Volume II, pp. 594–5.
[2] See Lee, *op. cit.*, p. 277.
[3] See *Letters*, Third Series, Volume I, p. 396.

A GLIMPSE OF THE QUEEN'S HOME LIFE—

THE QUEEN WITH PRINCESS HENRY OF BATTENBURG

From a painting by S. Begg

Illustrated London News

beneath his black eyebrows in a glowering manner, and making himself a general nuisance.[1] On the same day she received news that Prince Bismarck intended to resign owing to the fact that the Emperor and Empress of Germany favoured the engagement of their daughter Victoria to Prince Alexander of Battenberg. The Queen intended going to Berlin to see her daughter and dying son-in-law; but at this point Lord Salisbury became alarmed at the proposed visit, since he knew that Bismarck was in a state of great anger against the Queen because he believed, quite wrongly, that she was urging her daughter to insist on the marriage—and William was under Bismarck's influence. Lord Salisbury knew William, and he knew William's grandmother; and he told the Queen frankly that if any thorny subject should be mentioned the Prince might say something which would not do him credit, and if this drew down on him a rebuke from his grandmother he might take it ill, and this might in future be a cause of trouble between England and Germany.[2] But the Queen was not to be deterred, and on the 23rd of April set out for Berlin. She broke the journey at Innsbruck in order to lunch with the Emperor Franz Josef, who was waiting on the platform to receive her, having travelled from Vienna for seventeen hours for the purpose. The day was so hot and fine, the countryside so romantic, with villages like bunches of great waxen begonias among green baize leaves, that it seemed impossible she could be travelling to visit a dying man.

The Queen and Princess Beatrice and her husband lunched with the Emperor in a little room full of flowers, then the Queen continued her journey, and at 6 o'clock reached Munich where she was met on the platform by the Queen Mother of Bavaria, like a beautiful and sad shadow in her

[1] Private information.
[2] See *Letters*, Third Series, Volume I, pp. 390–8. Benson, *op. cit.*, p. 316.

deep and eternal mourning, worn in memory of the death of her son Ludwig, who was drowned two years before, and of the madness of her son the King who succeeded him. She gave the Queen a bunch of roses, but they were pale and had a strange and mournful smell. Then the train continued its journey, and the Queen watched the Alpenglühen over the Alps.

It was a quarter to eight next morning when she arrived at Charlottenburg and was met by her daughter, who was struggling to restrain her tears. Her life, since the moment when her husband had been stricken by illness, had been almost that of a hunted creature—pursued by the dark shadow of Bismarck, and the attacks of the Press, who contended that according to the constitution no Prince could succeed to the throne of Prussia if he were the victim of an incurable disease, since this would make him incapable of acting as Sovereign. But, above all, there was the behaviour of William. The breach between that prince and his mother was widening day by day; both were headstrong, both had a certain degree of arrogance, and both were determined to rule. The Crown Princess had complained already to her mother that he was "as rude and impertinent and disagreeable as possible",[1] that he interfered, and was officious. But, if we can judge from the character shown in the Empress's letters, it is probable that there were two sides to the question. It is, however, undoubted that his head had become a little swollen owing to the position in which he had been put by the death of his grandfather the Emperor and the illness of his father. Before the death of the old Emperor, his grandson signed all official papers, and although this was a necessity, yet, as Mr Benson[2] has pointed out, each time that a signature was required, both the Prince and his mother knew, one with arrogance, one with anguish at her heart, that the day

[1] See Benson, *op. cit.*, p. 312.
[2] *Op. cit.*, p. 313.

would soon come when the Prince would be signing his own name, as Emperor of Germany. And now the proposed marriage of his sister to Prince Alexander of Battenberg added bitterness to their relations, for William held the same views as Prince Bismarck, and was violently opposed to the match.

The Queen and the Empress drove to the Palace, and the Queen walked upstairs to her son-in-law's room. He was lying in bed, and his beloved face seemed to her to be unaltered; he raised up his hands in joy at seeing her, and gave her a little nosegay of flowers. Then his wife led her mother from his bedside into such a pretty little green room with rococo decorations in silver, and there they breakfasted with the Empress's three girls, Princess Beatrice, and Prince Henry of Battenberg. The three young Princesses looked so charming in their black high-necked dresses with bustles, and their fair hair done high up on the forehead in curls. The leaves round the window were not more green than the shadows that flitted round the room, and the Princesses' voices were high like those of birds, as they chattered to their grandmother. But it was all very dreadful, and the Empress cried almost without ceasing.

In the afternoon, the Queen drove through the hot dream-like streets of Berlin to visit the old Empress; and this, too, seemed like a bad dream; the Queen went up alone, and found the old woman shrouded in black, with a long black veil, seated on a chair in the middle of the room, quite crumpled up and ghastly pale.

Next day, at a little after twelve, the Empress brought Prince Bismarck to visit the Queen. As the door opened, Prince Bismarck, who, whilst she was safely in England, had been full of boastful self-confidence as to the outcome of any combat between himself and the little old widowed lady, who had talked of her as 'Mama' and 'the matchmaker', met the eyes of the Queen. Wellington, Peel, Palmerston,

Gladstone, each in turn had known that look. And now it was the turn of the unconquerable Prince Bismarck. He managed, somehow, to reach the chair she offered him, and to reply to her polite remarks, and she noted in her diary that she was agreeably surprised to find him so amiable and gentle. She does not appear to have understood the reason. He spoke to her long and earnestly of the great strength of the German army and of the immense number of men who could be put into the field if it were necessary; he told her that his great object was to prevent war—an object which, by a strange coincidence, was also that of England and France, as the Queen pointed out. The Prince agreed, but added that the French government was so weak it might be forced into anything. The interview lasted for half an hour, and then the Queen rose.

The time passed with such terrible quickness! And, although the Queen knew that it was probably the last time she would ever see her son-in-law alive, it did not seem possible. As she kissed him in her long farewell, she managed not to burst into tears, and told him tenderly that when he was stronger he must come to visit her, as he had done in the old happy days. Then she dressed and drove with her daughter to the station. As the train steamed out of Charlottenburg, she looked at the figure of her daughter, so lonely in spite of the courtiers surrounding her, standing in tears on the platform, and her heart melted within her.

Seven months later, on a dark November afternoon,[1] the waiting Court at Windsor heard the trumpet of the escort sound, and a woman dressed in the deepest black, shrouded in a thick crape veil that swept to her feet, stepped out of the carriage and shook them all by the hand. But she could not speak, for she was weeping too bitterly.

[1] See *Letters*, Third Series, Volume I, p. 451.

Chapter XXVIII

OLD AGE

Even before this time, the veiled warfare between the Queen and her grandson, the new Emperor, had begun. He had not changed much since the time when, a dear, good little boy, he had managed, at his uncle Edward's wedding, to extricate his cairngorm from his dirk and throw it across the chapel in order to annoy his young uncles. No sooner was his father dead than, with a curious mixture of arrogance and fear, he set about defying his grandmother as far as he dared. Yet, strangely enough, he never for a moment lost his affection and respect for her, and his replies to her gentle reproofs, though they had a jaunty air and were boastful in tone, bore signs of a wholesome terror. He seems, at one moment, to have taken a pride in his obstinacy, for he boasted to Sir Edward Malet[1] that his mother and he shared the same character, that good stubborn English blood which could not give way; and he added that, as a result, should his mother and he happen to disagree, the situation became difficult. He had forbidden the marriage of his sister to Prince Alexander of Battenberg, and now, in answer to his grandmother's gentle advice as to his conduct, he returned jaunty answers, stating his firm though respectful resolution to do exactly the opposite of what she suggested. For her advice, it seemed to him, savoured very often of interference.

[1] See *Letters*, Third Series, Volume I, p. 485.

His answer to her suggestion as to where his mother should live now that she was widowed,[1] her earnest request to him to bear with her if she were sometimes irritated and excited after her long and terrible ordeal: "*not to mind it*" (a phrase which showed, indeed, that the Queen understood that he had something to bear), her gently expressed hope that the rumours crediting him with the intention of paying visits to other sovereigns could not be true, since it was only three weeks since his dear beloved papa had been laid in his grave —these received a rather loudly expressed and slightly boastful answer. He was, it seems, doing his best to fall in with his mama's wishes, he had already stated his intention of making some of his capital over to her; but Uncle Bertie had been mistaken about her wishes as to where she should live. As for visits to sovereigns, it seemed that the Emperor himself was the best judge of his own conduct (though he did not tell his grandmother this). At the end of the month, he had every intention of inspecting the Fleet and of paying a visit to the Baltic, where he hoped to meet the Czar for the sake of the peace of Europe. Had it been possible to postpone the visit he would, naturally, have done so, but state interest must always go before private feelings. And then came a remark about "We Emperors".

The happiest moments in the relationship between the Emperor of Germany and his grandmother seem to have been those when he was provided with the means of dressing up, and of appearing in some fresh role, since whenever he received a new uniform he saw himself, immediately, in the character suitable to the costume. It is true that the battles were all over, and the man of war was at liberty to indulge in the pleasures of peace—but the battles were always in evidence, as a becoming background to the uniform. Nothing could exceed the Emperor's delight, for instance, on being informed by the British Ambassador that he was to be made

[1] See *Letters*, Third Series, Volume I, p. 423.

an admiral of the British fleet. "What a surprise!" he exclaimed. "Fancy wearing the same uniform as St Vincent and Nelson; it is enough to make one quite giddy!"[1] He was determined, however, in spite of the giddiness, to do his utmost for the service to which he was attached, and set to work accordingly to advise his grandmother as to the expenditure that was to be laid out on the Navy. At first, it appeared, the proposed grant of £21,000,000 would be sufficient for a seven years' programme; but after a while it became his duty to warn the Queen that seven new battle-ships must be built to add to the Mediterranean fleet; and, later still, that the estimate of £21,000,000 must be trebled, for fear lest France and America might combine against England.[2]

It is sad to think that eventually his pride and delight at being an admiral of the British fleet were dimmed, temporarily, by the prospect of being obliged to mount a horse in admiral's uniform and, in this garb, review the British army. Colonel Swaine told Sir Henry Ponsonby[3] that he had discovered that the Emperor would cherish a British military uniform, in order to avoid that contingency, and that, above all, he would like to wear Highland costume.[4] But for some reason the Queen could not see her grandson dressed in a kilt, and nothing would induce her to give way in the matter. In three months, however, he was made Honorary Colonel of the Royals, and became, as he explained to his grandmother, one of "the thin red line of England".[5] He was greatly delighted at seeing his new regiment, and at being able, he added, "to associate with so many nice comrades-at-arms".[6]

The Emperor was grateful for these opportunities, but he

[1] See *Letters*, Third Series, Volume I, p. 524.
[2] See Benson, *op. cit.*, p. 323. [3] 13th January 1894.
[4] See *Letters*, Third Series, Volume II, p. 345.
[5] *Letters*, Third Series, Volume II, p. 424. [6] *Ibid.*

feared as well as loved his grandmother, and there is an odd note about his letter to her on her seventy-third birthday, in which he prayed that she might still remain the Nestor or Sibylla of Europe's sovereigns, venerated and revered by all, feared only by the bad!

His relations with the Prince of Wales were not tinged by the awe in which he held his grandmother. His uncle Bertie had always, in the past, made him feel vaguely inferior—less urbane, less sure of himself and of his clothes. But now, whilst Uncle Bertie remained only the heir apparent to the throne of England, his nephew was the Emperor of Germany and intended, for the future, that Uncle Bertie should feel who was in the superior position. Shortly after the death of the Emperor Frederick, a painful incident occurred. It was reported to the Prince of Wales that his nephew the Emperor refused to meet him in Vienna, giving as reasons (though not to the Prince, since there was no communication between them) (1) that the latter had told a Russian grand duke, who had promptly repeated the remark, that if the Emperor Frederick had lived he would have made some concessions as to Alsace, as to North Schleswig, and as to the claims of the Duke of Cumberland; (2) that both the Prince and Princess of Wales had urged these latter claims on Prince Bismarck in private conversation, the latter had been forced by the presence of the Princess to reply amiably, and the Prince had taken advantage of this fact to make a memorandum of his replies and present it to him for confirmation; and (3) that the Prince of Wales treated him as a nephew, not as an emperor should be treated.[1] The Queen's indignation was great, and she told Lord Salisbury that the Emperor's complaint that he was treated by the Prince as a nephew instead of as an emperor was too vulgar and absurd to be believed. It was *perfect madness*. He was treated exactly in the same way as his beloved father, and as she herself had been treated

[1] See *Letters*, Third Series, Volume I, pp. 438–9.

by her uncle the King of the Belgians. "*If*", she added, "he has *such* notions, he had better *never* come here. The Queen will not swallow this affront."[1]

Eventually, the Emperor climbed down to a certain extent, and sent a message through Prince Christian stating that the assertion that he had not wished to see the Prince of Wales was an invention, and that he would be glad to know through whom the news was sent. The Prince replied mildly that he readily accepted the word of his nephew, and that he thought the best course would be for the Emperor to write him a few lines regretting that he had made such an impression—in which case the matter would be at an end.[2] The Emperor did not accept this suggestion, saying that he could not express regret for a remark that he had not uttered, but adding that he was anxious for a mutual understanding, and that he was looking forward to seeing the Prince in England —a fact which, as Sir Henry Ponsonby remarked to the Queen, rather aggravated than modified the situation. However, the Prince with his usual urbanity accepted his nephew's explanation, and eventually it was this affair which led to the Emperor obtaining his long-coveted admiral's uniform (since something had to be done to cement the re-established friendly relations), and led, also, to a happy family party.

Peace was restored, and the Queen's birthday the following year was the occasion of the usual effusive and enthusiastic congratulations from her grandson. For each birthday was a family event, and there were reunions of as many of the Royal House as could be gathered together, whilst the Queen was nearly smothered by bunches and bunches of lilies-of-the-valley, with their blond tight buds so like the blond curls of her little grandchildren, as they ran into her bedroom early in the morning, jumping on to her bed, throwing their arms round her neck, shouting "Many happy returns, Gangan,"

[1] *Letters*, Third Series, Volume I, p. 440.
[2] See *Letters*, Third Series, Volume I, p. 492.

and throwing lilies all over her. Then, a little later in the day, she would witness the Trooping of the Colour, and, in the evening, tableaux, with her little grandchildren and great-grandchildren acting in a piece called *Grandmother's Birthday* —which always brought tears to her eyes.

In the summer mornings at Osborne, the Queen breakfasted under a huge green umbrella on the lawn, and watched the shadows playing over the grass; when breakfast was over, she opened her despatch-case; then, a little later, would come her lesson in Hindustani from one of the Indian servants by whom, since the death of good Brown, she was constantly attended. For the Queen's imagination was much stirred by the Orient. We find her, for instance, despatching [1] a present consisting of *Leaves from the Journal of our Life in the Highlands, More Leaves*, and *The Life of His Royal Highness the Prince Consort* to the Emperor of China, [2] and learn that His Celestial Majesty was roused to such a frenzy of expectation by these promised gifts that he decreed that the audience at which these should be presented should take place at once, and the books were therefore despatched to the Palace in a sedan chair and laid on the table before the Emperor—this being the Chinese way of showing the highest honour and respect. Transported by a royal hand to the land of heather and of haggis, His Celestial Majesty could not fail to feel the bond between himself and our empire strengthened, the understanding enhanced.

Meanwhile, during the years which immediately preceded and followed the Queen's Jubilee, political troubles came and went, but now, with old age, she seemed more able to deal with them. Already, in 1886, the question of Home Rule had caused Her Majesty great anxiety, and she had gone so far as to appeal, personally, to Goschen and to "all moderate, loyal and *really* patriotic men who have the safety of the Empire

[1] In December 1892.
[2] See *Letters*, Third Series, Volume II, p. 195.

and the Throne at heart" to rise above party politics and be
true patriots. Mr Gladstone, as usual, incurred the wrath of
the Queen on this occasion, and the Queen told the same
correspondent that his duty to his Queen and country came
before his duty to Mr Gladstone who, by some alchemy,
was, it seems, able to persuade himself that everything he did,
every cause he espoused, was right, even though this entailed
calling black white, and wrong right. For nothing could
persuade the Queen that Mr Gladstone had the honour and
power of his country strongly at heart. Lord Palmerston,
with all his faults—so she told Lord Granville—had this great
quality, and so had Lord Beaconsfield. But Mr Gladstone,
in her opinion, put the welfare of the House of Commons
and the question of party politics first, although she acknowledged that he was actuated by the strongest sincerity.[1]

New phenomena had appeared on the horizon, and one of
the strangest of these was Mr Joseph Chamberlain, so lately a
Republican, but soon a strong Imperialist. The Queen could
not, at first, approve of him. In 1882 she told Lord Granville
that he was Mr Gladstone's evil genius, and although two
years later she was pleased with his firm attitude as regards
the policy towards Egypt, and found him decidedly more
pleasant and less obtrusive in manner than Sir Charles Dilke,
she was shocked when, some time afterwards, he made a
speech dealing with the future of the House of Lords. From
that moment Mr Gladstone found himself in the position of
being harried by the Queen to rebuke Mr Chamberlain, to
keep him in order, to restrain the violence of his speeches, and
as well to disown, or at any rate to separate, his own name
from that of his errant colleague. At last Mr Gladstone was
forced to tell Her Majesty that he had no power or jurisdic-
tion over the speeches of his colleagues, except where they
had offended against some assurance which, with their permission, he had given the Queen. As a result, Her Majesty

[1] See letter to Granville, 22nd October 1883.

complained to Sir Henry Ponsonby that Mr Gladstone was very shifty about Mr Chamberlain.[1] Noble and chivalrous, he could yet do no right in the eyes of the mistress whom he served so devotedly. They were divided by the impenetrable wall of their utterly opposed personalities, and by his unconquerable austerity of manner. And when, in 1892, he succeeded Lord Salisbury as Prime Minister, the Queen could see only the terrible danger to England, to her vast empire, to the whole of Europe, in having "such great interests entrusted to the shaking hand of an old, wild, and incomprehensible man of $82\frac{1}{2}$".[2] Perhaps the most cruel blow that the old man had yet received was that which befell him when, it being proposed that Lord Lansdowne should receive the Grand Cross Extraordinary of the Order of the Bath at the end of his term as Viceroy of India, Mr Gladstone reminded the Queen that the Grand Cross of the Order of the Bath (ordinary) had not been offered to himself until he had been a member of three Cabinets, and the Queen replied that she could not for a moment accept the fact that "political party services could be considered as equal to great political services to the Sovereign and the country".[3] It was then, perhaps, that he understood most fully how deep was the breach between them. Three weeks later, on the 27th of February 1894, he sent in his resignation, giving as a reason his great old age, his ever increasing blindness and deafness; and on the next day the Queen gave him an audience. She noticed that he looked very old, and seemed very deaf; she asked him to sit down, and told him that she was sorry for the cause of his resignation, but she did not say she was sorry he was leaving her service. He said very little, except that he found his blindness had increased since his recent stay at Biarritz. Then he spoke of conferring honours on

[1] See Hardie, *op. cit.*, pp. 87–8.
[2] Guedalla, *op. cit.*, Volume II, p. 70. Benson, *op. cit.*, pp. 337–8.
[3] *Letters*, Third Series, Volume II, p. 357. Benson, *op. cit.*, p. 354.

some of his colleagues, and then of other and indifferent topics.[1]

Three days after this time, Mr and Mrs Gladstone paid their last visit to Windsor, and after breakfast on the 3rd of March the Queen had an interview with Mrs Gladstone who, with many tears, said that, whatever the errors her husband might have committed, his devotion to Her Majesty and the Crown was very great. With tears she repeated this, with tears begged the Queen to allow her to tell him that she believed this. The Queen said that she did, and added, in her journal, that she was convinced it was the case, although at moments his actions had made it difficult to believe.[2]

It was the end. And nothing had been said to thank him for his devotion, for his unfailing chivalry, for his service. He could not believe that she had thus said good-bye to him, so, hoping perhaps for one comforting word, he wrote to her, thanking her for "the condescending kindness she had graciously shown him on so many occasions".[3] In reply, she said that she did not like to leave his letter unanswered, so was writing to say that she thought, after so many years of hard work and responsibility, he was right, at his age, in wishing to be relieved of his duties—and that she wished him peace and quiet with his excellent wife, health and happiness, and improved eyesight. She would gladly, she said, confer a peerage upon him, but she knew he would not accept it.[4] And that was all. Afterwards he wrote in his diary: "It was the kind and generous farewell from Ponsonby which had to fill for me the place of a farewell from my Sovereign."[5]

Three years afterwards, on the 22nd March 1897, the Queen and her faithful servant, now aged eighty-eight, met

[1] See *Letters*, Third Series, Volume II, p. 366.
[2] See *Letters*, Third Series, Volume II, p. 370. Benson, *op. cit.*, p. 344.
[3] *Letters*, Third Series, Volume II, p. 372.
[4] See *Letters*, Third Series, Volume II, p. 373.
[5] Viscount Gladstone, *op. cit.*, p. 348. Hardie, *op. cit.*, p. 101.

once again, and the old man noted that "her manner was decidedly kind, such as I had not seen it for a good while before my final resignation. She gave me her hand, a thing which was, I apprehended, rather rare with men, and which had never happened with me during all my life, though that life, be it remembered, had included some periods of rather decided favour."

Meanwhile, the position of Lord Salisbury as Prime Minister and Secretary of State for Foreign Affairs had proved to be by no means a sinecure. His difficulties were enhanced by the fact that His Majesty the King of the Belgians, son of the Queen's uncle Leopold, had inaugurated a new school of thought as regards foreign politics and was bent on making Lord Salisbury his confidant. His communications, indeed, were of so extraordinary a character that the bewildered, but delighted, Lord Salisbury was left almost breathless with astonishment. The affair began with His Majesty paying a visit to Lord Salisbury at the Foreign Office [1] and "plunging almost immediately into the Valley of the Nile".[2] His language was highly mysterious, and he hinted much at secrets that might not be divulged, and at opportunities that would never return. He was insistent that England should throw herself into the arms of France, paying no heed to Germany. For France, it seemed, carried Russia with her, and Russia carried Germany. The affair was therefore perfectly simple, since, if England obtained the support of France, it stood to reason that she would obtain that of Russia and Germany as well. As a result of the unparalleled popularity of the King of the Belgians in Paris, he had received certain information from France, and as a result he wished England to fix a date for evacuating Egypt; for, as the price of that policy and through the consequent favour of France,

[1] 5th December 1895.
[2] *Letters*, Third Series, Volume II, p. 578.

England would be able, by some mysterious means, without spending one shilling or losing a single man, to annex China to the Indian Empire. Should China by some unhappy chance fall to pieces, Egypt would, he assured Lord Salisbury, be returned to England. But, above all, for England's own sake it was necessary for her, in her dealings with Egypt, to persuade the Khedive to give a concession of the Valley of the Nile, from Khartoum upwards, "to some person who was *au courant* with the affairs of Africa". Lord Salisbury noted that His Majesty was too modest to mention the name of that person, but he told his correspondent, Sir Arthur Bigge, that it was obvious the King was up to some mischief, and that he suspected he had every intention of selling to France any rights of England on which he could lay hands in the Valley of the Nile. Lord Salisbury complimented His Majesty on his most interesting conversation, and the interview came to an end.

But matters did not rest there. On the 17th of January 1896, His Majesty visited Lord Salisbury once again, and reverted to the subject of a lease from the Khedive to himself (under British influence) of that part of the Nile which was, at the moment, in the hands of the Mahdists. This lease, it seemed, he was willing to undertake purely in the interests of Britain. Dwelling with fire and fervour on the great military qualities of the Mahdists, he pointed out the profit that England could derive from these, should they be at her service. And who was so fitted to train them to subservience as the King of the Belgians? When, he continued, he had "subdued them, and made them pliant instruments of England's will", they would be at the disposal of any work which she wanted done. England would have, of course, to pay them some money, but that was the only condition attached to the transaction. It would be a splendid idea, he continued, if they were used for the purpose of invading and occupying Armenia, and so putting a stop to the terrible massacres which were at that time horrifying the world. Lord Salisbury was much struck and delighted by "the idea of an English general at the head of an army of dervishes, marching from Khartoum to Lake Van, in order to prevent Mohammedans from mal-treating Christians". But although His Majesty made several pauses in his discourse, in order to give Lord Salisbury the opportunity of imploring him to bring about these desirable innovations, that imperturbable man preserved throughout the attitude of a listener, "and there was nothing left but for His Majesty to retire, despairingly, amid a shower of compliments".[1] The little old lady sitting under the green umbrella on the lawn at Osborne was much amused by Lord Salisbury's account of this visit.

As she sat there in the winter sunlight, warm as if with the promise of spring, the shadows passing over her aged face seemed as if they had been left there by the sorrows that had fallen upon her. Five years previously, soon after his engagement to Princess Mary of Teck, her young grandson the Duke of Clarence had been stricken with pneumonia and had died. Beloved and young, on the threshold of his happiness, he had been taken from the world which needed him. And now a fresh blow was to befall her. For the light of her house, her son-in-law Prince Henry, had left her to fight in Ashanti, and soon bad news, and then worse, was to reach her. On the 10th of January 1896, Princess Beatrice came into the Queen's room at Osborne, as she was dressing for dinner, and handed her a telegram. Prince Henry was suffering from fever—but the fever was slight. Days of anxiety, of anguishing hopes and fears, followed. Then came the note in the Queen's diary:[2] "A terrible blow has fallen upon us all," and she heard the voice of her daughter saying "The life is gone out of me," and then silence.

But the years, passing so swiftly, had brought her joys as well as sorrows. There had been that happy 3rd of May in

[1] *Letters*, Third Series, Volume III, p. 24.   [2] 22nd January 1896.

the year 1893, when her grandson George had telegraphed to
ask for her consent to his engagement to his cousin Princess
Mary of Teck, and five days afterwards she had a talk with
him about the arrangements for the wedding, as she sat in
her pony carriage in the gardens of Buckingham Palace,
under the starry heaven made by the boughs of pink and
white hawthorn.[1] And then came the 6th of July, the wedding day, bright and fine, but overpoweringly hot. The
Queen, while she was still in bed, could hear the hum of the
crowds, like the sound of a myriad hives. As she dressed, in
her wedding lace over a thin black stuff, and her wedding
veil under a small coronet, she felt as if the July sky were
made of blue flowers, forget-me-nots and speedwell, and
the bride's eyes were like a deeper heaven as she walked into
the Queen's room dressed in a simple gown of white satin
with a silver design of roses, shamrocks, thistles, and orange-
flowers. The flying summer lights were so white they might
have been snow, or the feathers of white doves, the crowds
were enormous, and everybody seemed happy. Then, after
the ceremony, came the large luncheon-party, at which
everybody was gay and the laughter flew like the little
feathers of the lights; and then at last the new Duchess of
York, looking sweet and young in her dress of white poplin
edged with gold, and her pretty little toque with roses, left
with her husband for Sandringham.

Sixteen months later, another grandchild, the daughter of
the dead Princess Alice, married. How strange it was, thought
the Queen on this wedding day, that gentle simple little
Alicky should be the great Empress of Russia.[2]

The Queen, in her wise old age, had attained to that complete control over her will which, with her strange foresight,
constituted her greatness. Gone were the underlining of the

[1] See *Letters*, Third Series, Volume II, p. 253.
[2] See *Letters*, Third Series, Volume II, p. 454.

letters, the mountains and gulfs showing a strong will that had broken free from discipline. And, having obtained this control over herself, she was able to curb the wild impetuosity of others. Her grandson William, she reflected as she read the report of his latest exploit, would have to be restored to some sense of what was due to his responsible position. He interfered, he gave unasked opinions, it was impossible to calculate what would be his next step. The year 1896 had begun with a storm in South Africa which caused the Queen and her Secretary of State for the Colonies, Mr Chamberlain, grave anxiety. Three days before the new year, Dr Jameson, the Administrator of the British South Africa Company in Rhodesia, crossed into the Transvaal with four or five hundred men, in order to obtain by force from President Kruger the civil rights that he had denied the Uitlanders. Mr Chamberlain telegraphed at once to Sir Hercules Robinson, the High Commissioner for South Africa, repudiating the raid, and ordering that it should be stopped. But Dr Jameson disobeyed the Commissioner's commands and continued his course until, on the 2nd of January, he met a force of Boers at Doornkop and, after a battle of some hours, was defeated and surrendered. Then came the moment for the Emperor William to strike a new attitude. Abandoning, for the moment, the role of a member of the Thin Red Line (which, by some mysterious means, he had succeeded in amalgamating with that of an apostle of peace, "working for the maintenance of peace and goodwill among all nations—*nota bene*, as far as possible"),[1] he appeared now as champion of the oppressed, and, to the unbounded astonishment of his grandmother, sent a telegram to President Kruger congratulating him on having "restored order against the armed bands that broke into his country as disturbers of the peace".[2] The indignation caused by this telegram was

[1] *Letters*, Third Series, Volume II, p. 51.
[2] *Letters*, Third Series, Volume III, p. 7.

immense, and the Prince of Wales expressed his (not infrequent) hope that the Emperor would not appear at Cowes that year. Her Majesty, remarking that it would not do to give her grandson too cutting a snub, since his faults came from impetuosity as well as conceit, and therefore calmness and firmness were the most powerful weapons in dealing with him, sent him a letter in which both these qualities were exceedingly prominent, and which met with the desired result, for the Emperor wrote and explained to his grandmother that the telegram was dictated purely by indignation because he considered the Jameson raiders rebels against his grandmother, and that he had acted only in the interests of peace and of German investments in the Transvaal. Lord Salisbury, when shown this letter, advised Her Majesty to accept all the Emperor's explanations without inquiring too narrowly into the truth of them,[1] adding that the Emperor had always shown the profoundest affection and reverence for the Queen and that he had probably written the telegram in a moment of excitement; and gradually peace was restored. But three years later we find the Queen writing to the Czar that she was sorry to say William was taking every opportunity of assuring the British Ambassador in Berlin that Russia was doing all in her power to injure Britain, was offering alliances to other powers, and had actually made one with the Ameer of Afghanistan against Britain. She added that neither she, Lord Salisbury, nor the Ambassador believed a word of these tales; but that she feared he might be saying exactly the same thing against Britain to Russia, in which case she hoped she would be told in order that such mischievous proceedings should be put a stop to.[2] And three months after this time the Emperor wrote in such terms to his grandmother, about Lord Salisbury, that she felt constrained to tell him that his letter had *greatly astonished* her,

[1] See *Letters*, Third Series, Volume III, p. 20.
[2] See *Letters*, Third Series, Volume III, p. 343   Benson, *op. cit.*, p. 373.

and that she doubted whether any sovereign had ever written in such terms to another sovereign, especially when that sovereign was his own grandmother.[1]

This behaviour occurred only a few months after he had told his most beloved grandmother that he could well understand how great must be her astonishment at finding that the "tiny weeny little brat whom she had so often held in her arms, and dear Grandpapa swung in a napkin" had reached the age of forty. He congratulated himself, however, on the love of a very, very kind grandmother, adding that he ventured to believe that "where the Sovereign will sometimes shake her head often over the tricks of her queer and impetuous Colleague" (a new role this, one of an Imperial Till Eulenspiegel) "the good and genial heart of his grandmother" would realize that, on those occasions where he might fail, it was never from want of truth or goodwill or honesty, and she would therefore "mitigate the shake of the head by a genial smile of warm sympathy and interest".[2] The shake of the head, however, predominated over the genial smile in his grandmother's comment in her journal: "William's fortieth birthday. I wish he were more prudent and less impulsive at such an age."[3]

The year that followed the abortive Jameson raid saw the Diamond Jubilee of the Queen, and it brought her gifts from all parts of the Empire. Amongst these, was the present of a bicycle from the Mayor of Coventry, on behalf of that city.[4] This proposed gift was the source of some worry to Lord Salisbury,[5] but in the end his objections were overruled by the Queen, and the bicycle was accepted.

On the 21st of June 1897, ten years after that last triumphal

---

[1] See *Letters*, Third Series, Volume III, p. 381.
[2] *Letters*, Third Series, Volume III, pp. 336–7. Benson, *op. cit.*, p. 373.
[3] *Letters*, Third Series, Volume III, p. 336.
[4] See *Letters*, Third Series, Volume III, p. 118.
[5] See *Letters*, Third Series, Volume III, p. 125.

ceremony with her people, the Queen drove through the crowded streets from Paddington, under a triumphal arch bearing the inscription *Our hearts thy Throne*, to Buckingham Palace. The night following was hot, and the Queen felt restless; it was a very different night to the one, sixty long years ago, when a young girl lying in a little white bed in Kensington Palace had listened to the distant music, speaking of love and of glory. Now, outside the Palace, there was no music except the sound of the voices of the gathering crowds.

Next morning she breakfasted with her widowed daughters the Crown Princess of Germany and Princess Beatrice in the Chinese Room, and then watched the procession for a little while. How disappointing it was! The head of the procession, including the colonial troops, had, unfortunately, passed the Palace before she sat down to breakfast. At a quarter past eleven the Queen started, in an open state landau, drawn by light cream horses, with the Princess of Wales, looking lovely and pale in a lilac dress, sitting opposite her, and the Prince of Wales riding beside her.... The crowds roared as if they had been a universe of lions, and the Queen's eyes were so dimmed she could scarcely see if those hundreds of thousands of faces were flowers or seas or stars. So had a little eighteen-year-old Queen seen the faces of her people, sixty years ago, as she drove from the Abbey after the heavy Crown had been pressed down upon her brow.

During the four years of life that remained to her, she was to see many changes; she was to meet the men who were building her empire, to see the blood of Gordon avenged by Kitchener, the British and Egyptian flags hoisted over Gordon's palace at Khartoum, and the tomb of the Mahdi destroyed. She who knew that to go to war was "an awful responsibility to God and man"[1] was, by saving the French from humiliation at the time of the Fashoda incident, able to avert war, though she could not save South Africa from

[1] *Letters*, Third Series, Volume III, p. 298.

the storm which, in October 1899, broke over her. On that occasion she was to see the Emperor of Germany, once more a member of the Thin Red Line, giving advice as to military matters, and lamenting to his grandmother, on Christmas Day, that though the angels had sung "Peace and goodwill among men" it seemed difficult for the latter to live up to those good and simple words.

With her failing eyesight, she was to see these things, but she was to see no day which so epitomized the splendour of her life as that day in which she drove in triumph among the love of her people.

Chapter XXIX

THE LAST DRIVE

O n the 15th of January 1901, a carriage containing two old ladies might have been seen driving through the violet dusk cast by the woods at Osborne. The dusk cast by the boughs was so deep that the woods seemed as if they were already preparing their dim sweet flowers for the early spring. But there were no buds upon the ground, nor had the first leaves begun to stir.

The Queen of England and the widowed Duchess of Saxe-Coburg-Gotha, sitting side by side, had fallen into a half dream, and the Queen was very tired, for the South African war had cast many burdens of grief and anxiety upon her. She, the queen of the working hive, the mother of her people, had, the year before, renounced her plans of wintering in the South of France in order to visit Ireland, which had given many recruits to her armies; the little intrepid figure drove through the streets, though it had been supposed an attempt would be made upon her life. She was eighty-one years of age, but her duty to her people was all that mattered; so she distributed medals to her soldiers, as she had done so many years before after the Crimean war, she entered into all the details of the campaign, the practicability of the uniforms, the nursing arrangements, she received Lord Roberts on his return from South Africa, she granted Mr Chamberlain, the Colonial Secretary, an audience in order to discuss

South African affairs; but now she was very tired and she longed to sleep.

Hers had been such a long life, and it had seen the beginning of a new era. On the day of the Diamond Jubilee, by means of touching an electric button, her message had been sent to her people of the Dominions. Hers had not been the same world as that which was known by her father and her uncles. She had used a telephone, travelled in a train, her voice had been recorded on a gramophone, her photograph was familiar to those over whom she ruled.[1] The whole of the hospital system had been reformed, the use of chloroform, which had so astonished Mr Greville, was now general; the sanitary system was now in good working order, so that the country was no longer swept by appalling plagues of typhus and cholera. The penal system, too, had been changed, and the horrors of transportation and of public executions were abolished. No longer were the workhouses the People's Bastille, nor did the terrible Debtors' Prison exist. The state of the workers was much ameliorated, their wages were put on a better scale; the divorce laws were less cruel, and there was some attempt to ease the hard lives of children born out of wedlock.

All these ameliorations of the human lot, these strivings towards the light, had been brought about in her lifetime. But now the Queen of England was tired, and she wanted rest. The trees were silent because of the secret of the coming spring that they held within them, and as the carriage drove beneath the violet boughs the shadows seemed to grow longer. Yet she knew that there was someone with whom she had made a tryst years ago, someone who was surely waiting for her round the bend in the forest where the trees were darkest.

Then, driving through the woods in that half dream, she

[1] See Hector Bolitho: "The Two other Jubilees", *Daily Mail*, April 1935.

THE LAST DRIVE

From a painting by S. Begg

Illustrated London News

saw a boy and girl walking hand in hand among the violet-coloured trees of winter. She could hear the boy's voice as he spoke, and it was a voice she had known—oh, many years ago, when she too was young. If only he would turn and look at her, she thought she would know the face.

Why, how strange! She had thought she was at Osborne, but, looking at the young figure, the young face before her, she knew she was at Windsor once again, and it was the day when Albert and she had joined their lives together.

BIBLIOGRAPHY

Ashley, A. E. M. *The Life and Correspondence of H. J. Temple, Viscount Palmerston.*

Benson, E. F. *Queen Victoria.* Longmans, Green and Co.

Bolitho, Hector. *Albert the Good.* R. Cobden-Sanderson, Ltd.

Creevey Papers, The, edited by the Rt. Hon. Sir Herbert Maxwell, Bart. John Murray.

Dalling, Lord. *The Life of H. J. Temple, Viscount Palmerston.*

Early Victorian England, edited by G. M. Young. Oxford University Press.

Engels, Friedrich. *The Condition of the Working Class in England in 1844,* translated by Florence Kelley Wischnewedzky. George Allen and Unwin, Ltd.

Fischel, Dr Oskar, and Max von Böhn. *Modes and Manners of the Nineteenth Century.* J. M. Dent and Sons, Ltd.

Fulford, Roger. *The Royal Dukes.* Gerald Duckworth and Co., Ltd.

Girlhood of Queen Victoria, The, edited by Viscount Esher. John Murray.

Gladstone, Viscount. *After Thirty Years.* Macmillan and Co., Ltd.

Greenwood, Walter. *Love on the Dole.* Jonathan Cape, Ltd.

Greville Memoirs, The. Silver Library edition.

Grey, Lieut.-General the Hon. C. *The Early Years of the Prince Consort.* John Murray.

BIBLIOGRAPHY

Guedalla, Philip. *The Queen and Mr Gladstone*. Hodder and Stoughton, Ltd.

Hardie, Frank. *The Political Influence of Queen Victoria*. Oxford University Press.

Journal of our Life in the Highlands, Leaves from the, from 1848 to 1861, edited by Sir Arthur Helps. John Murray.

Journal of a Life in the Highlands, More Leaves from the, from 1862 to 1882. John Murray.

Lee, Sir Sidney. *Queen Victoria: A Biography*. John Murray.

Letters of Queen Victoria, The, edited by A. C. Benson and Viscount Esher. John Murray.

Letters of Queen Victoria, The, Second Series, edited by George Earle Buckle. John Murray.

Letters of Queen Victoria, The, Third Series, edited by George Earle Buckle. John Murray.

Martin, Sir Theodore. *The Life of His Royal Highness the Prince Consort*. John Murray.

Maurois, André. *Disraeli: A Picture of the Victorian Age*, translated by Hamish Miles. John Lane, The Bodley Head, Ltd.

Monypenny, W. F., and Buckle, G. E. *The Life of Benjamin Disraeli, Earl of Beaconsfield*. John Murray.

Morley, Lord. *The Life of William Ewart Gladstone*. Macmillan and Co., Ltd.

Rattenbury, Owen, J.P. *Flame of Freedom*. The Epworth Press.

Scott, Sir George Gilbert. *Personal and Professional Recollections*.

Sichel, Walter Sydney. *Disraeli: A Study in Personality and Ideas*. Methuen and Co., Ltd.

Sitwell, Osbert, and Margaret Barton. *Sober Truth* and *Victoriana*. Gerald Duckworth and Co., Ltd.

Stanley, Lady Augusta. *Letters of Lady Augusta Stanley, 1849–1863*, edited by the Dean of Windsor and Hector Bolitho. Gerald Howe, Ltd.

BIBLIOGRAPHY

Strachey, Lytton. *Eminent Victorians.* Chatto and Windus. Harcourt, Brace and Co.

Strachey, Lytton. *Queen Victoria.* Phoenix Library edition. Chatto and Windus. Harcourt, Brace and Co.

Tennyson. *Alfred, Lord Tennyson: A Memoir,* by his son, Hallam, Lord Tennyson. Macmillan and Co., Ltd.

Ullathorne, Bishop. *The Catholic Mission in Australia.*

Ure, Dr. *Philosophy of Manufactures.*

INDEX

INDEX

INDEX

INDEX

INDEX

INDEX

INDEX

INDEX

INDEX

Gladstone,
> William Ewart, *(contd)*
> and son of, 199; opposes the
> Divorce Bill, 235; asked to
> form Ministry, 274; effect
> upon the Queen, *ib.*; character
> of, 275; as lover, *ib.*; the
> Bible and, 276; middle-class
> sympathies of, *ib.*; speech
> quoted, 276, 277; idealism of,
> 278; meeting with Disraeli,
> *ib.*; seriousness of, 279; visit
> to Tennyson, *ib.*; conversation
> of, *ib.*; Lord Morley quoted,
> *re*, 280; reading of, *ib.*; as
> adviser to the Queen, 281;
> Prince Consort and, 281, 282;
> Balmoral and, 283; his manner
> with the Queen, 284; bores
> the Queen, 285; persistency
> of, 286; displeases the Queen,
> 287; reforms, and the Queen,
> 288; the Queen's treatment of,
> 289; goes out of power, *ib.*;
> grant to Princess Louise, and,
> 308; as the Queen's champion,
> 309; Sir Charles Dilke's re-
> publican speech and, 310, 311;
> the Prince of Wales and, 318;
> his policy, and the Queen,
> 321; second administration of,
> *ib.*; "Woman's Rights" and,
> 322, 323; attacked by a cow,
> *ib.*; Home Rule and, 324;
> Gordon's death and, 326, 327;
> Queen's allusions to, 335; re-
> buked by the Queen, 349;
> the Queen, Mr Chamberlain,
> and, 349, 350; succeeds Lord
> Salisbury, 350; the Order of
> the Bath and, *ib.*; resignation
> of, *ib.*; visit to the Queen at
> Windsor, 351; last meeting
> with the Queen, 351, 352

Glassalt Shiel House, 254
Glenlyon, Lord, (afterwards 6th
> Duke of Atholl), 161
Gloucester, Duchess of, 42, 54, 69,
> 101, 136
> Duke of, 102
Gold-fields, The, 81
Gordon, General, description of,
> 324; enters Khartoum, 325;
> action in the Sudan, *ib.*; death
> of, 326; Gladstone and, 327;
> alluded to, 328, 359
Goschen, Viscount, 348
Graham, Sir Gerald, 325
> Sir James, 117, 154, 155
Gramont, Duc de, 296
Granville, Earl, 289, 296, 300, 335,
> 349
Graves, Lord, 42
Gravesend, 234, 256
Great Exhibition (1851), The, 200,
> 216 *et seq.*, 262, 266
Greece, 105; British Fleet des-
> patched to, 205; Lord Pal-
> merston offends, *ib.*
Green Park, The, attempt to
> assassinate the Queen in,
> 147
Greville, Charles Cavendish Fulke,
> quoted, *re* William IV, 49;
> *Memoirs*, quoted, 53, 64;
> alluded to, 75; railway journey
> described by, 82, 83; the
> Queen's Court and, 83, 84;
> mentioned, 86; Tolpuddle
> martyrs and, 92; quoted, *re*
> the Queen's unpopularity, 113;
> quoted, 114, 122; Sir Robert
> Peel described by, 117
Grey, General, 245, 251, 259
> Lady, 69
Grimston, Lady Mary, 99
Grinders (of Sheffield), The, work-
> ing conditions of, 168

INDEX

INDEX

Juvenile offenders, Miss Murray's asylum for, 89; the Queen and, 90; Lord Melbourne and, *ib.*

Kemble, Charles, 67
Fanny, 48
Kensington Palace, Duke and Duchess of Kent arrive at, 27; Princess Victoria's christening at, 28, 29; alluded to, 31; Princess Victoria at, 34, 35, 44 *et seq.*; Princess Victoria's visitors at, 57 *et seq.*; King William visits, 63; unrest at, 66; Princess Victoria's eighteenth birthday at, 67; allusion to, 245
Kent, Edward Augustus, Duke of, last hours of, 17, 18; debts of, 19; Robert Owen and, 19, 20; charities of, 20; hobbies of, 21; Mr Creevey and, 21, 22; Madame St Laurent and, 23; marriage of, 25; his occupations at Amorbach, 26, 27; Alexandrina Victoria born, 28; removes to Sidmouth, 30; death of, 31, 41
Victoria Mary Louisa, Duchess of, Lanark and, 20; marriage of, 25; poverty of, 25, 26, 27; Sir Walter Scott and, 37; alluded to, 42; Princess Victoria's tuition and, 45; William IV and obduracy of, 49, 51 *et seq.*; Sir John Conroy and, 56, 65, 66, 67; quarrel with King William, 62–66; morning visit to Princess Victoria and, 72; disillusioning realizations of, 75, 76; penchant for whist, 86; Lehzen's triumph and, 86, 87; emotion at the Queen's Coronation, 99, 100; Lady Flora Hastings and, 107–111, 122, 123; mentioned, 139; at the Queen's wedding, 142; the Princess Royal and, 178; re-instatement of, 181, 182; a letter to, *re* Balmoral, quoted, 219; at Frogmore, 232; at Abergeldie, 233; Princess Beatrice and, *ib.*; illness and death of, 238, 239, 240; the Queen's grief for, 240; mentioned, 257

Khartoum, 324, 325, 326, 327, 353, 354, 359
Khedive Ismail, The, 285, 353
Kirchbach, General, 299
Kitchener, Lord, 359
Knight, Dr, (Sheffield), quoted, 168
Koh-i-noor diamond, The, 301, 302
Koller, Baron, 206, 207
Korin (artist), 191
Kossuth, visits England, 207
Kruger, President, 356
Kuch Behar, Maharanee of, 334

Lablache, Signor, 194
Labour, the industrial revolution and, 81; Lord Melbourne and child-, 90; the Tolpuddle martyrs, 91 *et seq.*; conditions of, 167 *et seq.*
Lacemakers, 170
Lamartine, 198
Lamb, Lady Caroline, 88, 227
Lanark, 20
Lancashire, 81
Landseer, Sir Edwin, 45, 195
Lansdowne, Lady, 97
Marquis of, 77, 350
"League of the Just, The", (afterwards "The Communist League"), 149

[379]

INDEX

INDEX

Manufactures, 81, 166, 167, 168, 169, 170, 171

Marlborough, Duke of, 252

Martin, Sir Theodore, the Queen and, 285, 291

Marx, Karl, privations of, 149, 150; early activities of, 149; Engel assists, 150; *The Communist Manifesto*, and, *ib.*

Mary, Queen, engagement to Duke of Clarence, 354; marriage to Duke of York, 355

Maslin (Duchess of Kent's page), 233

Mecklenburg-Strelitz, Augusta, Duchess of, 187

Frederick, Grand Duke of, 187

Melbourne, Lord, Princess Victoria's letter to, quoted, 74; his audience of the Queen, *ib.*; speech quoted, 75; the Queen's first Privy Council and, *ib.*; alluded to, 77; attends upon the Queen, 84, 86, 89, 95; characteristics of, 87, 88; agricultural rioters and, 90, 91; the Tolpuddle martyrs and, 91, 92, 95; at the Coronation, 99–102, 106; the Lady Hastings scandal and, 108, 110, 111, 112; resignation of, 115–122; the Queen and personality of, 125, 126; consulted by the Queen, 129, 130; the Queen's marriage intentions announced to, 135; the Queen's wishes for Prince Albert told to, *ib.*; Prince Albert's reclusion and, 140; at wedding of the Queen, 141; dines with the Queen at Windsor, 143; the Queen's will and, 144, 145; quoted, *re* Prince Consort's boredom, 145; the

Chartist riots and, 154, 155; alluded to, 160; fading influence of, 177, 178, 179, 180; and Sir John Russell, 181; death of, *ib.*; allusions to, 253

Memoirs of Colonel Hutchinson, Princess Victoria's opinion of, 48

Mendelssohn, Felix, melodies of, 182; description of, 192; the Queen, Prince Albert, and, 193, 194

Mensdorff, Count, 38

Mersey, The, 81

Meyerbeer, 230

Midland Railway, The, 248, 261

Mines, The, 81

Mohammedans, The, 354

Molesworth, Sir William, 153, 154

Monck, Lord, 252

Montreal, 20

Montrose, Duchess of, 113

Mordaunt, Sir Charles, 337

Morir, The Thakur of, 334

Mulgrave, Lady, 97

Munich, 339

Murray, Miss Amelia, 89, 98

Nail workers, The, living conditions of, 168

National Gallery, The, 67

New Age, The, rise of the middle class, 80; machinery in, 80, 81; capitalism and industrialism, 80, 81; manufactures, 81; labour conditions in, *ib.*; steamboats and railways, 81, 82, 83; the gold-fields, 81

New South Wales, 153

New York, 238, 252, 322

New Zealand, 36

Newcastle, 310

Duke of, 238

Newgate Prison, 154

INDEX

INDEX

INDEX

INDEX

INDEX

INDEX

INDEX

INDEX

INDEX

INDEX

A NOTE TO READERS

We hope you have enjoyed this Cresset Library edition and would like to take this opportunity to invite you to put forward your suggestions about books that might be included in the series.

The Cresset Library was conceived as a forum for bringing back books that we felt should be widely available in attractively designed and priced paperback editions. The series themes can be loosely described as social, cultural, and intellectual history though, as you can see from the list of published titles at the front of this book, these themes cover a broad range of interest areas.

If you have read or know of books that fall into this category which are no longer available or not available in paperback, please write and tell us about them. Should we publish a book that you have suggested we will send you a free copy upon publication together with three other Cresset Library titles of your choice.

Please address your letter to Claire L'Enfant at:-

> Century Hutchinson
> FREEPOST
> London
> WC2N 4BR

There is no need to stamp your envelope.

We look forward to hearing from you.

THE CRESSET LIBRARY